The Democratic Value of News

The Democratic Value of News

Why Public Service Media Matter

Stephen Cushion

Lecturer, Cardiff School of Journalism, Media and Cultural Studies

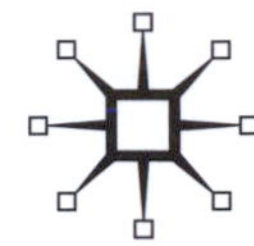

First published 2012 by
PALGRAVE MACMILLAN

Palgrave Macmillan in the UK is an imprint of Macmillan Publishers Limited, registered in England, company number 785998, of Houndmills, Basingstoke, Hampshire RG21 6XS.

Palgrave Macmillan in the US is a division of St Martin's Press LLC, 175 Fifth Avenue, New York, NY 10010.

Palgrave Macmillan is the global academic imprint of the above companies and has companies and representatives throughout the world.

Palgrave® and Macmillan® are registered trademarks in the United States, the United Kingdom, Europe and other countries.

ISBN: 978–0–230–27152–4 hardback
ISBN: 978–0–230–27153–1 paperback

This book is printed on paper suitable for recycling and made from fully managed and sustained forest sources. Logging, pulping and manufacturing processes are expected to conform to the environmental regulations of the country of origin.

A catalogue record for this book is available from the British Library.

A catalog record for this book is available from the Library of Congress.

10 9 8 7 6 5 4 3 2 1
21 20 19 18 17 16 15 14 13 12

Printed and bound in Great Britain by
CPI Antony Rowe, Chippenham and Eastbourne

Contents

Tables

We are witnessing, in this sense, a "McDonaldization" of news values (Franklin 2005).

News audiences, from this perspective, are treated as consumers rather than citizens. If news is seen by journalists and scholars as "the hard-wiring of our democracy" (Hargreaves and Thomas 2002: 4), equipping citizens with the information to understand politics and public affairs, the lurch towards consumerism is seen to diminish the prospects of informed citizenship. Operating within a neo-liberal framework, it has been argued that global news media networks work towards enhancing market economies, as opposed to fourth estate principles that foster democratic interests or engender citizen engagement (McChesney 2004). Although a voluminous literature has grown around the marketization of news in recent decades or the neo-liberal spell under which journalism operates (Fenton 2011a; McManus 2009), underlying many of these critiques is the assumption that another system of ownership – a publicly rather than privately funded news service – could better serve the democratic needs of citizens. And yet, while many studies have drawn distinctions between these media systems, there is little systematic evidence bringing together internationally comparative empirical studies of public and market-driven news programming (with notable exceptions, of course: see Aalberg and Curran 2011).

In the context of a widely perceived decline in the concept of public service broadcasting (Hoynes 1994, 2003; Jacka 2003; Tracey 1998; Tambini and Cowling 2004), this book will explore an important facet of its mission – asking whether public service journalism is distinctive from market-driven news. The aim will be to interpret the democratic value of a news service citizens help fund compared to market-driven systems. After all, why should citizens pay for news provision that the market has made more widely available than at any other point in history? Of course, news of democratic value can be difficult to interpret and classify. Chapter 2 discusses how scholars have typically evaluated the quality of news and subsequent chapters will define how the democratic value of news is interpreted more specifically to the topic under examination. But, broadly speaking, throughout this book *the democratic value of news will refer to news that, above all, has informative quality, enhancing people's understanding of the world on issues likely to empower them as citizens in a democracy.*

Before introducing the methodological framework this book employs to develop a cross-national comparative analysis of news media operating under different funding models, a wider context into recent inquiries about the role of public service media is necessary to establish how this study will offer a new perspective about a system of ownership increasingly threatened by market forces in recent decades.

Crisis in public service media? The commercialization of the media industries

According to many scholarly accounts, public service broadcasting has experienced varying levels of crisis over recent decades (Lowe and Bardoel 2008; Lowe and Jauert 2005; Iosifidis 2010; Tracey 1998). There are, of course, many conflicting reasons why publicly funded media appears precariously placed within the media industry, but most studies have tended to focus on the increased threat of commercial values and market-led direction of media policy-making. While a tension between, on the one hand, state ownership and intervention and, on the other hand, market freedom and liberalization, has plagued the history of media policy-making over many decades, for many countries around the world in the 1980s the pendulum swung decidedly in favour of the market. Advancements in new technologies permanently changed the broadcasting infrastructure. Where once "spectrum scarcity" limited how many broadcasters could fill the airwaves, new cable, satellite and digital technologies made a multi-channel media environment possible. A lucrative commercial market soon opened up and many governments began relinquishing control of the media industries, deregulating them to encourage growth and investment independent of the state. This deregulation of the broadcasting industry needs to be interpreted as part of wider political and economic changes in many countries, since a wide range of industries, throughout the 1980s and 1990s, were denationalized and free-market principles of globalization embraced.

However, the commercialization of media industries has not followed a globally uniform pattern. The balance between state, public and market-driven media models varies considerably in different regions around the world. Nor have governments carried out a wholesale retreat from state ownership or regulation, since there remains a strong public service presence in many countries and robust regulatory structures. But, as Chapter 1 explores, there has been a broad trend in which the market gradually challenged the state monopolization of the media industries in the 1980s and 1990s.

Even in countries where the media is censored by national governments, the state's firm grip on broadcasting has been challenged by transnational news channels or the World Wide Web (WWW). When the Middle Eastern/North African anti-government protests emerged in January and February 2011, many political leaders chose state television to broadcast their message but found it hard to shut down foreign news channels, websites, Twitter, Facebook and SMS phone messaging. In other words, in countries diametrically opposed to relinquishing state control of the media industries and embracing commercial choice, market forces have proved almost unstoppable, impacting on national broadcasting cultures and political events.

The liberalization of broadcasting in countries once tightly controlled by state forces has generally been interpreted as a powerful antidote to governments operating under autocratic rule or, worse still, outright dictatorship. Days after the Egyptian president resigned in February 2011, attention turned to how state media had been complicit with the outgoing government's failure to secure human rights. A journalism professor, Nailah Hamdy (2011), suggested:

> We're going to see major political alterations in the coming months, and that means altering the media landscape as well. In a democracy I can't imagine that there will be any role to play for state TV channels or official newspapers which take diktats from a Ministry of Information; they will have to look to other models, such as BBC-style public broadcasting, to survive. (cited in Shenker 2011)

But while some countries rebuilding democracies have turned to the market or long-standing public service broadcasters like the BBC as models when considering how to establish editorially independent media systems, in more developed nations publicly funded media have had to justify their role in increasingly market-driven economies. The role of publicly funded journalism and the purpose of state regulation have come under a great deal of scrutiny as commercial media markets have expanded. So, for example, Syvertsen (2003: 155) has observed that the "question of whether public broadcasting should be sustained and protected is at the heart of current media policy debates in Europe". As commercialization has intensified in the digital era, scholars have begun to explore how public service broadcasters negotiate the role they should play in an increasingly multimedia, multichannel environment (Lowe and Bardoel 2008; Lowe and Jauert, 2005; Iosifidis, 2010). In doing so, public service broadcasting has been redefined as public service media (Iosifidis 2010: 1) or public service communication (Lowe 2010), since broadcasting only encompasses television and radio services. Where once broadcasters were exclusively focused on national audiences and faced minimal competition, the media market has since internationalized and rapidly expanded, fragmenting audiences and reducing the reach and influence of public service media. In this context, scholars have suggested a new era of "minimal effects" (Bennett and Iyengar 2008) is diminishing the impact individual broadcasters can have in society. In the context of these debates, this book explores how public service broadcasters have adapted to the multimedia environment, developing online and digital strategies, asking how they can justify and legitimize continued public subsidy and remain distinctive in the face of increasing competition from commercial media.

To accurately reflect the contemporary multimedia environment in which broadcasters operate, *this book will primarily refer to them as public service media rather than public service broadcasters*. While countries with a long history of public service broadcasting might be familiar with what this system of ownership represents in a digital, online age, elsewhere (such as in the US), it holds less resonance. But since debates about the history and philosophy of public service media have largely been understood in a broadcasting culture, the terms "media" and "broadcasting" will sometimes be used interchangeably throughout the book, most notably in the opening chapters to introduce the conceptual principles of this media system. Either way, each refers to a publicly funded system of media ownership.

While the principle of public service media remains championed in many countries, in practice talk of a continued "crisis" is ongoing. So, for example, in the UK, home to arguably the most well-known public service broadcaster, the BBC, the opening words of a 2009 House of Lords Committee review began with: "This report responds to the current crisis in public service broadcasting" (Communications Committee 2009: 1). Within academic scholarship, according to Enli (2008: 106), a "crisis discourse" pervades "current recent literature on public service broadcasting" as "a result of deregulation and competition". Likewise, Jacka (2003: 178) has stated unequivocally that "there is no doubt that PSB [public service broadcasting] is under threat around the world". Padovani and Tracey (2003), by contrast, have suggested that the crisis of public service broadcasters has subsided in recent years. They point to the growth of public service media, such as in children's programming, the emergence of a digital infrastructure and the healthy audience ratings maintained by many public broadcasters. While they conceded that an "inherent contradiction between the public service mission and commercial imperatives" exists, in their view these new developments "point toward a positive future" (Padovani and Tracey 2003: 140). In many countries public opinion polls have shown high levels of support for public service media (Cushion 2009), with governments reluctant to be seen attacking well-regarded public institutions. But while many public service broadcasters may appear on relatively safe ground, new licence fee contracts or budget negotiations are always on the horizon and threaten future programming arrangements. The financial crisis that began in late 2007, for example, has led many Western national governments to seek ways to radically reduce levels of public expenditure and public service broadcasters have had their share of budget cuts.[2]

Although many public broadcasters have suffered budget reductions, in the late 1990s and 2000s it is possible to detect a scholarly renaissance in the role of public service broadcasters and a wider recognition of the value public service media brings to societies. The increasingly commercialized media and digitalized environment has prompted many inquiries from a variety of cultural, economic and legal perspectives into the *general* impact on public service structures and their wider values. Having to justify state subsidies, many national and international regulators have sought to develop public service value tests where the cost, quality of media content and audience impact are measured against scales that vary from one country to the next (Donders and Pauwels 2010; Moe 2010).

The titles of anthologies about the contemporary state of public service broadcasting have tended to be broad in scope, largely examining media generally such as *Public Service Broadcasting in the Age of Globalization* (Banerjee and Seneviratne 2006), *Public Service Broadcasting in Transition: A Documentary Reader* (Price and Raboy 2003), *Cultural Dilemmas in Public Service Broadcasting* (Lowe and Jauert 2005), *The Public in Public Service Media* (Lowe 2010), *From Public Service Broadcasting to Public Service Communications* (Tambini and Cowling 2004), *Public Service Broadcasting: Change and Continuity* (Ward 2004), *From Public Service Broadcasting to Public Service Media* (Lowe and Bardoel 2008), *Public Broadcasting and the Public Interest* (McCauley *et al.* 2003) and *Making a Difference: Public Service Broadcasting in the European Media Landscape* (Nissen 2006). Special editions on public service broadcasting have been published in academic journals, such as *Television and New Media* (2003), *Convergence* (2008) and *Interactions: Studies in Communication & Culture* (2010). Many of the book titles, chapters and articles in academic journals feature (sub)titles implying change and recovery such as Petros Iosifidis's (2010) edited book, *Reinventing Public Service Communication* or Mary Debrett's (2010) *Reinventing Public Service Television for the Digital Future*. All of which, in short, demonstrates the fact that public service broadcasting remains an enduring presence in academic scholarship.

However, while much academic literature has debated at length the contributions public service media make to culture and democracy, many of these collections review programming, management structures, funding mechanisms and market impact more *generally* (e.g. Iosifidis 2010; Lowe 2010). In addition, key texts in public service media have tended to discuss their political history, contemporary performance or immediate future within the context of what Moe and Syvertsen refer to as "policy studies" (2009: 400–1) without meaningful engagement with the *content* produced. There have, in other words, been edited viewpoints on the legalistic or policy-related condition of state or public service media either in a particular nation or on a comparative basis of two or three countries. The intention in this book is to comprehensively examine a particular aspect of public service media – the supply of news – and to compare the quality of publicly funded journalism with market-driven news media.

It is also important to assess the relative strengths and weaknesses of contemporary public service media cross-nationally since different broadcast models and regulatory environments shape the delivery of news. But the focus in the book, throughout, is on how changing media ecologies and shifting regulatory frameworks impact on the production of *news*.

Understanding media systems and internationally comparative research: towards a comprehensive review of empirical news studies

To explore journalism operating under different ownership structures, regulatory systems and wider media cultures, it is necessary to develop an internationally comparative framework of analysis. Cross-national research into media systems has, in the previous decade or so, grown more prominent within the disciplines of journalism, communication, media and cultural studies (Livingstone 2003). While there have been pockets of comparative research in recent decades, studies spanning many countries that have been informed by robust data sets are thin on the ground. Blumler and Gurevitch (1995: 73) pointed out well over a decade ago in *The Crisis of Public Communication* that comparative research is the "extending frontier" in understanding the future of political communications studies. As the forces of globalization have impacted on journalism scholarship (Löffelholz and Weaver 2008), cross-national research within relevant disciplines has begun to appear more regularly in a range of international academic journals and, to a lesser extent, book-length endeavours, with publishers eager to capture the lucrative global market. Consequently, much theoretical understanding of media systems is driven by American, European and Australian empirical observations or analysis. Or, to put it another way, Western trends have tended to dominate the interpretation of media systems within the broader academic literature.

It is in this context that Curran and Park (2000) argued that media studies should be "de-Westernized". Their book, *De-Westernizing Media Studies*, was intended, in their words, to counter " the self-absorption and parochialism of much Western theory" (Curran and Park 2000: 1). Of course, since there are close to 200 countries worldwide, developing a truly global comparative study is, in most cases, practically impossible, not just for logistical reasons but due to financial constraints. Very early attempts to characterize the global characteristics of media systems appear almost farcical when even a flicker of empirical light is shed on the sample used to represent the global population. So, for example, in *Four Theories of the Press*, Siebert *et al.* (1956) set out to demonstrate that media systems tended to reflect their political identity. Primarily dealing with the US, Russia and England, they argued that four theoretical models – authoritarian, libertarian, Soviet and social responsibility – characterized the media systems of regions around the world. While their book is much cited and intended as a normative rather than empirical mapping of world media, it has largely been dismissed within the literature for not capturing the character and complexity of global communications (Curran and Park 2000; McQuail 1987). McQuail (1987) has since extended the four models to six – adding development and democratic-participant models – to recognize third world countries and the democratization of many countries since the 1950s. But, in more recent years, scholars have largely moved on and developed new comparative frameworks of cross-national research into media systems.

Hallin and Mancini's (2004) *Comparing Media Systems: Three Models of Media and Politics* developed a more systematic approach to understanding international patterns of journalism in different Western European/North American contexts. Their aim was not to offer any new empirical material but to draw on "existing published sources" in order to "propose a theoretical synthesis and a framework for comparative research on the media and political systems" (Hallin and Mancini 2004: 16). Examining journalism in 18 countries, they identified three models – liberal, democratic corporatist and polarized pluralist – that characterized the political and news media structures in these regions. The liberal model, evident in Britain, Ireland and the US, was "characterized by a relative dominance of market mechanisms and of commercial media"; the democratic corporatist model, representing Northern Europe, "by a historical co-existence of commercial media and media tied to organized social and political groups, and by a relatively active but legally limited role of the state"; and, finally, the polarized pluralist model was interpreted as reflecting the character of Southern European countries by "the integration of the media into party politics, weaker historical development of commercial media and a strong role of the state" (Hallin and Mancini 2004: 11). They arrived at these categories by examining in each country:

1 the type of media markets, most notably the strength of the press readership;
2 the relationship between media systems and political parties;
3 journalistic professionalism; and
4 the extent to which the state intervenes in media regulation. (Hallin and Mancini 2004: 21)

Hallin and Mancini's (2004) study has since sparked further engagement with international comparative research into media systems (Aalberg and Curran 2011; Dobek-Ostrowska *et al.* 2010). In particular, their attempt to pattern news media structures according to relevant historical and political dimensions, and to develop interpretive frameworks to compare media systems is often used by scholars to explore whether certain countries conform to or deviate from the three models (see Curran 2011 for critique). This point was taken up by Hallin and Mancini in a foreword to Dobek-Ostrowska's (2010) edited volume, *Comparative Media Systems: European and Global Perspectives*. They stated that:

> Our models [in *Comparing Media Systems*] are not intended as universal patterns that are somehow inherent in the nature of media and politics. We conceive them as concrete, historical patterns that can be observed in the groups of countries we studied. We have always hoped that people studying other regions would not try to apply them unmodified, but instead would follow our approach, in the sense of developing models of their own ... the main goal of our research was to propose an interpretive

> framework for comparing systems of the relationship between the mass media and politics, not to label particular systems in different parts of the world. (Hallin and Mancini 2010: xi–xiv)

It is in the latter sense that this book attempts to develop a greater understanding of media systems cross-nationally. While Hallin and Mancini explored media systems generally, "with particular emphasis on strong or weak development of a mass circulation press" (2010: 21), the focus in this book is on a comparative assessment of public service and market-driven broadcasters (and online platforms) and the wider regulatory frameworks within which they operate.

Of course, as Chapter 1 explores in depth, public and private broadcasting cannot be crudely made into a dichotomy since broadcast ecologies have in recent years evolved into complicated multi-platforms with hybrid funding models operating in changing regulatory environments. Complex cross-national variations in the ownership and culture of news production thus bring inherent tensions and challenges for researchers when attempting to understand and identify the broad characteristics of news in different regions around the world. As Livingstone (2003: 480) has observed, in "cross-national comparative research .... Folk wisdom cautions against comparing apples and oranges. Anyone who has conducted comparative research will have been berated for attempting to compare unlike objects or categories." But in acknowledging the complexity of different media systems and accepting that comparative international research inevitably brings many sampling headaches, this should not invalidate or discourage ways and means of comparing communications beyond the safer confines of national boundaries. The aim of the cross-national comparative exercise in this book is to broadly map the type and nature of journalism produced by different media systems and to weigh up the relative merits of news coverage on a range of subject matter vital for citizens in a democracy.

Since news can mean reporting potentially anything going on in the world, a degree of semblance is necessary to ensure journalism is consistently analyzed on a comparative cross-national basis. Thus, whatever topics are explored need to be internationally relevant for points of comparison as well as broad areas already sufficiently researched so that existing publications can be pulled together and compared cross-nationally. Perhaps most importantly, however, the framework of analysis needs to revolve around topics where the democratic value of news is most evident. After all, a global case study of sports or celebrity-driven news would not, as Chapter 2 discusses, typically inform democratic choices about what is happening in the world or, to put it more grandly, empower citizens in the public sphere.

To address internationally relevant topics that can be compared cross-nationally, four broad areas of journalism will be explored. First, relatively routine periods of news media coverage will be examined, at a time when no major events, accidents, disasters or conflicts occurred (Chapter 3). The aim will be to generally assess public and market-driven news, examining what stories typically feature, how local, national and international news agendas are balanced, which actors regularly appear, and, in the context of the rise in "citizen journalism", the role citizens themselves play in making and shaping news. To interpret the performance of news media at a more critical juncture, the second area of journalism explored will be election news over the campaign period (Chapter 4). Since elections are considered to be key democratic moments, it will explore their prominence in the news agenda over the campaign period, the approach taken towards covering politics and the type of reporting pursued. The third topic includes another critical time for journalism – during moments of war and conflict, when news "on the ground" is difficult to establish and when concerns about objectivity or independence are raised as propaganda distorts the informational climate (Chapter 5). The fourth and final area of journalism that will be examined is the rise of 24-hour journalism or, more specifically, the editorial agendas of dedicated news channels on public and commercial stations (Chapter 6). The aim will be to explore the type of information conveyed in a fast-moving format and whether journalistic ideals about objectivity, accuracy and analysis can be sustained in a 24/7 environment. At a time when journalism is increasingly shaped by the speed of its delivery, the chapter will seek to evaluate whether accuracy or analysis have been compromised to break news first.

Like Hallin and Mancini's (2004) study, the book does not deliver new empirical pearls of wisdom but draws extensively on existing empirical research into news coverage that distinguishes between public and market-driven journalism. This will bring together evidence cross-nationally to paint a "big picture" analysis of the prevailing patterns and longitudinal trends across broadcast and online journalism. Since journalism studies has rapidly expanded over the previous decade, with more publishers interested in book-length endeavours, more dedicated journalism journals arriving on the scene, more established scholarly networks emerging (see Cushion 2012), the intention of this book is to draw extensively on the rich tapestry of research from around the world to develop a globally relevant case study about whether news ownership matters.

While the broad purpose of this book is to explore whether public or market-driven media produce distinctive news of democratic value, the wide-ranging nature of the inquiry examines different aspects of journalism that require more specific questions. In doing so, making nuanced distinctions between media systems cross-nationally and establishing the democratic value of news does not lend itself to a quantitative conclusion whereby the sum of all empirical news studies can be aggregated to answer a specific question. Instead, the book will qualitatively interpret the prevailing trends of journalism, mapping the characteristics of coverage and identifying where public and market-driven news is distinctive. While Chapters 1 and 2 provide a broad context to different media systems by drawing on relevant sources about government regulation, broadcasting guidelines, professional codes, journalistic cultures and public service charters, *the comprehensive review of empirical news studies carried out in Chapters 3 to 6 is primarily based on unpacking the key conclusions reached in academic studies*. After all, relying on the latest scholarship, most of which is peer-reviewed, offers the most robust methodological credibility to cross-national comparative studies about the democratic value of news operating under different media systems.

On the face of it, carrying out a comprehensive review of empirical news studies perhaps seems a methodologically easy option. Rather than having to carry out a fresh empirical study, the hard work of other scholars can be heavily drawn upon, entering key term searches into a library database and downloading relevant books and articles to generate a sample. However, the sample of scholarship brought together for this book was far from simple to assemble. In order to locate studies that compared public and commercial news studies, tools which included Google Scholar and the author's own library search engine were utilized, including the use of metalib – an electronic database that systematically locates key terms in a wide range of academic journals from a variety of disciplines. But while finding empirical studies about specific periods of time such as during elections and wars made life easier, the book also explores normal periods of time across different media. This involved trawling through hundreds of academic journals and book chapters to find articles that *could* contain empirical comparative data about public and commercial journalism. In this respect, the approach taken in this book is replicable, since almost all data sets drawn upon are publicly available subject to subscription charges for journals or access to sometimes expensive academic books.

This approach also included proactively locating empirical studies that compared public and commercial news media. So, for example, the author contacted a wide range of scholars for relevant material, having found publications on their web profiles or in the bibliography of a study that included such comparative data. Empirical findings were particularly difficult to identify in the case of book chapters sometimes hidden in volumes not always obviously relevant to news studies, since search engines often only locate journal articles by relevant key words. Part of this proactive approach also included asking scholars for their raw data sets where the public-commercial data had not been compared in a particular study. In Chapter 4, for instance, use was made of an SPSS file kindly emailed to the author by Professor David Deacon of Loughborough University on media coverage of the 2010 General Election, which revealed some striking differences between BBC and commercially driven journalism. Likewise, data were generated using SPPS files available at the PIREDEU data centre (www.piredeu.eu) and the author is grateful to Ingo Linsenmann for her guidance on downloading the relevant data sets about how different EU countries reported the 2009 EU elections. All of this took considerable effort and was extremely time-consuming. Had it not been for the study leave granted in 2011 by Cardiff University it would not have been realistically possible for the author to undertake such a comprehensive review of empirical news studies. But due to an exhaustive search for academic articles and books in a range of search engines and from proactively generating comparative data sets, *the evidence amassed in this book was based on over 250 sources and a wider review of academic literature.*[3]

While an extensive review of existing academic literature was undertaken, the study remained handicapped by a variety of practical limitations that need to be acknowledged. First, the author, with only English as a mother tongue, could not read non-English publications and translation was beyond the scope of the book's budget. Second, while the attempt was to compare public and commercially funded news media, many of the empirical studies located were based on television rather than radio or online samples. Third, in encountering these obstacles, it is difficult to claim that a balanced assessment of public and commercial news media from right around the world or in every part of their journalism has been achieved. The partiality in the review of literature, in other words, is driven by the inherent bias of journalism and communication studies already present in academic scholarship, which privileges Anglo-American authors, Western concerns and anxieties, and comparative empirical studies of television news above that of radio and online journalism (Curran and Park 2000; Cushion 2008).

Although the book was intended to be as globally ambitious as possible, with these limitations acknowledged above, many of the cross-national studies throughout the chapters that follow are published in developed countries such as the US and UK, in particular, but also in several European countries, notably the Scandinavian nations. But throughout the book data sets from other countries around the world will be explored together with transnational news media serving large geographic regions (this is particularly the case in Chapters 4 and 6). Of course, even among the most developed countries in the world there are many national social, economic and political differences shape the culture of news production. In comparing and contrasting the many hundreds of empirical news studies examined in this book, it was not always possible to unpack the wider context of why news is shaped uniquely from one country to the next nor was it feasible to generate the same level of discussion as the original article under examination. While this may frustrate some readers, this is an inevitable consequence of carrying out such an internationally diverse review of empirical news studies in a wide range of countries. Readers, in this respect, are encouraged to consider the primary purpose of this book – *to deliver an aggregate assessment of a large body of scholarship and reach broad conclusions about the weight of academic evidence overall*. Readers are invited to go back and revisit the original studies if they require more information or discussion or are curious about a particular national news culture.

However, the study does not claim to be a definitive or finished account of interpreting how far news coverage is shaped by different media systems. There will inevitably be gaps, areas of journalism less researched than others, and moments with clear, neutral or contradictory patterns of coverage. The intention is not to form simplistic distinctions but to track broad empirical patterns of news coverage, relating them back to news media ownership, with a view to mapping and understanding what existing scholarship tells us about the quality and value of journalism operating under different media systems, from different regions around the world. However, while the book is unapologetically evidence-based, it is not shaped entirely by an empiricist prism. In making sense of the many empirical studies in broadcast and online news drawn on throughout the book, wider academic debates in journalism about news values, election coverage, war reporting and rolling news practices will inform the discussion about the relative merits of news media operating under different media systems.

Chapter-by-chapter outline

Chapter 1 begins by introducing the philosophy and economics of public and commercial broadcast systems. The concept of public service broadcasting is defined and the hybrid funding models that have evolved over time briefly examined. This includes drawing on normative assessments of public service broadcasting, in particular the relationship a public model of media ownership is seen to have with democracy and citizenship. It will be explained how the infrastructure of programme-making on public service media is, in theory, driven by citizen needs rather than consumer demands. In respect of maintaining high editorial standards of journalism, Chapter 1 compares and contrasts the regulatory checkpoints broadcasters are subject to in many countries, asking how news is policed to ensure values of impartiality, objectivity, accuracy and balance are upheld. Beyond the formal mechanisms regulating the supply and content of news, the importance of cross-national journalism cultures to editorial standards is also discussed since journalistic values are not uniformly shared around the world. The final part of the chapter explains how public service broadcasters have evolved from the analogue to digital age, developing digital channels and expanding their journalism to online news media communications, prompting new regulatory questions and challenges. Since public service media operate in a crowded commercial market beyond just broadcasting, it will explore how they have exploited new technologies and faced criticisms about impeding the growth of the commercial media market-place.

Chapter 2 begins by considering how the news-making process is influenced by journalists. It explores cross-national differences in news cultures, levels of professionalization and ethical considerations that inform and shape the production of news beyond formal regulatory checkpoints. The chapter then turns more specifically to evaluating journalism, unpacking what is meant by "quality" news or news of "democratic value". In doing so, it compares how news values are made sense of by journalists and scholars, and asks what intrinsic democratic value news brings to citizens. As part of this the chapter draws on scholarly debates about how informed citizens need to be to maintain a healthy democracy. To sustain a vibrant and diverse news culture, the concept of pluralism is critically examined. It is suggested that regulatory controls to prevent the concentration of media ownership have often been inadequately designed by drawing on the plurality test developed by a UK regulator after Rupert Murdoch's attempted bid for full control of BSkyB in 2011. Chapter 2 then connects democratic theory with how to research the supply and content of news. While the methodological framework of the book has already been explained, this final section of the chapter briefly introduces readers to quantitative and qualitative approaches to studying news, explaining how the democratic value of news has tended to be measured in academic research.

Subsequent chapters focus on shedding empirical light on the comparative strengths of public and market-driven journalism. Chapter 3 examines the balance of local, national and international news reporting across media systems, asking if a distinctive "window on the world" is evident or whether a similar routine agenda is pursued. It draws on studies before wider trends of deregulation and commercialization had taken place and compares them to later studies to ascertain whether any longitudinal patterns can be traced. Contemporary trends are then explored, with public and commercial news agendas and sources used to inform stories compared and contrasted to assess if journalism can be routinely distinguished according to ownership patterns. More specifically, it then compares the supply and content of local and international news reporting, since public service media tend to have more regulatory obligations to cover more of the world, locally and globally. Finally, it asks if online news media have enhanced a more diverse news agenda and whether citizen journalism has contributed to this.

Moving from routine news coverage to election reporting, Chapter 4 asks whether public and commercial media remain distinctive at a critical moment in any democracy. Because of their perceived significance, elections are one of the most empirically researched areas in journalism studies. To do full justice to the depth of studies addressing the analysis of elections this became the longest chapter in the book. Chapter 4 begins by examining the regulatory frameworks across broadcast models during election time, asking if statutory requirements are likely to make and shape differences in election reporting. Longitudinal trends in election reporting are then explored cross-nationally, to once again assess whether commercial or deregulatory changes in broadcast ecologies have coincided with patterns in news coverage. It looks, in particular, at trends of Americanized election reporting and assesses how far these commercialized conventions have spread to other regions around the world where more robust regulatory checkpoints and public service media structures are in place. Coverage of televised leaders' debates – a familiar part of elections in the US but relatively new to many other advanced democracies – and the role of online news during the campaign will be examined in detail, notably in whether it has shifted more attention away from covering policy to reporting game-type conventions. The conclusion of the chapter compares the volume and nature of public and commercial coverage of "second order" elections, such as local, regional/state or European electoral campaigns, since these remain important democratic moments but tend not to be considered as significant as national elections by citizens.

Another significant democratic moment occurs during war and conflict, a time when journalists struggle to make sense of the facts in the face of much misinformation and propaganda. In order to be able to compare public and market-driven news coverage during wars and conflict, Chapter 5 examines first how each reported the aftermath of 9/11 and the run-up to the wars in Iraq and Afghanistan. Since the terrorist atrocities of 9/11 had global significance, cross-national differences are examined in detail to assess whether the relationship many countries had with the US, in particular, shaped news coverage subsequently. It then unpacks the reporting of the war in Iraq more specifically, comparing how far coverage about the military conflict, casualties, diplomatic efforts or wider international context was balanced by different media systems cross-nationally. It asks, above all, if journalists in countries such as the US and UK could remain independent at a time when their nations were at war. The chapter examines the role of embedded reporters, a technique more widely used in the war in Iraq and compares Western news coverage with reporting by Middle Eastern channels, most notably Al-Jazeera.

The last area of journalism explored in empirical detail is that of 24-hour news channels. Chapter 6 develops a comparative assessment of news channels operating under different media systems. While rolling news coverage deals with routine coverage, elections, wars and conflicts also, this chapter focuses on how different media have extended their journalism to the platform of 24-hour news and asks whether the democratic value of news has been enhanced. It begins by charting the rise of public and commercial dedicated rolling news channels since the launch of CNN in 1980 to establish how they have evolved around the world. Chapter 6 first explores channels with a global reach, comparing routine international news coverage of not just public and commercial broadcasters but state rolling news channels, since many new stations have emerged in recent years and it remains questionable how independent they are from government control. National news channels are then examined, comparing their rolling scheduling, news agendas and conventions used to report 24/7 journalism. Indeed, the last part of this chapter unpacks, in detail, the widespread use of live broadcasting or "breaking news" reporting on 24-hour news channels, asking whether these conventions enhance or compromise the quality of journalism.

The final chapter asks what impact public and commercial broadcasters have had on people's knowledge and understanding of politics and public affairs; whether they have encouraged citizens to participate in civic life by, for example, voting in elections or in raising political interest; and if audiences trust them to report what is happening in the world. It compares, in short, to what degree public and market-driven news media have helped to promote an active and informed citizenry. The last section of the book reflects on the significance of the conclusions established throughout each chapter to generate a wider discussion relating to the central question posed in this study – what is the democratic value of news produced by public service media compared to that provided by their commercial rivals? Put another way, it asks whether public service media matter to the future of news and whether citizens should continue to subsidize services already supplied by the market.

Chapter 1

The philosophy and economics of different broadcast models

How do funding models and regulatory frameworks shape the democratic value of news?

Introduction

Broadcast ecologies operate in unique ways around the world, having developed under political, economic and cultural contexts that reflect wider histories and traditions embodied within nation states. There are, of course, similarities and continuities in broadcasting across particular regions and neighbouring countries which have subsequently spread to other parts of the world. Western Europe, for example, has the strongest regional commitment to public service broadcasting and a robust regulatory environment, reflecting a longer history of government intervention (Collins 2002; Humphreys 1996). In the US, by contrast, the government has provided limited public subsidy for broadcasting, and its broadcast media have grown up in a free-market environment with a regulatory framework that has loosened in recent decades (Aufderheide 1999; Barkin 2003; Cushion 2012; Douglas 1987; McChesney 1993; Ouellette 2002). Since minimum government funding or intervention are needed for a market-driven broadcasting system to flourish, the commercialized model has become the dominant system in many countries (Hallin and Mancini 2004; Thussu 2007).

However, even in countries that have cultivated a US-style free-market system or within Western Europe where public service broadcasting is at its strongest, there remain important distinctions between media organizations. Around the world broadcasters have developed hybrid models sometimes unique to a nation, since many operate under different funding systems, financial resources, political interference, editorial autonomy, ethical standards, regulatory frameworks, technological capabilities, journalistic cultures and audience expectations. As broadcasting has moved towards multi-platform communications (Debrett 2010; Iosifidis 2010; Lowe 2010), shifting economic models of broadcasting, audience fragmentation, more commercialized editorial values and less robust regulatory frameworks have all impacted on national and international media ecologies. Against this backdrop, the culture of news production, the delivery of journalism and the consumption of information are being reshaped as broadcasters adapt to a far more competitive, multimedia environment.

Before interpreting the impact changing media ecologies and shifting regulatory frameworks have had on the democratic value of news (Chapter 2), it is necessary to introduce the different models and regulatory environments that shape the delivery of news programming cross-nationally. The philosophy of public service broadcasting, of course, stretches well beyond news and current affairs, offering a diversity of programming, most notably in the form of "quality" drama and minority or niche programming. This chapter will explain how, in most countries, the public contribute to public service broadcasting by paying for programming that, at least in theory, caters for a range of citizen needs rather than consumer demands. It will begin by comparing cross-national media systems generally before examining how state, public and market-driven models are sustained economically. The concept of public service broadcasting is then explored in more depth, unpacking its main characteristics cross-nationally and introducing some of the normative claims made about its relationship to enhancing democracy and informed citizenship. To maintain high editorial standards of impartiality, objectivity, accuracy and balance, the regulatory frameworks policing news will be critically examined. While these problematic concepts are discussed further in the next chapter, this section considers how formal regulatory powers can safeguard editorial standards.

Beyond the formal mechanisms regulating news provision, a wider discussion of journalism cultures is also required since many countries interpret these editorial values differently. Moreover, the professional practice of journalism and the ethos of public service are discussed in the context of understanding the production of news cross-nationally. Finally, the chapter will explore how public service broadcasters have evolved in the "digital age". No longer confined to analogue space, it will show how public service media have developed digital channels and expanded into online communications, prompting new regulatory questions and challenges. In the context of a post-broadcasting democracy, the legitimacy of public service media in a crowded commercial market will be examined along with the way journalism has been able to exploit opportunities opened up by new technologies.

The philosophy and economics of broadcasting: defining the theory and practice of public service media

In comparing different media systems around the world, it is important to acknowledge the diverse ways in which broadcast models have evolved over the course of the twentieth century into the new millennium. As the "Introduction" to this book pointed out, since *Four Theories of the Press* was published in 1956, scholars have increasingly begun to recognize the diversity of media systems not just around the world but within regions of it. Indeed, Hallin and Mancini's (2004) *Comparing Media Systems* has not only become an important book for proposing three models that characterise media systems in countries from Western Europe and North America, it has also developed into a reference point for *disputing the generality of comparing media systems in advanced democratic nations*. These three models – liberal, democratic corporatist and polarized pluralist (introduced in the previous chapter) – have been criticized by scholars for too broadly conveying the 18 countries' political and news media structures. So, for example, Curran (2011: 43) has observed that:

> To accept the Liberal Model at face value requires us to overlook the fact that the North Atlantic group of four nations includes different geopolitical entities (a world superpower and a former colony (Ireland), whose party system and political culture are still profoundly influenced by the events surrounding its struggle for national independence), different types of state (federal, multinational and unitary, different political systems (presidential and parliamentary), different electoral systems (proportional and majoritarian), different political structures (where the political party is central and where it is not), different television systems ... .

The many categories that define a media system, in other words, can often be difficult to apply cross-nationally even in advanced democracies, since they represent a range of structural, cultural and political differences.

Blum has sought to extend Hallin and Mancini's categorization of media systems to countries beyond North America and Western Europe (cited in Thomass and Kleinsteuber 2011). These revised models are worth quoting at length as his aim was to describe the characteristics of media systems central to this book's inquiry – namely, media ownership, funding of media, state control of media and media orientation (among others, including dimensions explored by Hallin and Mancini) (cited in Thomass and Kleinsteuber 2011: 32–3). In the process, Blum identified six categories that help paint a picture of where state, public and commercial broadcast models are located around the world and the extent to which they are found in countries that pursue a broadly liberal or regulated philosophy, or somewhere in between (see Table 1.1 and list below).

Six types of media system

1 *The Atlantic-Pacific liberal model* – with A grades in every dimension – has a media system which is orientated to commerce, is autonomous and

Table 1.1 Categories of media systems

	A Liberal	*B Middle*	*C Regulated*
Government system	Democratic	Authoritarian	Totalitarian
Political culture	Polarized	Ambivalent	Concurring
Media freedom	No censorship	Cases of censorship	Permanent censorship
Media ownership	Private	Private and public	Public
Funding of media	Market	Market and state	State
Parallelism of media and political parties	Low	Moderate	High
State control of media	Low	Moderate	High
Media culture	Investigative	Ambivalent	Concurring
Media orientation	Commercial	Divergent	Public service

investigative. A typical example is the United States; Australia and New Zealand may also belong to this model.

2 *The Southern European clientelism model* – with a domination of B grades, which is typical of ambivalence – has a commercial-populist orientation in TV and an elitist public service-orientated print sector. Blaum finds it in Portugal, Spain, Greece, Malta and Cyprus, and possibly in Eastern Europe.
3 *The Northern European public service model* – with a strong mixture of A and B grades – has a public service orientation in broadcasting and the print sector. It includes Germany, Scandinavia, the Benelux states and France, as well as modernized Eastern European countries such as Estonia.
4 *The Eastern European shock model* – with dominating B grades – includes a strong state control of the media within a formal democratic frame, which represents a media system where the government interferes and breaches media freedom, as is the case in Russia, Belarus, Iran and Turkey.
5 *The Arab-Asian patriot model* – located between the B and C grades – postulates that the media are obliged to support development aims and are subject to censorship. Blaum names Egypt as typical for this model, as well as Syria, Tunisia, Morocco and Asian countries like Indonesia.
6 *The Asian-Caribbean command model* – with a majority of C grades – represents countries where the government has absolute control of the media, except that the market is used for funding them. China is representative for this model, which also fits North Korea, Vietnam, Burma and Cuba. (Adapted from Thomass and Kleinsteuber 2011: 33 citing Blum 2005; *original emphasis*)

It is in the Arab-Asian patriot model and Asian-Caribbean command model where either state funding or tight state control is most prevalent. These models tend to prevail in authoritarian or totalitarian political systems although since the 2011 Arab spring some of the countries falling into these models may need to be reassessed. Despite Blum identifying public service orientation and media ownership with some of the more oppressive media systems, it is important – and this is explored further in this chapter – to remember that a defining feature of public service media, in theory, is their editorial autonomy and independence from state control. The relationship between state and market forces is also more complicated than sometimes assumed. While the Asian-Caribbean model dominates in countries with largely state-controlled media systems, the market still plays a role in sustaining them economically under close government oversight.

In the more liberal media systems, commercial broadcasting is sustained by advertising without heavy-handed government regulation; products on television, radio or online media are sold to fund what programming is commissioned. Thus the commissioning of programming is largely a commercial exercise because it needs to appeal to the needs of advertisers. Since advertising tends to be aimed at particular demographics such as students, housewives or businessmen/women, programming is most often pitched at consumers with disposable incomes or affluent lifestyles. Most commercial media have to abide by advertising caps allowing a certain amount of minutes of advertising per hour that differ cross-nationally. But again commercial freedom varies. While there are no restrictions for advertising on US television, a pan Television without Frontiers Directive operates for EU members allowing nine minutes on average per hour, or up to 12 minutes in a particular hour. Many EU countries, such as France and Sweden, however, police advertising times more strictly (see Anderson 2005).

The mix between liberal and regulated media systems, notably in Northern Europe, is where public service broadcasting is most prominently located. According to Blum, these tend to be countries where there are divergent media orientations and more ambivalent media cultures, with moderate state control of the media and a combination of private and public ownership. The combination of these arrangements means that public service media are financially sustained under a complicated and diverse set of conditions cross-nationally. While commercial broadcasters have to rely primarily on market forces to survive, public service media tend to be funded by a variety of mechanisms either directly or indirectly by state subsidy. Table 1.2 indicates the level of public subsidies across European countries in pounds with the relevant euro exchange rate.

Since contributions to public service broadcasting have been converted without controlling for inherent economic differences (cost of living, GDP etc.) cross-nationally, Table 1.2 needs to be interpreted cautiously. But even after taking this into account, the annual contributions public media receive does differ in countries with similar economies. The Scandinavian countries, in particular, have comparatively higher levels of funding. In the US, by contrast, there is no compulsory licence fee and limited funding is via a federal grant and private contributions made to its 348 affiliate member stations.

Table 1.2 Comparative funding for public service broadcasters in 12 European countries in 2009/2010

Country	*Funding*
Switzerland	£277.32
Norway	£265.53
Denmark	£261.98
Austria	£232.25
Finland	£202.96
Germany	£189.53
Sweden	£186.45
UK	£142.50
Republic of Ireland	£140.51
France	£103.65
Italy	£95.75
Czech Republic	£73.31

(Adapted from the BBC http://www.bbc.co.uk/aboutthebbc/licencefee/; euro exchange rate £1=€1.14)

Benson and Powers (2010) carried out a 15-nation study of public media in some of the most advanced democracies and, compiling data from a range of sources,[4] found that the US per capita had the least-funded system by some margin (see Table 1.3). They calculated non-public funding as licensing fees, sponsorships, programme sales along with advertising and, in the US, this also included business sponsorships, foundation grants and subscriptions.

In the chapters that follow, the analysis of news cross-nationally should be interpreted in the context of the public service model that produced it and the level of funding public media receive.[7] As explored so far, commercial, public and state media systems operate under different but sometimes overlapping economic, political and cultural models which will influence the production of news examined throughout this book. While public media or broadcasting are often understood *generally*, around the world they can operate under different financial constraints and editorial independence that may impact on the quality of journalism. But despite the difficulty in defining the institutional role of public service broadcasting, what it broadly represents is the recognition that in the cultural industries public funding in some form is necessary, since left alone to market forces the content of media is unlikely to fulfil the programming needs of *all* citizens in a democracy.

It is important, then, to move beyond funding mechanisms to recognize the philosophical purpose of public service broadcasting and consider how scholars have theorized the contribution it can make to society. In doing so, we can examine the normative claims often associated with public service broadcasting, which can be interpreted in light of the extensive empirical data drawn on in later chapters about the democratic value of publicly

Table 1.3 Funding public media in the US and 14 leading democracies

Country[5]	*Year*	*Public funding (millions in dollars)*	*Non-public funding (millions in dollars)*[6]	*Total revenue (millions in dollars)*	*Per capita public funding (converted into dollars)*	*Per capita total revenue (converted into dollars)*
Australia (ABC)	2008	728.9 (82.3%)	157.0 (17.7%)	885.9	34.01	41.34
Belgium (VRT/RTBF)	2008	805.1 (77.8%)	229.8 (22.2%)	1,034.9	74.62	95.92
Canada (CBC)	2008	1,013.3 (63.6%)	579.7 (36.4%)	1,593.0	30.42	47.83
Denmark (DR)	2008	717.0 (91.0%)	70.9 (9.0%)	787.9	130.52	143.42
Finland (YLE)	2007	526.0 (95.0%)	27.7 (5.0%)	553.7	99.00	104.21
France (F2/F3)	2008	3,211.1 (74.0%)	1,128.2 (26.0%)	4,339.3	51.56	69.68
Germany (ARD/ZDF)	2008	10,778.5 (86.2%)	1,721.5 (13.8%)	12,500.0	131.27	152.23
Ireland (RTE)	2008	317.1 (45.6%)	378.3 (54.4%)	695.4	71.65	157.3
Japan (NHK)	2009	6,900.0 (100%)	–	6,900.0	54.03	54.03
Netherlands (NPO)	2007	822.3 (68.0%)	386.9 (32.0%)	1,209.2	50.00	73.53
New Zealand (TVNZ/NZoA)	2008	126.5 (38.5%)	202.4 (61.5%)	328.9	29.63	77.05
Norway (NRK)	2007	636.9 (95.0%)	33.6 (5.0%)	670.5	133.57	140.62
Sweden (SVT)	2008	533.5 (93.0%)	40.1 (7.0%)	573.6	57.87	62.22
United Kingdom (BBC)	2009	5,608.8 (77.9%)	1,593.4 (22.1%)	7,202.2	90.70	116.43
United States (PBS/NPR)	2008	1,139.3 (40.0%)	1,710.0 (60.0%)	2,849.3	3.75	9.37

(Adapted from Benson and Powers 2010)

produced news. According to Christians *et al.* (2009: 76), "Normative theory attempts to link our everyday communication activities in the public sphere to a broader system of values that will help eliminate some of the contradictions in our actions." Moreover, it is a philosophical pursuit concerned with what communication *could* theoretically achieve as opposed to what it empirically delivers. This should not entirely divorce the real from the fantasy but open up a philosophical discussion about, in the case of this book, the democratic values that underpin contemporary news culture (explored in Chapter 2) and the public structures that can shape the architecture of high-quality journalism. While this book is primarily an empirical investigation into the role of public service news compared to commercial media, underpinning the inquiry is an attempt to measure whether the normative claims scholars associated with the concept of public service broadcasting stand up to empirical scrutiny. Although McQuail (2005: 179) has observed that "there has never been a generally accepted 'theory' of public service broadcasting", a broad understanding of the ethics and ideals underlying public broadcasting prevails. Moreover, these ethics and ideals can be contrasted with how state and market-driven media systems operate. Normative theory can thus help not only in understanding the origins of public service broadcasting, but can also act as a conceptual accomplice throughout this book to evaluate the democratic value of contemporary news across media systems.

Many scholars have defined the purpose of public service broadcasting by drawing on Jürgen Habermas's (1989) concept of the public sphere, since public media are seen to embody the normative possibilities of communication, counteracting the incursion of commercial values or preventing the state from disseminating government propaganda. In *The Structural Transformation of the Public Sphere*, German philosopher Habermas (1989) developed a normative set of conditions in which democracy could thrive if citizens had access to a diverse range of viewpoints, free from state influence or market interference. Democracies with a pluralistic informational infrastructure, according to Habermas, could reach rational decisions about the burning issues of the day, having formed conclusions based on an understanding of current events from a variety of perspectives. By the late nineteenth and twentieth centuries the media began to constitute the public sphere since first newspapers, then radio and television were where most people learnt about the world in order to deliberate about politics and public affairs. But as capitalism grew, most societies became more market-driven and the idealized democratic conditions – once present when information was protected from commercial corruption – began to deteriorate.

In what has become recognized as a neo-Habermassian approach, public service broadcasting is seen to encapsulate the normative democratic ideals of the public sphere. As Dahlgren (1995: 13) has observed:

> In Europe, the most explicit appropriation of Habermas' public sphere concept has been within the British debates where it has been utilized as a

> platform from which to defend public service broadcasting. There was a strong effort from the left to associate public service broadcasting with the realization of the public sphere, and to portray commercial broadcasting and the market model of financing as a serious threat.

So, for example, Garnham has argued that public service broadcasting delivers an egalitarian approach to informing, entertaining and engaging audiences. Whereas the market was made to fit consumer choices, public service broadcasting provides "all citizens, whatever their wealth or geographical location, equal access to a wide range of high-quality entertainment, information and education" (Garnham 1990: 120). For Scannell (1989: 140), the emergence of public broadcasting in the 1920s created public life, since prior to this "there were public events that took place in particular places for particular publics". While a mass newspaper industry was in operation, it did not imagine the world in *the same way for all* viewers as a public broadcaster (first radio, then television). Indeed, in Curran's (1991: 42) Habermassian understanding of public service broadcasting, he contrasts the "reasoned discourse ... its ideology of disinterested professionalism, its careful balancing of opposed points of view and umpired studio discussions" with "the polemicist and faction-ridden London press of the eighteenth century, operating in the context of secret service subsidies, opposition grants and the widespread bribing of journalists". Public broadcasting, put simply, is seen as operating above market manipulation or proprietorial propaganda, conveying a more rational "window on the world" for citizens to deliberate and form public opinion.

The historical interpretation of the public sphere has been criticized from a range of theoretical, historical and feminist perspectives (see Calhoun 1992 for overview). After all, the emergence of public service broadcasting coincided, according to Habermas, with a time when the public sphere was being "refeudalized" in the twentieth century. But in normative terms, the public sphere embodies many of the ideal communicative qualities necessary for a healthy democratic culture. Murdock (1992), for example, has suggested that, just as citizens have political and economic rights (to vote, to have access to state welfare), public service broadcasting represents – or, at least, promises – a set of cultural rights. These include rights to information, experience, knowledge and participation, which Murdock (1992) has suggested the increasing privatization of the communication industries are diminishing.

These conceptual rights have been practically applied in Michael Tracey's (1998) *The Decline and Fall of Public Service Broadcasting*. To fulfil conditions necessary for a healthy and sustainable public sphere, Tracey argued that public service broadcasting should be universally accessible, with universal appeal but catering to minorities and groups; further still, it should reflect the nation and its communities; it should inform and educate, allowing producers to innovate free from commercial constraints; and it should be funded by all citizens without relying on the market to sustain its income. In Tracey's (1998: 29) own words:

> Public broadcasting's very nature is ... to nurture the public sphere as a means of serving the public good. It understands that while within civil society individuals pursue their own private self-interests, it is within the public sphere that they function as citizens. It is a fundamental principle then that public service broadcasting must motivate the viewers as citizens possessing duties as well as rights, rather than as individual consumers possessing wallets and credit cards.

From this perspective, public service broadcasting adopts an almost paternalistic role in state affairs, with a self-appointed *raison d'être* to act in the "national interest".

It is in this context that public service broadcasters have found it difficult to shake off their laudable mandate of working in the "national interest". For acting on behalf of "the nation" public broadcasting can appear an anachronistic institution; in an age of consumer choice, top-down imposed programming is interpreted as anti-democratic – a reflection of middle- to upper-class priorities as opposed to what "the people" want. As Collins (2004: 43) has argued, "Rather than a democratic public sphere, in which the actual experience and interest of a real empirical public was represented, monopolistic European public service broadcasters too often addressed the public experience and interests, the public sphere, of elites." Since the proliferation of commercial media in the late 1980s and 1990s, a democratization of broadcasting culture is claimed to have taken place. John Hartley (2005: 111) has suggested "In commercial democracies, long-term trends have encouraged citizenship itself to become a creative act. People are making themselves up as they go along ... I have called this phase of modern identity formation 'DIY Citizenship'." Freed from state control, market forces in broadcasting appear to have broken down relativistic values of snobbery telling audiences what they *should* watch, read or listen to.

In one of the most commercialized media landscapes, the US's public broadcasting service – PBS – has struggled to gain popular appeal among the multiplicity of television channels, capturing just 3 per cent of the audience (Miller 2010: 62). Ouellette (2002) has suggested that PBS in the US has largely failed because it promoted itself in opposition to the fun, entertainment-based genres on commercial television. It has become a worthy channel, where serious topics about politics and public affairs are aired, but it has failed to meaningfully connect with audiences. In other words, while viewers could enjoy the sense of being a "good citizen" if they tuned in, the channel's self-conscious attempts to stamp its public service credentials on programming have prevented an editorial agenda more attuned to mainstream audiences from developing.

But while PBS has long had to compete in a highly competitive media market, for many public broadcasters the emergence of cable, satellite and online media has brought new challenges to their identity and purpose. For the well-intentioned ethos behind public broadcasting – to act as the social glue that binds a country and to promote an understanding of the world from the perspective of "the nation" – appears somewhat quaint in an increasingly globalized media culture. As Dahlgren (1995: 14) noted even before the emergence of the Internet,

> public service broadcasting is so strongly linked to the nation-state. As a political unit, the nation-state is by no means on its death bed, but the growth of transnational economic and financial flows, coupled with migration and other forms of globalization, have contributed to eroding much of its former sphere of power.

While public service broadcasting aims to supply media content consistent with the philosophical aims previously discussed, creating programming that is viewed as relevant and important to "the nation" can prove problematic.

Of course, since public service broadcasting operates, in theory, with a guaranteed source of income, its financial security should allow for the delivery of a wide range of programming without having to cater for a particular demographic taste or conform to populist demands (Tracey 1998). As already outlined, a key philosophical aim of public service broadcasting is to make services accessible to all citizens, to remain appealing to all audiences while ensuring minority tastes and cultures are served since these tend to be marginalized in market-driven programming (Tracey 1998). This has typically included, among other genres, children's programming, science, religion, arts, current affairs and news. While fiction dominates, news programming across most European broadcasters makes up a reasonable share of the total spent on television genres (from 6 to 23 per cent). See Table 1.4 for a breakdown by genre in 2008.

Table 1.4 Percentage of time afforded to different genres across European public service channels in 2008

	UK	*France*	*Germany*	*Italy*	*Poland*	*Spain*	*Netherlands*	*Sweden*	*Ireland*
Other	7	17	11	3	4	2	–	5	14
Arts and music	3	22	13	16	9	6	5	9	1
Education	4	–	–	–	–	–	–	–	–
Sports	8	4	8	6	5	16	11	11	7
News	**14**	**8**	**9**	**13**	**6**	**20**	**23**	**8**	**11**
Entertainment	13	18	10	20	13	14	9	13	9
Fiction	25	17	30	20	51	27	21	22	54
Factual	27	14	19	19	10	15	32	32	3

(Adapted from Ofcom 2009)

In some countries commercial broadcasters are also legally required to deliver a quota of programming as opposed to only commissioning populist programming – sports, game shows, soap operas etc. – that appeal to advertisers. In the Netherlands, for example, the Media Act of 1987, revised in 2008, stipulates that at least 50 per cent of all public and private programming must be news, cultural and educational (Almiron *et al.* 2010). While for some commercial broadcasters there may be minimal commitments or none whatsoever, other commercial stations – such as those in the UK, including ITV, Channel 4 and, to lesser extent, Five – operate as *commercial public service broadcasters*. And, like fully fledged public service broadcasters, they have to negotiate future broadcasting licences by agreeing to fund and schedule particular types of programming at certain times.

The next section now turns to how the editorial standards of news on public service media are monitored and, moreover, the regulatory framework different media systems operate under when producing journalism.

Impartiality and regulatory bodies: shaping the production of broadcast journalism

News and current affairs have historically been central to the identity of public service broadcasting, a genre where values of accuracy and impartiality have been championed (see Chapter 2), making state interference or commercial pressure threats to the integrity of journalism. In many countries, public service broadcasting has been established to prevent state corruption and to act as a safe haven from market manipulation. In countries previously governed by corrupt regimes or autocratic leadership, the transition to democracy is often associated with a strong public service broadcasting infrastructure and a robust regulatory framework needed to uphold values of journalistic independence. So, for example, immediately after the end of South African apartheid, according to Barnett (1999: 650), there was "a dramatic upheaval of the broadcasting environment, involving the transformation of the South African Broadcasting Corporation (SABC) from a state-controlled broadcaster into an independent public service broadcaster, the establishment of a new independent regulatory body". While SABC has struggled to gain the kind of editorial freedom many public broadcasters in Europe have historically enjoyed (Dumisani and Siphiwe 2009), laying down public service broadcast foundations represents, at the very least, *an attempt* to create a more democratic culture in South Africa. More recently, countries in and around the Middle East and North Africa have sought to construct a more independent system of broadcasting modelled on BBC foundations (Ayish 2010a). Indeed, the public service broadcasting credentials established over many decades in countries such as the UK and Norway have influenced the type of broadcast systems adopted in other countries around the world. International bodies, such as the EU and the United Nations Educational

Scientific and Cultural Organization (UNESCO), have sought to transfer suitable criteria to countries where new public service broadcasters are being established. Afghanistan, Cambodia, India, Kyrgyzstan, Malawi, Panama and Sri Lanka are countries UNESCO has worked with in recent years to develop public service media frameworks (Stiles and Weeks 2006). Of course, news alone does not define the concept of public service broadcasting, but in up-and-coming democracies establishing an editorial charter independent of the state has served as an important shield from government control and propaganda.

Within many developing countries, in particular, it is important to acknowledge that different countries institutionally police regulation more [illegible] others. Where democratic institutions are in their infancy, for [illegible] practices set up to regulate broadcasting might have been [illegible] or be part of self- or co-regulatory codes of conduct, but this [illegible] translate into journalists complying with legislation or infor[illegible]ns. Nor, of course, does it mean media watchdogs are tenaciously holding journalists to account. There may be well-intentioned declarations from broadcasters to conform to new and improved standards in journalism or, conversely, grand promises from regulators to robustly monitor the production of news. But a historically unregulated culture will struggle to instantly conform to top-down rules and structures. The regulation of news media content is also shaped by the resources within a nation. Whereas well-established legal institutions operate to assist watchdogs or defend media organizations in many Western nations, in more developing regions around the world the resources are not always available to routinely monitor or intervene if illlegal acts are committed. In other words, caution must be exercised when comparing regulatory rules cross-nationally, since the wider environment might not be equipped to effectively regulate the content of media.

In broadcasting, well-established democracies tend to legally enforce journalistic conventions such as objectivity, impartiality, balance, accuracy and fairness. Needless to say, these principles are conceptually problematic when put into practice and scholars have operationalized them in different ways (see Hopmann *et al.* 2011 for review). Beyond preventing outright bias and partisanship, they are often invoked to achieve media pluralism. However, pluralism has also been difficult to theoretically define and empirically substantiate. Chapter 2 will examine the concept of pluralism and how it has been operationalized in the context of interpreting the democratic value of news. But if the problematic nature of pluralism is put to one side temporarily, notions of impartiality or goals of plurality are generally invoked to represent a widely held recognition that news should be regulated, in some form, to prevent journalism being distorted by state or private interests. It is in this sense that a UNESCO (2005) report suggested values of public service broadcasting to be distinguishable from other broadcast models. It stated: "While state-controlled broadcasting systems do perform certain public service functions, their control by governments, funding models, lack of independence and impartiality in programming and management, prevent them from being identified as PSB" (UNESCO 2005: 15). Likewise, the Council of Europe's Television Commission has asserted that public service broadcasting should deliver a "Strong sense of independence and impartiality, authoritative news, a forum for public debate, ensuring a plurality of opinions and viewpoints" (cited in UNESCO 2005: 17).

Of course, public service missions or codes of ethics can be *general* principles of intent or broad advisory guidelines for editors to follow as opposed to rigorously enforced regulatory requirements. Even in advanced democracies, public service broadcasters remain under threat from government influence. When analyzing journalism produced at sensitive political moments in subsequent chapters, most obviously during wars and elections, the book will evaluate whether news media operating under different media systems are able to withstand government pressure and abide by regulatory frameworks to safeguard their independence and editorial values.

However, the regulatory environment policing journalistic standards varies across different media systems. Moe and Syvertsen (2009) have identified three types of public service models with varying degrees of intervention into the broadcasting market. First, in countries where public service broadcasters have broad interventionist aims, they tend to be well funded and historically supported. This type is most prominent across Northern Europe, such as in the Scandinavian countries, the UK, Germany, Belgium and the Netherlands, but Japan's NHK is also classified. Second, public service broadcasters with some interventionist instincts, used to protect markets in national cultures, notably the case in France, Canada and Australia. Third, minimalist intervention tends to be found in countries where public service broadcasters are not well established or supported, and are "seen as a supplement to commercial services, and not as core national broadcasters" (Moe and Syvertsen 2009: 398–9). Greece, Italy, New Zealand, Portugal, Spain and the US have been identified as falling within this category. While these classifications provide a broad understanding of how interventionist particular nations are in broadcasting, to what extent has media regulation changed in recent decades?

Meier (2011) has developed a set of binary oppositions which characterize the prevailing trends between new and old systems of media regulation (see Table 1.5). Meier usefully displays the shift in regulatory power from a robustly policed state control to a softer mode of governance by a wider range of vested interests, most notably powerful media companies themselves, via informal means. While this was once viewed as largely a job for top-down state regulators, political institutions, such as the European Commission, appear to favour less state-imposed regulation and more flexible models of co-regulation or self-regulation (Trappel and Enli 2011). Bardoel and d'Haenens (2008) have likewise summarized regulatory trends in a European context identifying:

> a change from protectionism to promotion of competition; the separation of political and operative tasks (i.e. independent regulatory authorities);

Table 1.5 Old vs new: control, regulation and/or steering modes

Old, "hard" governance rules	*New, "soft" governance rules*
Statutory regulation by strong state	Co-regulation, regulated self-regulation or self-regulation
State and administrative actors as dominant players within institutionalized processes by law	All stakeholders participate within open proceedings and ongoing decision-making processes
Centralized structure and steering mechanism	Decentralized structure and steering mechanism
Vertical-hierarchical processes: ruling by command and control (coercive)	Open and horizontal-heterarchical processes: agreement by deliberations (discursive)
Irreversible, final decisions	Provisional decisions
Non-transparent (CHECK) power games behind closed doors	Transparent power games in different arenas with different stakeholders

(Adapted from Meier 2011)

> the shift from vertical (sector-specific) to horizontal regulation; the transition from national to supra and international regulation; and the change from state to self- and co-regulation in which private and societal partners are becoming more actively involved in regulation.

While general observations about changing macro regulatory models have been discussed among European scholars in particular, less attention has been paid to how *public service or market-driven news is regulated on a micro-level cross-nationally*. It is important, in other words, to assess what type of specific regulation is used to maintain journalism standards cross-nationally; how robustly it is enforced; and whether it has any legal basis. Table 1.6 lists key public service broadcasters across Europe, showing the legal regulatory framework they operate under and whether an external control body polices regulation.

Almiron *et al.*'s (2010) study examined how different broadcasting regulatory frameworks operate to ensure political pluralism. Of the ten countries examined, four have internal regulatory checkpoints to police their content (Finland, Germany, the UK and Spain to an extent) and the remaining countries largely rely on regulatory authorities to police pluralism (the Flemish community in Belgium, France, Italy, the Netherlands and Sweden). All the countries have regulatory codes relating to safeguarding pluralism and, in most cases, the impartiality of news. Again, as Chapter 2 explores more thoroughly, pluralism can be conceptualized and quantified in different ways. In Italy, for example, RAI's 2004 Act contains general statements advising RAI broadcasting outlets to provide content representing pluralism. In doing so,

Table 1.6 Public broadcasters' legal frameworks across European countries

Country	*Regulation*	*Public broadcasters' control bodies*
Belgium (Flemish community)	Constitution, Broadcasting Act, Federal Acts, Protection of Philosophical and Ideological Associations Act, VRT's Editorial Statute	Vlaamse Regulator voor de Media (VRM) (Flemish Regulator for the Media)
Finland	Constitution, Government Activity Transparency Act, Mass Media Act, YLE and Yleisradio Acts, Parties Act, YLE's Internal Code	Internal control
France	Constitution, Media Freedom Act, CSA control mechanisms	Conseil Supérieur de l'Audiovisuel (CSA) (Superior Council of Audiovisual Material)
Germany	Constitution, Interstate Broadcasting Treaty, State Broadcasting Acts, ARD/ZDF/Deutschlandradio Statutes and Recommendations	Internal control
Italy	Constitution, Parity of Access to the Media in Electoral Periods Act, Gasparri Act, RAI's Service Agreement and Ethical Code, AGCOM Statements	Autorità per le Garanzie nelle Comunicazioni (AGCOM) (Authority for Guarantees in Communications)
Netherlands	Constitution, Media Act	Commissariaat voor de Media (CvdM) (Dutch Media Authority)
Portugal	Constitution, Radio and Television Act, Electoral Acts, Journalistic Coverage of Candidates Act	Entidade Reguladora para a Comunicação Social (ERC) (Broadcasting Regulatory Authority) and Comissão Nacional de Eleições (CNE) (National Electoral Commission)
Spain	Constitution, State Broadcaster's Act, Autonomous Communities Broadcasting Acts, General Electoral Regime Act	Junta Electoral (Electoral Board). One central and three regional authorities
Sweden	Constitution Acts, Radio and Television Act, SVT-State Charter, SVT's internal guidelines	Granskningsnämnden för radio och TV (GRN) (Swedish Broadcasting Commission)
United Kingdom	Communications Act, BBC's Royal Charter and Agreement, BBC Editorial Guidelines	Internal control

(Adapted from Almiron *et al.* 2010)

RAI television channels offer a "plurality of partialities": meaning choice is seen as fostering necessary levels of pluralism.

Where pluralism is policed quantitatively (France, Italy and Portugal), political balance is largely achieved by allocating time quotas proportionate to the distribution of seats parties acquired after the election. France's CSA, for example, rigorously quantifies the appearances of political actors on news and other programming on a monthly basis to parliament, while in Italy AGCOM likewise records (by both quantitative and qualitative measures) minutes that are routinely scrutinized by a parliamentary committee (Commissione parlamentare per l'indireizo generale e la vigilanza dei servizi radiotelevisivi).

Within a European context, then, most broadcasters are legally obliged to ensure impartiality in news and journalism or, at the very least, operate safeguards to protect pluralism. Commercial broadcasters, in some cases, are regulated by the same regulatory bodies as public service broadcasters. France's CSA, for example, regulates political pluralism for private and public broadcasters. Many of the rules pertaining to balance and impartiality legally apply to commercial broadcasters.

In the UK, Ofcom regulates commercial broadcasters and, irrespective of whether commercial broadcasters have to fulfil public service responsibilities (as ITV, Channel 4 and Five do), all broadcast news programming is subject to the strict "due impartiality" guidelines. Indeed, while the satellite broadcaster, BSkyB, has no legal requirement to schedule *any* news or current affairs, like other commercial public service broadcasters it has to adhere to rules on "due impartiality". To quote Ofcom at length, broadcasters must

> ensure that news, in whatever form, is reported with due accuracy and presented with due impartiality ... . Impartiality itself means not favouring one side over another. "Due" means adequate or appropriate to the subject and nature of the programme ... presenters of "personal view" or "authored" programmes or items, and chairs of discussion programmes may express their own views on matters of political or industrial controversy or matters relating to current public policy. However, alternative viewpoints must be adequately represented either in the programme, or in a series of programmes taken as a whole. (Ofcom 2011)

In other advanced democracies around the world, distinctions remain between media regulatory bodies and practices. According to their regulatory bodies, for example, Canada, New Zealand and Australia appear to have different priorities in how they police the impartiality of news. According to the Canadian Broadcast Standards Council, it should

> be the responsibility of broadcasters to ensure that news shall be represented with accuracy and without bias. Broadcasters shall satisfy themselves

> that the arrangements made for obtaining news ensure this result. They shall also ensure that news broadcasts are not editorial.

Meanwhile in New Zealand there are clear guidelines on accuracy that oblige all broadcasters to "make reasonable efforts to ensure that news, current affairs and factual programming: is accurate in relation to all material points of fact and/or does not mislead" (BSA 2009). More specifically, it is stated that:

- The accuracy standard does not apply to standards which are clearly distinguishable as analysis, comment or opinion.
- In the event that a material error of fact has occurred, broadcasters should correct it at the earliest appropriate opportunity.
- News must be impartial. (BSA 2009)

In Australia public and commercial broadcasters adhere to different regulatory principles. The Australian Communications and Media Authority (ACMA) role is "to encourage providers of commercial and community broadcasting services to be responsive to the need for a fair and accurate coverage of matters of public interest and for an appropriate coverage of matters of local significance".[8] The public broadcasters, by contrast, have more robustly worded practices shaping their impartiality requirements in news production. For ABC this includes:

> a statutory duty to ensure that the gathering and presentation of news and information is impartial according to the recognized standards of objective journalism.
>
> Aiming to equip audiences to make up their own minds is consistent with the public service character of the ABC. A democratic society depends on diverse sources of reliable information and contending opinions. A broadcaster operating under statute with public funds is legitimately expected to contribute in ways that may differ from commercial media, which are free to be partial to private interests.

For the other Australian broadcaster, SBS, the principles seem a little less stringent but rules of impartiality nonetheless remain in place:

> SBS is committed to achieving the highest standard of news and current affairs presentation. To this end, all reasonable effort must be made to ensure that the factual content of news and current affairs programs is accurate, having regard to the circumstances, and facts known, at the time of preparing and broadcasting the programs ... . The requirement for accuracy does not mean that an exhaustive coverage of all factual material relating to matters broadcast must be presented. While the emphasis in news is the reporting of factual information, news programs, as well as

current affairs programs, may include comment and analysis. Reasonable effort should be made to ensure news and current affairs programs are balanced and impartial, having regard to the circumstances at the time of reporting and broadcasting, the nature and immediacy of the material being reported, and public interest considerations.

For commercial broadcasters, then, it can be observed that in some countries they appear less obliged to strictly follow formal legal requirements of impartiality in news or, if they are, their ethical guidelines on balance and objectivity are not necessarily policed as robustly as public service broadcasters are by their regulatory bodies. This is strikingly the case in the US, for example, where rules governing impartiality were abolished in 1987 after the Fairness Doctrine was considered an affront to free speech in the Reagan administration. Since a 1949 *Report on Editorializing* established the Fairness Doctrine, "US broadcasters had to 1) devote a reasonable percentage of air time to the coverage of public issues and 2) be fair in the coverage of providing an opportunity for the presentation of contrasting viewpoints" (Chamberlin 1978: 361). The relaxation of the Fairness Doctrine has not led, of course, to all US broadcasters entirely abandoning aspirations to be objective since many journalists remain ideologically committed to values of balance, impartiality and objectivity within their profession (explored further in the next chapter). PBS, for instance, continues to exercise strict impartiality guidelines and its journalists are expected to remain publicly non-partisan. Subsequent chapters will explore whether a lack of regulatory requirements relating to impartiality shapes a qualitatively different approach to journalism in routine times or at critical moments in wars and elections.

Within the commercial market in particular, many countries have adopted what is sometimes referred to as "light-touch" regulation. While "light-touch" is quite a vague term, generally speaking it implies a minimalist, hands-off approach to media regulation (Cushion *et al.* 2012). There are, of course, degrees of "light-touch" regulation cross-nationally, but what it represents is a broader trend in media policy-making that increasingly favours forms of self- or co-regulation as opposed to heavy-handed, top-down state intervention. The US has long pursued a light-touch approach to the regulation of news programming, promoting either a form of self- or co-regulatory solution. To a much lesser extent, it has been observed that many European countries have also increasingly pursued a *laissez-faire* approach under the auspices of audio-visual policy-making at the European Commission (see d'Haenens and Saeys 2007 or Trappel *et al.* 2011 for more detailed overviews of EU media regulatory policy). All of this makes it necessary – and the primary propose of this book – to *empirically examine the nature of news coverage operating under different media systems* in the context of how heavily or lightly they are regulated.

The next section now explores further how broadcasters have evolved in the digital, interactive era. In particular, it asks whether the current regulatory arrangements need to be reformulated to take into account the way journalism operates in the digital age.

Post-broadcasting future? Building and regulating online public service news media in the digital age

By the end of the twentieth century, television and radio faced new challenges in a far more competitive, market-driven and multimedia environment. No longer constrained by limited analogue airwaves, broadcast culture moved from an era of "scarcity" to "plenty" (Ellis 2000). A new digital and online era had not only made more broadcast channels possible, it had moved public service broadcasting into public service media (Iosifidis 2010) and communication (Lowe 2010).

In making sense of the technological shift in communication, scholars have suggested we live in a "post-broadcast democracy" (Prior 2007; Cohen 2010). Since a broadcast system has been surpassed by an online, digital media environment, the implication is that a new means of communication has displaced its predecessor. Of course, it would be hard to dispute that a new digital and online environment *has* evolved after the "old" broadcasting model. But whether or not this meaningfully warrants a radical democratic departure from the broadcast age remains open to question (see Cushion 2012). Television remains, in the budget of most public service broadcasters, the most funded medium. So, for example, Table 1.7 shows the BBC's breakdown of the 2009/10 licence fee resources by media, demonstrating that online services account for just 6 per cent of the total budget whereas television accounts for two-thirds of it.

On a more global level, television remains the most consumed form of media internationally and television news is where most people turn to understand the world (Cushion 2012). In this context, characterizing contemporary media culture as "post-broadcasting" does appear somewhat premature given the continued impact of "old" broadcasters such as television. If

Table 1.7 A breakdown of where the BBC spends its licence fee by media

Media	*Cost as a proportion of licence fee per month (£11.88)*	*Percentage overall*
Television	£7.85	66
Radio	£2.01	17
Online	£0.67	6
Other	£1.35	11

(Adapted from 2009/2010 BBC Trust Review)

anything, the Internet is likely to morph into the television set in future years, integrating its services into the TV box and, in the process, redefining how online media is routinely consumed.

In recent years there have been many promises that new media will revolutionize the communications industry. Considerable commercial investment has been ploughed into capturing the money-making technologies of the post-broadcasting future. But amid a fiercely competitive market, public service broadcasters have also sought to adapt and respond to the challenges of the digital, multimedia and online age. This is not a "new" development – as is sometimes implied by observers making sense of broadcasting in the twenty-first century – but included in strategies dating back to the early 1990s. Indeed, according to Debrett (2010), we have already reached the second phase of the digital era. Summarizing the new technologies available to broadcasters a decade into the twenty-first century, in *Reinventing Public Service Television for the Digital Future*, she argued that we have moved on from a "digital infrastructure by telephone companies, internet service providers (ISPs), and governments" since the new age "is being driven by content provision and user take-up" (Debrett 2010: 24). Facilitated by broadband connection, the second phase brings on-demand services like television via the Internet (Internet Protocol TV – IPTV) but is evident more widely "across a range of platforms – TV, computer, mobile phone and [the] personal digital assistant (PDA)" (Debrett 2010: 24). Public service broadcasters have sought to adopt new digital services to multiple platforms with varying success. Leurdijk (2006) has provided a useful typology of digital services used by public service broadcasters, demonstrating the range of media beyond conventional forms of broadcasting (see Table 1.8).

The process of platforms overlapping, sharing technologies, employers, audiences and content has become known as media convergence (Dwyer 2010). So, for example, podcasting – "distributing digitalized audio files to subscribing audiences" – has been embraced by public broadcasters around the world, converging media platforms to cultivate relationships with audiences (Murray 2009: 198). Likewise, broadcasting on TV is no longer reliant on real-time experiences; technologies like the iPlayer on the BBC or i-View on ABC allow viewers to go online for a period of days after a programme was first broadcast to "catch up" on anything missed.

For news more specifically, technological developments have made new forms of journalisms possible, including user-generated content or citizen journalism. In some countries, notably the UK and Australia, public service broadcasters have been at the forefront of experiments with how new technologies can engage and interact with audiences via a range of new or social media (Flew 2011; Harrison 2010; Wardle and Williams 2010). When relevant, subsequent chapters in the book will assess the impact new media forms have had on journalism, asking whether they have reshaped conventional understandings of production, content, distribution and reception. In doing

Table 1.8 Typology of digital services by public service broadcasters

Types of digital services	*Description*
Digital television channels	Simulcasting of general interest channels and new thematic or niche channels. Often broadcasting archive programme material in carousels, but sometimes also containing extended versions of programmes on the main channels and some new productions
Internet, channel and programme-related websites	Websites containing programme guides, channel information, links to programme-related websites or genre portals (drama, news, education, youth, multicultural etc.)
Interactivity	Text messaging, voting for candidates, playing in quiz and game shows
Video on demand, podcasting, vodcasting, timeshifting	Mostly in streaming format, making available archived programmes for time-shifted viewing and listening. Sometimes limited to the day after, in other cases whole seasons of series or programmes are available. Limited to material over which PSB's own copyrights and underlying or secondary rights. Little downloading of audiovisual material
User-generated content	Providing access to archive material for reuse by viewers and providing spaces for users to upload their own films and stories
Mobile television	Experiments with news, previews, extra information and other brief formats, usually related to open-channel television programmes
Digital radio channels	Simulcasting of general interest channels and new thematic or niche channels

(Source: Leurdijk 2006)

so, they will explore how existing news services have been integrated online since many journalists in the age of media convergence move from one medium to the next to report what is happening in the world.

In trying to make sense of media convergence, there has been a renewed scholarly interest in examining the infrastructure and digital ambitions of online public service media (Bardoel and d'Haenens 2008; Brevini 2010; Brugger and Burns 2011; Debrett 2010; Flew 2011; Lowe 2010; Lowe and Jauert 2005; Moe 2008, 2011; Murdock 2005; Murray 2009; Tambini and Cowling 2004). Within these accounts, general debates surface about the role public service broadcasting can play in the context of continued commercialization of the media industries, the breakdown of national audiences into fragmented consumers, together with the potential exclusion of online and digital technologies, since many marginalize users unable to take advantage of the avenues opened up by new technologies.

While Murdock (2005: 227), among many other scholars, shares these concerns about the possible exclusion effects of online media, he has argued that public service broadcasting could be "the central node in a new network of public and civil institutions that together make up the digital commons, a linked space defined by its shared refusal of commercial enclosure and its commitment to free and universal access, reciprocity, and collaborative activity". Although Murdock points to the democratic possibilities of a "digital commons", public service broadcasting has to negotiate these ideals in a far more commercialized environment compared to that existing when most were born.

Indeed, many public service broadcasters cross-nationally have struggled to adapt to the new digital environment and incorporate online technologies since wider social, economic and political forces have created inequalities of access – or a "digital divide" as it has widely become known – and have thus challenged the principle of universality in public service provision. While the EU, for example, set up principles as far back as 2001 endorsing online public service facilities, the national level of investment, time and energy in digital and online accessibility is what primarily drives levels of penetration in digital television and broadband technologies.

Table 1.9 gives a flavour of the disparity in digital and broadband penetration levels across some of the most advanced democracies. While some countries have struggled to move from analogue to digital technologies, many social, economic and political obstacles have impeded the establishment of a broadband infrastructure. If broadband penetration levels are examined on a more global scale, far greater inequalities of access are evident in the emerging democracies around the world, such as India (4 per cent), Brazil (21 per cent), China (26 per cent) and Russia (29 per cent). All of which, in short, makes it

Table 1.9 Percentage of broadband and digital penetration across advanced democracies

Country	*Broadband penetration (% change in brackets since 2004)*	*Digital penetration (% change in brackets since 2004)*
UK	70 (45)	91 (33)
France	69 (43)	81 (58)
Germany	62 (45)	48 (33)
Italy	49 (29)	71 (45)
USA	71 (40)	83 (37)
Japan	64 (25)	69 (31)

(Adapted from Ofcom 2010a)

important to consider the context of the wider digital and online infrastructure within a country, since public service broadcasters operate within different technological environments. While some broadcasters may be able to influence national infrastructures – the BBC, for example, was granted increased funding to encourage digital take-up many publicly funded media remain at the mercy of forces well beyond their control. In the chapters that follow, comparative studies of online news need to be interpreted within this context, along with the resources at the disposal of such services to deliver high-quality journalism.

Brevini (2010) has explored the relatively shortlived histories of online public service provision across the UK, Spain and Italy and found considerable differences in resources, editorial direction and content management. She found that the UK's online infrastructure was by far the most developed, having established an online presence since the 1990s and, in particular, an online news service that is widely used around the world. The BBC is the dominant online news provider in the UK but its success – as explored later in the chapter – has had to be scaled back in recent years by regulators because it has ostensibly stifled commercial growth in the market. By contrast, Spain's RTVE's online infrastructure has historically been under-resourced since its launch in 1996. According to Brevini (2010: 353), a "proper workforce, resources and funding" was not in place in Spain until 2008 but since then RTVE's journalism has been vastly improved by a multimedia website and iPlayer type capabilities. It, nonetheless, lags behind many commercial online services such as El Mundo. Italy's RAI, likewise, has been a slow starter in the online world, partly because its "expansion was never a priority for RAI executives or for the political majorities in power" (Brevini 2010: 353). RAI NET, which develops much of its online activity, is funded by just 0.2 per cent of RAI's overall budget. Since Italy's online presence remains understaffed and under-resourced, Kataweb and RCS (online publishers for the commercial news outlets *La Repubblica* and *Il Corriere della sera* respectively), are the dominant sources of online news (Brevini 2010: 354).

Trappel's (2008) analysis of Austria, Germany and Switzerland also demonstrates a disparity in online market dominance from commercial or public service outlets. While Austria's ORF is the most popular news source, in Germany a joint tabloid/telecommunications venture – Bild.T-Online – is the most visited site. In Switzerland, meanwhile, the public service broadcaster only initiated its online services in 2005, which has allowed the popular newspapers, *20 Minuten*, *Blick*, *Tagesanzeiger* and *Neue Zürcher* to capture the online news market.

This brief comparative analysis of six countries historically committed to public service broadcasting, then, reveals in each nation varying levels of commercial/public service dominance in the online news market. Of course, whereas most public service broadcasters were born into an era when the state monopolized the market, in highly sensitive market-driven economies state-assisted media face far tighter trade restrictions on what services they can provide without being commercially anti-competitive. Despite the regulatory freedom with which the Internet is often associated, public service broadcasters in Europe have had the scale, scope and purpose of their online expansion increasingly scrutinized in a crowded commercial market. As part of a European Commission initiative to limit state interference in broadcasting – known as "State Aid" – public service broadcasters have had to develop online public service principles, on the one hand, while ensuring they do not distort the market on the other hand. In doing so, they have had to tread carefully with digital and online expansion as the EU increasingly polices the boundaries of their impact on the wider commercial market (Brevini 2010: 359). While many scholars point to how broadcasters have evolved in a global context, it is also important to recognize that they remain firmly anchored by national or regional market forces.

In particular, the BBC's online expansion has proven commercially controversial since it began in 1994 (although it was officially rebranded to include a news service in 1997). Its vast online infrastructure is estimated to have more than 2 million pages of information available and reaches 38 per cent of the UK population per week. As a result, it has been argued within the commercial sector that the BBC's online infrastructure is stifling competition and discourages new market-led online news sites. Most recently, the BBC News iphone application was subject to BBC Trust approval to ensure that it would not distort the emerging commercial market of news via mobile-phone technologies (Plunkett 2010).

The BBC, of course, is not alone: public service broadcasters around the world have been accused of encroaching on commercial territory or being anti-competitive in developing new digital channels, online sources or mobile-phone accessories. Some scholars have recently suggested that more clearly defined principles of public service broadcasting are needed in the digital world to assess the specific role they play in the market (Brevini 2010; Donders and Pauwels 2010; Moe 2008, 2010; Trappel 2008).

In this context, public service broadcasters have had to sharpen up their own regulatory tools and demonstrate "public service value". Germany, the UK and Norway, for example, have sought to measure what value public service brings to the communication market. While cross-nationally this has led to competing definitions about what constitutes "value", more broadly it is an attempt "to define a legitimate remit for comprehensive public service media beyond broadcasting" (Moe 2010: 220). This enters into debates about public service broadcasters having to legitimize their presence in a crowed twenty-first-century media landscape (Moe 2011).

While the provision of news has been part of a general discussion about the "value" and "legitimacy" in twenty-first-century public service broadcasting, it has not been subjected to close critical attention cross-nationally. As this chapter has shown, in the digital age the commercial media market has grown rapidly and public service broadcasters have been part of this, experimenting with new technologies, and moving their journalism onto multimedia websites and wider mobile communication platforms.

The next chapter explains how this expanding range of journalism will be critically examined throughout the book. In doing so, it explores how scholars have previously set out to assess the quality of journalism and explains how subsequent chapters will evaluate the democratic value of news.

Journalism cultures and public service ethics

Chapter 2

Evaluating the democratic value of news

Introduction

In a speech to graduates at the University of Virginia in May 2010, the US president, Barack Obama, warned students they were:

> coming of age in a 24/7 media environment that bombards us with all kinds of content and exposes us to all kinds of arguments, some of which don't always rank that high on the truth meter. And with iPods and iPads; and Xboxes and PlayStations – none of which I know how to work – information becomes a distraction, a diversion, a form of entertainment, rather than a tool of empowerment, rather than the means of emancipation. So all of this is not only putting pressure on you; it's putting new pressure on our country and on our democracy. (Obama cited in Frisch 2010)

Ordinarily, when a politician attacks the latest technology, it can be easy to dismiss their view as being "out of touch" with the current generation's use of media. But since President Obama is often caught up in debates about the democratic potential of the Internet after running a media-savvy 2008 election campaign, his words resonate more than most. For what President Obama was alluding to is how the evolving choice of media culture can paradoxically lead to a reduction in diversity and freedom for citizens in a democracy. While audiences may be mesmerized by the latest mobile-phone accessory or computer console, the president was suggesting that amid the many pleasures these afforded, their underlying values and impact on democratic culture should not be overlooked.

The aim of this chapter is to critically examine the changing information environment in the context of assessing the impact on the *democratic value of news* for citizens. News, after all, is the dominant genre citizens turn to for reliable information about what is happening in the world. It can empower citizens by informing them about the social, political and economic events and issues that shape their lives. News, put more simply, is the informational fuel considered vital for a democracy to remain healthy.

Of course, not all news is necessarily "good" for a democratic diet. As this chapter will explore, in recent years journalism has been subject to a good deal of criticism for pursuing news that is more entertaining than informative, or for compromising on values of accuracy and balance to boost ratings and remain competitive. As the previous chapter outlined, in the face of commercial pressure, many public service broadcasters have sustained their commitment to the supply of journalism. But to what extent have they had to compromise editorial standards in order to remain competitive and justify their public funding? The purpose of this book is to shed light on the democratic value of news produced by public service media by drawing on a comprehensive range of empirical studies to develop a comparative analysis of journalism operating under different media systems.

This chapter begins by looking at the influence of journalists on the news-making process. It moves beyond the formal regulatory checkpoints examined in Chapter 1 to consider cross-national differences in news cultures, levels of professionalization and ethical considerations, all of which inform and shape the production of news. Attention then turns to identifying what is meant by "quality" news or news of democratic value. While journalism is often made sense of by a set of news values, it will be suggested that a more critical understanding of its democratic value is needed. Value-loaded terms such as "tabloid" or "broadsheet", "hard" or "soft" news can sometimes obscure rather than enlighten debates about what journalism can potentially deliver. Gans's (2009) conception of popularization will be drawn on to assess how news can be appealing but remain of democratic value. For, in assessing the quality of journalism, it will be seen that news can be entertaining as well as informative. After all, if news only appeals to a select few, its democratic value is limited to an elite sphere as opposed to a far wider constituency of citizens. Or, put more bluntly, journalism should be able to remain popular without being populist. In exploring the democratic value of news, wider debates in political science about how informed citizens need to be to act rationally in the public sphere will be addressed.

Since Western societies have become more information rich, delivering news from a multiplicity of sources, it is perhaps easy to conclude that citizens can pick and choose from a healthy market-place of news. However, a key part of the chapter will explore this pluralist perspective and how debates about pluralism have shaped an understanding of how news media diversity is measured. It will critically examine what is meant by pluralism, and suggest that its application tends to be invoked in broad conceptual ways that are both empirically elusive and open to much contention. The plurality test triggered in the UK by Rupert Murdoch's proposed bid to buy further shares in BSkyB in 2011 will be used to illustrate how pluralism can be narrowly defined by almost exclusively examining media ownership or audience reach as opposed to *editorial content*. It will be suggested that, to interpret media pluralism, studies need to also empirically examine, in detail, the editorial diversity of the news produced, also investigating whether the proliferation of media sources has brought more democratic choice and if knowledge has generally been enhanced.

The meanings of news "quality", "democratic value" and "pluralism" are discussed in the chapter to empirically inform the central question in this book – is public service journalism distinctive from market-driven news? But beyond an analytical approach to the democratic value of news, a wider discussion about researching news empirically is necessary. Many methodological tools exist to help researchers capture what constitutes news and how it is packaged and presented. Method guidebooks describing how texts – including the genre of news – can be broadly classified (e.g. content or framing analysis) or more closely deconstructed (e.g. discourse or semiotic analysis) are widely available today on academic bookshelves. But within the literature, it is often the methodological rules that are central to the discussion rather than an understanding of the wider democratic purpose of empirical pursuits.

The chapter, overall, is an attempt to connect democratic theory with how to practically research news. It develops an analytical framework which the book will broadly follow and includes a brief discussion about quantitative and qualitative approaches to researching news reporting. Subsequent chapters will draw heavily on empirical news studies, making it important to be aware of the methodological limitations shaping journalism research. After all, it is important to be aware of how scholars conduct research into news, since this is primarily the evidence used in this book to compare public and market-driven news media.

News, professional journalism and public service ethics: beyond the enforcement of top-down regulation

In understanding the impact of regulation and, in particular, interpreting how impartial news is practised and policed cross-nationally, the legal documents or general editorial codes explored in Chapter 1 do not tell the whole story. The professional values journalists hold cross-nationally and how they approach their job of news-making remain important agents in understanding the nature of journalism produced under different media systems. Cross-nationally, as Hallin and Mancini (2004) have pointed out, what is meant by professionalization can vary considerably. Moreover, they have argued that, the boundaries of professionalism "are ambiguous and their core definitions have been subject to repeated reinterpretation" (Hallin and Mancini 2004: 33). Consequently there has been much debate about what professionalization constitutes within national journalistic cultures, which strikes at the heart of what it means to be a journalist (Weaver *et al.* 2007). Since gaining employment as a journalist depends on nationally idiosyncratic institutions, traditions, experiences and educational levels, defining the values of journalism cross-nationally is deeply problematic. This was compounded in the last decade or so, with the very definition of "journalist" extended in some cases to anyone with Internet access and a basic level of software to develop their own brand of journalism in blogs and websites, or on new social media networks.

The expanding definition of journalism has often cast ordinary members of the public as "citizen journalists" or suppliers of "user-generated content". Debates involving citizen involvement in news often focus on the new technologies that facilitate greater interaction or freedom to make and shape the news. But the motivation for the public's participation in and contribution towards journalism can be generated by broader democratic interests. Take, for example, the movement for public or civic journalism that grew most prominently in the 1990s. On the one hand, the public journalism movement was a reaction to the increasing marketization of US news media over recent decades: many political economy analysts have shown that the increasing concentration of media ownership has created less localized journalism and cultivated a more corporate culture of news-making. These trends were – critics argued – contrary to the pursuit of a public service style journalism (Baker 2007; Croteau and Hoynes 2001; McChesney 2000). On the other hand, while the idea of public journalism was promoted as an alternative to mainstream media, it went beyond enhancing the supply of more publicly owned news or fashioning new journalistic values (Glasser 1999). As Christians's (1999: 75) vision of public journalism displays:

> The focus ought to be not on professional practice but on the general morality. How the moral order works itself out in community formation is the issue, not first of all what practitioners consider virtuous. The challenge for journalists is not to limit their moral perspective to their own codes of citizenship but to understand ethics and values in terms of everyday citizenship.

From this perspective, the purpose of public journalism is to develop a morally self-reflexive news culture in order to satisfy the needs of citizens in a democracy rather than consumers in a market-place.

In this context, measuring with any tangible precision what is meant by public service values is not only empirically challenging but theoretically awkward. Among journalists working in established media organizations, there have nonetheless been attempts to systematically explore what is meant by values of "public service" journalism. Beam *et al.*'s (2009) longitudinal study of US journalists measured changing attitudes towards the ethos of public service by asking questions such as how well they think they inform the public; how well they think their news organizations serve the public interest and all socioeconomic groups in society; whether a public service ethic has been compromised by the ownership status and locality of a news organization. Other questions were also posed about assessing the value they and their owners ascribed to journalism and whether market factors such as generating profit impacted on the quality of journalism (see Beam *et al.* 2009 for full questions). While they found "many journalists remain committed to public service as a core professional value" (Beam *et al.* 2009: 749), many also indicated that their resources and working environment were diminishing. Thus, overall they concluded by asking: "can that commitment [to public service] be sustained as new workers adjust to a changing technological and economic environment in which the people and resources for doing journalism grow more scarce?" (Beam *et al.* 2009: 749).

However, this cannot be entirely understood by corporate greed or increasing market pressures. As Beam *et al.* (2009: 747) pointed out, "it is hazardous to make sweeping generalizations about the impact of ownership characteristics on media performance". Indeed, the previous chapter showed both public and commercial media can have nationally unique public service responsibilities, orientations and regulatory frameworks which prevent straightforward correlations between news ownership and editorial standards. In this respect, it is important not to examine the ownership and regulatory structures that shape journalism in isolation; the practice of journalism must be understood in the wider cultural context in which it operates.

Zelizer (1997) has suggested we should not only attempt to understand how journalists operate by their professional status and editorial codes, but should seek to address their collective social experiences in becoming journalists and their everyday interaction with one another. She argues that journalists function in "interpretative communities", sharing similar experiences, knowledge and understanding of events and issues, and by constant interaction and negotiation collectively interpret what is happening in the world. To quote Zelizer at length:

> Reporters use discourse to discuss, consider, and at all times challenge the reigning consensus surrounding journalistic practice, facilitating their adaptation to changing technologies, changing circumstances, and the changing stature of newswork … . They come together not only through training sessions, university curricula, or formal meetings, but through stories that are informally repeated and altered as circumstances facing the community change. The collective discourse on which such a community emerges may thus be as important in understanding journalism as the formalized cues through which journalists have traditionally been appraised. (Zelizer 1997: 416)

As Zelizer makes clear, this is not to imply that professionalization does not have a role in shaping journalists' interpretation of news and application of journalism. Nor, for that matter, should it marginalize the significance of the regulatory environment in which journalists operate cross-nationally. The point is that journalists navigate their practices and understandings *collectively*. Hence when assessing the production of news it is important to recognize that "interpretative communities" (Zelizer 1997) exist among journalists nationally and internationally.

Hanitzsch *et al.* (2011) carried out a large-scale survey of journalists across 18 countries – Australia, Austria, Brazil, Bulgaria, Chile, China, Egypt, Germany, Indonesia, Israel, Mexico, Romania, Russia, Spain, Switzerland, Turkey, Uganda and the United States – and found that, while many journalists share an understanding of how journalism is conceptualized and practised on a global scale, many differences also remain. They concluded that:

> Being a watchdog of the government, to a lesser extent, business elites, as well providing political information do ... belong to the functions that have universal appeal. In terms of epistemological foundations of journalism ... personal beliefs and convictions should not be allowed to influence reporting. Reliability and factualness of information as well as the strict adherence to impartiality and neutrality belong to the highly esteemed professional standards of journalism around the world ... . Interventionist aspects of journalism ... are much less supported ... the active promotion of particular values, ideas, groups and social change is generally not a characteristic of Western journalistic cultures ... . Similarly controversial is the role of subjectivity ... . The ideal of the separation of facts and opinion does also account for substantial differences between countries ... journalists in the United States exhibit a remarkable tendency to let personal evaluation and interpretation slip into news coverage. (Hanitzsch *et al.* 2011: 14–15)

Thus, cross-nationally, while there are some uniform patterns in the way journalists understand their role, epistemological outlook and ethical concerns, there remain divergent understandings brought about by the different journalism cultures they inhabit. So, for example, Hanitzsch *et al.*'s survey (2011: 15) revealed that US journalists appeared to place less importance in the notion of objectivity, since many consider it acceptable to allow interpretation and evaluation to "slip into" everyday news coverage. Put another way, abiding by journalistic conventions of balance and objectivity – concepts unpacked later in the chapter – appeared less significant to US journalists than in other parts of the world. Historically, however, this has not always been the case. Tuchman (1978) once suggested that US journalists practise "strategic objectivity" when reporting news and justifying their news selection, drawing on well-established conventions, such as balancing opposing views, as a means of defending their independence and credibility when faced with criticism about biased media coverage. Over time it has been suggested that objectivity became the accepted ideological norm in US journalism and to a large degree shaped the professional identity of many journalists (Schudson 2001).

What Hanitzsch *et al.*'s (2011) survey suggests is that previous norms of journalistic objectivity in the US might be diminishing in a changing media and regulatory environment. As seen in Chapter 1, while in most advanced democracies around the world some form of state-imposed regulatory body remains in place to maintain editorial standards of accuracy, balance and impartiality, in the US these requirements have been significantly relaxed in recent decades, most notably with the termination of the Fairness Doctrine in 1987. Of course, this does not mean that all journalism produced prior to the Fairness Doctrine news was necessarily impartial or objective. Nor does it mean that all journalists have subsequently followed the same editorial codes of conduct, since there are different values policing the boundaries of competing news and current affairs programming. An NPR executive, for instance, was forced to resign in 2011 after allegedly calling Tea Party activists "racist" and suggesting that the Republican Party had been "hijacked" by the Tea Party movement. In doing so, Vivian Schiller, president and CEO of NPR, said the "remarks are contrary to what NPR stands for and are deeply distressing to reporters, editors and others who bring fairness, civility and respect for a wide variety of viewpoints to their work every day" (cited in Szalai 2011). Regulation, in this context, is not about formal obligations but the ideological environment in which broadcasters have to operate to maintain their editorial integrity.

But whereas many other advanced democracies around the world have a more resourced and healthy infrastructure of public media where robust regulatory checkpoints police the accuracy and impartiality of news carefully, in the US's market-driven landscape commercial media in the 1990s have rapidly expanded on cable, satellite and online platforms in a self-regulatory environment. In the chapters that follow, the cross-national analysis of different media systems needs to be interpreted not just in the context of formal statutory regulation, but by comparative news cultures and contrasting professional ethics that help shape journalism around the world.

Journalism, news values and informed citizenship: understanding the democratic value of news

When evaluating contemporary news agendas, scholars often turn to a set of news values to explain how journalists routinely select, shape and structure what is happening in the world. Journalists themselves, of course, tend to downplay a conveyor-belt interpretation of news-gathering since it diminishes their own editorial autonomy. But scholars have demonstrated that news is far from the "window on the world" it has set itself up to be. Instead news delivers a highly partial prism through which to view and understand the world, consisting of a select few characters and countries, with a familiar set of conventions and practices and a relatively predictable agenda of concerns and anxieties.

A voluminous literature stretching back to Galtung and Ruge's (1965) classic taxonomy of news criteria has long debated what values different news media subscribe to and what stories are most commonly reported (Brighton and Foy 2007; O'Neil and Harcup 2009). Values, in this sense, refer primarily to the type of news story most frequently pursued, such as reporting negative, predictable and unusual occurrences, covering elite nations or people, capturing an exclusive or being first on the scene. But news values tend also to be driven by what impact a news report will have. So, for example, a story is more likely to be selected if it is easy to understand, concerns a recent event or issue, or already holds currency or continuity for an audience without needing too much in the way of explanation (Galtung and Ruge 1965).

Needless to say, these news values are not uniformly found across different news media nor are they immune from change or renegotiation (Brighton and Foy 2007). The issue of what is "newsworthy" has become more debatable, varying between different media as news agendas become a cherry-picking exercise for segmented audiences in an "increasingly fragmented news market" (O'Neil and Harcup 2009: 171). In recent years, for instance, celebrities, whether pop stars, footballers or reality game-show contestants, have become "elite people" (Harcup and O'Neil 2001), while the priority granted to "breaking news" stories has enhanced the value of immediacy in broadcast and online journalism (Cushion 2012; Lewis and Cushion 2009). Cross-nationally, too, news values can vary and Western trends of "down-market" agendas should not be assumed to have spread right around the world. Nevertheless, by analyzing news values over many decades, scholars have broadly ascertained what typically constitutes "newsworthiness" according to different news media and journalism genres.

But while many decades of research have led to a broad consensus about the type of news values that meet the needs of journalists, there is less agreement about the values citizens need from news in a healthy democracy. Put another way, the "value" of news appears relatively clear-cut for journalists but its democratic value for the wider citizenry is more opaque. As Norris (2000: 32) has pointed out, "There are many approaches to defining appropriate standards that can be employed to evaluate the performance of news media." At the same time, when scholars interpret the normative value of mass media, they tend to connect democratic theory with the wider purpose and function of journalism (McQuail 2005). In doing so, many would not philosophically disagree with the classic liberal theory espoused by John Stuart Mill where the market-place of information promoted by mass media plays a normative role in promoting freedom of speech, holding power to account and, perhaps most recited, informing citizens about politics and public affairs. In most journalism or media textbooks, enlightenment philosophies are referenced (at least in the introductory chapters) or the notion of the public sphere invoked (addressed in Chapter 1) to generate a discussion about why journalism is important and what it delivers democratically. The democratic value of news, in this context, is often painted in the abstract, a celebration of its normative role established many centuries before.

But the reality of a busy newsroom culture or the economic imperatives shaping journalism should not be divorced from an understanding of the democratic value of news in a contemporary context. As classic liberal orthodoxy has evolved, information is far more readily available and citizens have access to a proliferating range of news media to help them understand what is happening in the world. In an increasingly information-rich culture, this inevitably raises questions about the "quality" of news and how it can be evaluated to deliver informed democratic citizenship. After all, while more information is available than ever before, it is important to critically interrogate what democratic value different media bring to a citizenry. The latter part of this chapter explores how "quality" news can be measured empirically, for now a wider discussion about the meaning of the term and the ways it has been understood in scholarship is needed.

In understanding "quality", media scholars have tended to focus on cultural rather than democratic value, drawing on eighteenth-century writers like Matthew Arnold to critique what is widely regarded as an elitist understanding of "culture" (Corner 1998). "Quality", in this sense, is reserved for "high" cultural texts such as Shakespearian plays, arthouse films and period dramas. In the 1980s some cultural studies theorists challenged these snobbish preconceptions, launching a fierce defence of "popular" or "mass" tastes (see McGuigan 1992 for discussion). No longer were "low" cultural texts, such as soap operas or reality game shows, dismissed in academic circles but rather they became celebrated with today's university library shelves full of scholarly interpretations of programmes like *Sex in the City* and *Buffy the Vampire Slayer*.

While a creeping sense of cultural relativism has entered into journalism studies in recent years, there remain relatively crude distinctions about the "quality" of news that can obscure rather than illuminate an understanding of the value of news. Crudest of all, accusations of "dumbing down" news coverage – launched, incidentally, by journalists themselves – have tended to distort serious debates in journalism scholarship (Cushion 2012). The "dumbing down" of news tends to represent a retreat from "hard", "serious" or "broadsheet" coverage (e.g. politics, business, economics and international affairs) and a more populist turn towards "soft", "light-hearted" or "tabloid" coverage (e.g. crime, sports, royalty and celebrity-driven reporting). While these binary positions have some merit in broadly tracing shifts in news agendas over time, they can reduce the democratic value of news to a simplistic dichotomy where a step in the direction of "tabloid" coverage is automatically interpreted as diminishing the "quality" of journalism (Lehman-Wilzig and Seletzky 2010). By the same token, a tabloid story can blur "soft" with "hard" news (an exposé of corporate crime), and a broadsheet story can conflate "hard" with "soft" news (an exposé of a politician's extramarital affairs). Characterizing trends in news coverage entirely by a hard/soft distinction can thus simplify the complexity of what journalism delivers, or distort its democratic value.

Thus, for example, where once tabloidization was widely viewed as a pejorative development, scholars have recently suggested that the term can encompass conventions and practices that enhance rather than diminish the democratic value of news. Sparks and Tulloch's (2000) edited book, *Tabloid Tales: Global Debates over Media Standards*, found that, outside Anglo-American circles, the concept of tabloidization was not used to portray commercialization or cultural degradation. Far from it, as one US contributor to the book has since claimed: "[in countries like] Mexico and the former Eastern bloc ... snappier, more accessible writing, concerns about engaging the reader ... were acting as positive forces for social change and democratic participation" (Bird 2010: 13). By contrast, while some public media have attempted to rebrand themselves in recent years to shake off a reputation of serving elite rather than popular tastes (Hoynes 2003), when news programming has sought to appeal to a wider constituency of audiences (beyond conventional news and public affairs), it has inevitably led to concerns that "hard" news is being debased by populist news values. As Lewis (2006: 310) bluntly put it, "the pursuit of the popular is somehow in contradiction with serious public affairs content". From this perspective, journalism is constrained by "hard" and "soft" news conventions that could impede rather than enhance democratic citizenship.

But while adopting a more popular form and mode of address should be welcomed if it engages citizens in journalism, whether it enhances the democratic value of news should remain open to question. For while entertaining, emotionally driven and colloquially presented news need not be instantly dismissed as tabloid trash, if a "popular" brand of journalism is misinforming citizens about the world, cultivating apathy or breeding cynicism, its values may run counter to those concerned with enhancing democratic citizenship. So, for example, while the comedy news programme, *The Daily Show* (1996), has rightly been celebrated for engaging younger citizens in politics and public affairs, it has been argued that – like Fox News – its popular appeal is perpetuating a trend in US journalism that sees audiences increasingly tuning into news ideologically consistent with their own views (Cushion 2012). As many studies have shown, this does not mean *The Daily Show* is without democratic currency. But whether pursuing a comic or serious approach to journalism, seeking popular approval or addressing largely elite audiences, irrespective of "soft" or "hard" news labels, the democratic value of what news is produced and its wider impact need to be carefully interrogated. If journalism is not subject to critical evaluation, it invites a degree of cultural relativism where no judgment is made about its democratic quality and contribution to citizenship. If news is popular, in other words, it must be inherently democratic since audiences keep turning to it.

Herbert Gans (2009) has sought to theorize how popularization can be useful for journalism but draws a clear distinction between cultural and democratic value. He has written that:

> The news audiences' "need to know" as citizens should not vary by taste, culture or class; after all, facts and explanations are the same in elite as in popular news media. Consequently, the *substance* of the news should not vary by taste or class. However, such variation is acceptable for the *presentation* of news, for example, in the language and the level of detail. (Gans 2009: 21; *original emphasis*)

To put it another away, while the form and style of journalism should be moderated in order to be comprehensible to audiences, the empirical value of news (like remaining accurate or supplying interpretation) should not be sacrificed for populist purposes. By not compromising these journalistic standards, what is being implied here is that a shared sense of "quality" news exists together with a core set of values to which journalists should subscribe in order to advance an understanding of the world. However, to what extent *all* citizens "need to know" about the world, as Gans (2009: 21) has put it, has been the cause of contention in recent years.

Most scholars, of course, accept the general liberal orthodoxy that democracy relies on an informed electorate. But within political science in particular, it has been argued that citizens can reach rational decisions based on a limited model of knowledge. Citizens, in this context, can ration their intake of news by making rational choices about what they need to read, watch or listen to in order to remain sufficiently informed. Rather than making sense of the breadth and depth of the day's events, Schudson (1999) has proposed the notion of a "monitorial citizen", whereby individuals keep abreast of what is happening in the world by picking and choosing the news most relevant to their own needs. In doing so, citizens can take what have become known as "information short-cuts", reaching rational conclusions and remaining well informed to sustain the conditions liberal theorists deem necessary for a healthy democracy (see also Zaller 2003).

Since the availability of news in the digital, online environment has rapidly expanded in recent years, in theory citizens have far more information at their disposal and a wider range of sources to select from. But if, on the face of it, more information implies more choice, it should not be assumed that news media have become far more plural, delivering a diversity of views about the world or reshaping conventional news values. For while the acquisition of knowledge might appear easier in the "information age", it is a premise that rests on the quality of news being equally distributed across media systems. And yet, as Chapter 1 posited, many different media systems operate around the world, under different economic, political and cultural conditions. In this context, the structures that shape journalism are likely to impact cross-nationally on the wider information environment. We cannot divorce, in other words, the political economy of media systems from an understanding of the quality of news and the wider informational climate citizens inhabit. To explore how information-rich societies help shape journalism, it is necessary to critically examine how an understanding of pluralism shapes regulatory debates about establishing a diverse culture of news media.

Towards a healthy democratic news culture? Interpreting pluralism in information-rich societies

While plural, in a literal sense, means more than one, within media and communications studies *pluralism* has been used to interpret to what extent different perspectives are routinely drawn on by different news media. Since, to paraphrase Stuart Hall, the meaning of things, people, events and relationships can be constructed in radically different ways, media representations have the power to profoundly shape the way we view the world. And, if this power is held by just the state or the concentration of ownership is dominated by a select few companies, it potentially diminishes the diversity of information in the public sphere. Ensuring plurality in mass media is thus central to classic liberal theory, for it delivers a market-place of viewpoints and competing perspectives, from which citizens can rationalize and deliberate about politics and public affairs.

But while most scholars would approve the philosophical pursuit of pluralism, its application in debates about journalism tends to be invoked in broad conceptual ways, remaining empirically elusive. So, for example, politicians can often be heard championing a "pluralistic media culture" or conversely complaining about a lack of "pluralism in the media". When used in relatively vague terms, pluralism is always likely to elude definition, since it becomes an abstract construct or subjective judgment often politically motivated to highlight a perceived "left"- or "right"-wing structural bias in the media. As the media industries have rapidly expanded in recent decades, academic studies have examined patterns of media ownership, the consequences of market forces and approaches in regulation to interpret plurality in contemporary news cultures (Baker 2007). Legislators have begun to recognize the threat to media pluralism and, in some countries, have responded by re-regulating media ecologies to sustain a diversity of content (see Chapter 1). The European Commission has, for example, developed an extensive research project into risk assessment indicators for media pluralism, examining what plurality constitutes and how observing the diversity of media culture generally can be monitored by nation states.

And yet, despite many scholarly endeavours into media pluralism or proposed regulatory frameworks to police market power, ascertaining with any kind of tangible precision what news plurality represents has proven contentious. In Rupert Murdoch's attempted wholesale acquisition of BSkyB in March 2011 (his company, News Corporation, owned 61 per cent), for example, several months of external review and wider consultation by Ofcom (2010b) drew on a range of approaches to measure whether the bid would breach news plurality in the UK. Since Murdoch already owned a considerable share of national newspapers, and BSkyB supplied news for many commercial radio stations and TV's Five, and ran a 24-hour news channel, Sky News, News Corporation's complete control was interpreted as a threat to news plurality in the UK. While Murdoch's bid eventually failed (not because of the plurality threat but due to the phone-hacking scandal uncovered at the *News of the World*), it remains important to remember how pluralism was measured and understood. The terms of the review warrant brief unpacking and can be applied to broader conceptual and methodological debates about media plurality.

Ofcom conducted the review based on internal and external plurality tests. By internal plurality, it asked whether News Corporation would ensure sufficient plurality within its organizations e.g. would journalism be editorially diverse across Murdoch's own news-media platforms. External plurality, by contrast, asked how many organizations owned by different individuals were operating in the wider news-media environment and what influence and impact on audiences each had in the market-place e.g. were citizens consuming journalism editorially supplied by numerous different owners? To evaluate the impact and influence of different news organizations, three measures of audience consumption (share, reach and claimed use of news) were considered. In each case, news plurality was assessed by whether News Corporation would appear to dominate the market if the acquisition of Sky News was allowed. The review concluded that News Corporation's bid did potentially pose a threat to news plurality but this was resolved in subsequent negotiations with the government after it was agreed that Sky News would operate under external editorial independence.

Many possible criticisms can be levelled not just at the government's decision but at Ofcom's plurality test. Much of the attention towards Ofcom's (2010b) plurality test focused on Sky News and the extended audience reach the wholesale ownership of this channel would give News Corporation organizations as a proportion of the UK market. The possible infringement on plurality was thus narrowly defined around one news channel. In doing so, the cumulative impact of Murdoch's portfolio of news across different media platforms (national newspapers, television, ISP and online) was not meaningfully challenged or subject to critical review by Ofcom. This may be because it is more difficult in cross-media ownership to establish precise measures indicating a lack of plurality. But if these and other criticisms are left aside temporarily,

Ofcom narrowly defined plurality by almost exclusively focusing on audiences as opposed to the *editorial content* of News Corporation's many outlets or the wider environment of journalism in the UK. While relative measures of impact (primarily interpreted by audience share and reach) provided some insight into interpreting plurality, it neglected the *editorial diversity* of news supplied by different media owners. To define plurality by the *range* of media owners, in other words, appears to assume every owner pursues different editorial agendas.

For commercial news outlets, it is perhaps understandable that this has become accepted wisdom since many have distinct owners and separate editorial boards. However, powerful public service broadcasters, like ABC, BBC and NHK, tend to be narrowly defined because they are huge monolithic institutions. But what this conceals, as Chapter 1 explained, are the internal regulatory frameworks underpinning most public service broadcasters, a diversity of content in journalism and wider media services. Commercial broadcasters, by contrast, are market-driven, with editorial policy primarily determined by advertiser needs without such internal mechanisms to ensure programming is delivered to appeal to a wider demographic.

Compared to other genres, while news is closely policed internally and externally, its regulatory scope is not geared towards guaranteeing plurality. Instead, when assessing the diversity of news, impartiality guidelines are often developed to monitor the editorial direction of journalism. While this may prevent outright partisanship or sustained overrepresentation of one view over another, it does not deliver any diversity of content since every news outlet has the freedom to pursue its own unique set of news values. News agendas may thus appear innocently selected on the face of it (a tendency to run crime stories, say, or a propensity to source former military commanders). But news values, over time, can have profound political implications (encouraging a punitive response to crime that is shown to be on the rise or framing debates about the military tactics of a conflict as opposed to interpreting the wider reasons why war has been waged).

What was missing from Ofcom's review, then (and observable in the wider literature about media pluralism too) was an empirical assessment of the *diversity in news content* – not audiences – across the UK news landscape. For, while the 156-page review measured, in detail, audience impact and influence across a variety of media platforms, there was no sustained analysis of routine editorial output of UK news media. By excluding editorial content from an analysis of news plurality, the review potentially obscured how the diversity of journalism can be interpreted and evaluated on a comparative basis.

From an impressionistic point of view, the rapidly changing media environment appears to encourage choice and competition, and the availability of news media has dramatically expanded in the digital, online era. But it remains unclear whether more sources of information have enhanced people's interest in and knowledge about what is happening in the world. So, for example, since the market-place of news media has rapidly expanded in previous decades, it might be expected that levels of public knowledge have increased, with far more choice being delivered. In one of the biggest media markets – the US – where *choice* has been the operative word since the 1980s after multi-channel television arrived and, more recently, the WWW brought a plethora of information online. A Pew Research Center for the People and the Press (2007) report has suggested that levels of public knowledge changed little between 1989 and 2007. Drawing on longitudinal data asking normative questions that attempted to measure engagement in politics and public affairs, they found that "today's citizens are about as able to name their leaders, and are about as aware of major news events, as was the public nearly 20 years ago". Even if one argued this knowledge is not necessary for citizens in a healthy democracy, the survey suggests that the "information age" has not meaningfully enhanced what citizens know about politics or current events. While the generic boundaries of news have changed and become more entertaining in recent years, the report further added "that changing news formats are not having a great deal of impact on how much the public knows about national and international affairs".

The Pew study raised many questions about why public knowledge has not been enhanced by the proliferation of news sources now available in the public sphere. As already discussed in this chapter, some scholars have suggested that citizens are able to rationalize and understand politics in a way not necessarily measured by a civic-style approach to the acquisition of public knowledge. But perhaps most obviously, simply because more information is accessible now than in previous decades it does not follow that *more* people are turning to these new sources. According to Prior (2007), as media have expanded in recent decades the visibility of news programming has been clouded by the ready supply of entertainment channels and genres. Whether consciously or not, politics and public affairs can thus be more easily avoided (where once, when viewers had a handful of TV channels to choose from, citizens might have inadvertently watched news while waiting for a film or soap opera to start). Media choice, in other words, appears to have mesmerized many citizens, distracting them from serious news genres and potentially acquiring important knowledge about public affairs.

In this context, it is important to understand the wider culture of media consumption when interpreting how citizens routinely use the news and how they make sense of contemporary journalism. News, after all, has not evolved in a generic vacuum but in an increasingly competitive and commercialized environment. Writing at the turn of the millennium, Norris (2000) has argued that the proliferation of news sources has made news more appealing to contemporary tastes and values. She has written that:

> in post-industrial societies the news media has diversified over the years, in terms of channels, availability, levels and even the definition of news, this means that today information about public affairs (broadly defined)

> reaches a wider variety of levels and interests in the audiences. (Norris 2000: 317)

Pluralism, in this context, is interpreted not just by the multiplicity of platforms carrying news, but a wider understanding of what "news" is and how it can enhance a healthy democratic culture.

Over the last decade, it could be argued that the elements constituting "news" have diversified further, redefining and renegotiating what "news" is in an increasingly competitive and crowded market-place. For while news was once a largely serious business, today it is increasingly hybrid, splicing together conventions from various genres to inform and engage viewers and listeners in politics and public affairs. In the process, what is considered newsworthy, how news is covered and, moreover, how accurate or impartial it is, can vary substantially across news channels and programming. In contemporary journalism, after all, news values can involve highbrow political coverage and investigation of public affairs to entertainment, human interest and celebrity-driven stories (Harcup and O'Neil 2001; O'Neil and Harcup 2009).

At the same time, previous sections in this chapter have shown that democratic value is not necessarily enhanced by *more* platforms supplying journalism or mixing *more* serious news and entertainment conventions and values. Or, put another way, neither media choice nor cultural relativism can presuppose pluralism and extend the editorial diversity of news in the public sphere. To move beyond this conventional view of pluralism and explore the central question in this book – what is the democratic value of public service news compared with market-driven journalism? – a more sustained empirical analysis of *editorial content* is required cross-nationally. The next section now examines the ways in which scholars have studied news and generates a broad framework for how subsequent chapters will evaluate the democratic value of news in domestic reporting, in times of war and conflict, during elections and in rolling news journalism.

Measuring the democratic value of news: the methodological tools behind empirical studies

Since the aim of the book is to examine the democratic value of news across different countries and, importantly, between different media systems, a brief methodological introduction to the tools scholars typically draw on to research journalism is needed. As this chapter has already outlined, understanding what is meant by "quality" news or news with democratic value is problematic and contested. As Norris (2000: 33) has pointed out, the "reason for the lack of consensus about appropriate standards for the political performances of the news media is that values often are only loosely linked to broader notions embedded in democratic theory". While journalists conform to a relatively routine and familiar set of news values, these are not necessarily conducive to establishing news with democratic value. News, as previously discussed, can be entertaining, pleasurable and comical but if little to no understanding about politics and public affairs is advanced, its democratic value is less obvious. Conversely, if news distorts information, compromises on accuracy or objectivity, its own democratic value can be compromised, since citizens could be misinformed about what is happening in the world.

Needless to say, there remains much debate about how people become informed. Cultural relativists would dispute a normative interpretation of democratic value and point towards the unprecedented range of sources of information available to citizens. From another perspective, scholars have warned against dismissing the value of media devoid of news or current affairs. It has been argued that trivial shows can inadvertently redirect traffic towards more serious news media in a gateway effect for citizens. Nonetheless, few would dispute the need for all citizens to have access to information, analysis and context on issues that identify audiences as citizens rather than consumers. If news empowers democratic intercourse (Lewis 2006), access to coverage of the notable issues of our age – from the environment, ongoing wars and human rights violations, to elections and the economy – remains relevant to all, irrespective of specialist interests or entertainment value. What is selected as "news" and how it is constructed in journalism are, in short, critical to informed citizenship.

In unpacking the construction of news, scholars draw upon a set of methodological tools that can reliably capture and closely analyze the types of stories journalists routinely report. Academic literature about methods in journalism research, in this respect, often describes how texts – including the genre of news – can be broadly classified (e.g. content analysis) or more closely deconstructed (e.g. semiotics or discourse analysis). These approaches adopt what is known as a quantitative and qualitative approach to the study of news respectively. Since the book is primarily informed by previous empirical news studies, a brief methodological note on the aims of quantitative and qualitative approaches is needed.

Quantitative analysis would tend to examine a large output of coverage in order to be able to generalize from the sample what a "typical" period of routine reporting represents. The volume of news is determined by either the amount of news media (e.g. six international news channels) or the length of time (e.g. over four weeks) examined. The sample media or sample period tends to be determined by the resources available to each study, which in turn delimits the extent it can claim to be "typical" or "representative". So, for example, while an extensive study of a range of news media over a day provides a broad comparative picture of coverage, if a smaller sample of content is examined over a longer period of time its reliability is enhanced. To generalize the significance of news studies beyond a one-off time period, projects can be longitudinal in scope, examining trends in coverage over successive years. This is most evident in elections, where the same media over the *same* period of time are analyzed and compared to previous campaigns (see Chapter 4). By considering the volume of media examined and the duration of the study period in a quantitative news study, it is possible to evaluate how comprehensive it is.

To examine a quantitative pattern of news media, scholars generally employ a content analysis, defined as a "research technique for the objective, systematic and quantitative description of the manifest content of communication" (Berleson 1952: 147). Put more explicitly for news studies, the aim of content analysis is to quantify what is reported over a predetermined period without bias. On the face of it, this appears relatively straightforward, but establishing what aspects of news coverage to quantify reliably can prove problematic. Many content analyses explore trends longitudinally, sampling news every month or year, to assess whether the news agenda has broadly changed over an extended period. But content analysis can also trace, in some depth, underlying elements of journalism that determine what kind of democratic value it brings. *This is the central empirical goal of this book – to comprehensively explore previous news studies and develop a comparative analysis between different media systems.* For an interpretation of balance, impartiality, objectivity and news diversity – all values, as this chapter has explored, likely to enhance journalism's democratic functions – can be empirically measured by content analyses of news.

Using relatively clear coding measures such as news topic, prominence, length (in time or words), location, reporter location and source selection, these elements combined can begin to convey a general picture about what kind of journalism is routinely produced by different news media. By collating a range of studies cross-nationally, the book can thus generate significant comparative data about which news stories are consistently chosen (and ignored or marginalized); what prominence they are granted; which parts of the world they cover; which regions around the world journalists report from; and which actors (such as politicians, celebrities or citizens) routinely feature in journalism, to shape how issues and topics are discussed. While these comprise the standard set of coding categories used to explore the quantitative character of news coverage, content analyses can be more complex in scope. The many studies drawn on in the book do more creatively explore the quantitative character of news, attempting to measure the diversity of journalism from a variety of perspectives on different topics and issues.

Like any methodological approach, a quantitative approach can only tell part of the story. In weighing up the democratic value of news, many nuances elude content analyses and it is important to acknowledge the limitations of quantitative studies. The main criticism of content analysis, in particular, is that it provides more breadth then depth, quantifying news content in a relatively crude way. To explore coverage in more discursive detail, studies of news need to be more qualitative, selecting a smaller sample and unpacking its content in more depth. This moves from the selection to construction of news, where the language and style of particular stories are given more prominence in analysis. Framing analysis, in this respect, can incorporate some quantitative emphasis but the main aim is qualitative, interpreting the salient features of a news story. Or, as Entman has put it, to "frame is to select some aspects of a perceived reality and make them more salient in a communicating text, in such a way as to promote a particular problem definition, causal interpretation, moral evaluation, and/or treatment recommendation" (Entman 1993: 52). The purpose of frame analysis, then, is to empirically identify the frames that shape the news and to then uncover their meaning and wider significance (see D'Angelo and Kuypers 2010).

Discourse analysis, an exclusively qualitative method in news studies, shares many similarities with a framing approach. News, put simply, is treated as discourse, and deconstructed with critical interpretation about its underlying social, political and economic meaning. From an analysis of what journalists write or talk about, to a close textual reading of well-rehearsed news conventions and practices (Montgomery 2007), discourse analysis does not attempt to "objectively" uncover the news but to actively interpret the latent meaning of how the world is presented in journalism. Semiotic analysis, likewise, is a qualitative method where news is put under the microscope less for what information it literally delivers, and more for how visual clues in news stories, conventions and practices operate to communicate a message (Bignell 2002; Hartley 1982). For semiotics is the study of signs and, in studies of news, scholars act as meaning-makers to decode why news is constructed in certain ways and how this shapes our understanding of what is happening in the world.

This very brief discussion of qualitative approaches to news – framing, discourse and semiotic analyses – does not do full justice to the complexity of each method nor to what many scholars have established in journalism studies. While qualitative studies into news are drawn on throughout the book, for the most part quantitative evidence is explored in greater detail. This is not because qualitative studies of news texts are not significant to understanding journalism or informative about interpreting the democratic value of news. As already mentioned, quantitative analyses of news cannot always capture the nuance of news stories or explain how information is communicated. But the book, in this respect, is hamstrung by the available evidence of empirical news studies. Since most of these studies are quantitative in scope and need to be evaluated cross-nationally, the primary method drawn upon in this book is large-scale media content analyses of broadcast and online journalism. Where qualitative studies are relevant and instructive, they will be readily used to inform or shape the discussion.

The next section now turns to the first area of journalism explored in the book – namely, the comparative coverage of local, national and international news across different media systems.

Chapter 3

Reflecting a "window on the world"?

Reporting local, national and international news

Introduction

From decisions made in local councils to famine crises in remote African states, the "window on the world" many news media outlets claim to represent has become a more difficult "beat" to keep an eye on. While the availability of cheap technology has enabled journalists to report from remote locations more easily, maintaining an infrastructure of roving reporters right around the world remains, for many broadcasters, financially unsustainable. Paradoxically, covering what is local can also be highly costly for national broadcasters, many of whom are based in capital cities, making it a challenging prospect to reflect the diversity of countries which are geographically large or densely populated. What is more, as news has become more niche – sold to entice a specific demographic, or customized so people only watch or read stories in which they are interested – developing a news agenda that represents "national priorities" can prove problematic as shared national identities have grown increasingly diverse and complicated.

But while many scholars have begun theorizing the implications of an interconnected world (Rao 2009; Reese 2010; Wasserman and Rao 2008), what is less understood is how far contemporary journalism empirically reflects the everyday world (Cottle 2009; Thompson 1995). How far, in other words, do news media cover what is happening locally as well as globally? The aim of this chapter is to explore the balance of local, national and international news reporting on different media systems, asking if public service media convey a distinctive "window on the world" or whether they broadly share the same routine news agenda as market-driven news outlets?

Making sense of what routinely makes and shapes the news agenda should, on the face of it, be relatively straightforward to establish. After all, the voluminous literature concerning news values that now exists might conceivably be expected to occupy itself centrally with understanding which types of journalism are consistently pursued by different news media. In practice, however, when researching this chapter, it soon became apparent that many scholars discuss the relative merits of news values in academic books and journal articles *without* empirically assessing the content of journalism (instead tending to rely on previous data sets, e.g. Galtung and Ruge 1965; Golding and Elliott 1979; Harcup and O'Neil 2001) or by exploring atypical issues or events. Devoid of any fresh empirical understanding, academic engagement with news selection can sometimes be largely theoretical, making news values appear conceptually abstract. Or, more commonly, previous studies of news values are contrasted with practitioner accounts of journalism, which invariably challenge the academic premise of any kind of news taxonomy since journalists rely on "sniffing out" a "good" story.

When news content is examined, it tends to be aytpical moments, special events or topical issues that are subject to empirical analysis. Research funding, in this respect, perhaps drives what scholarship is produced, since empirical studies about elections – where grants are more freely available – overwhelmingly dominate the literature. But wars, terrorist attacks or certain topics in health, politics and crime are either sample periods or generic issues more likely to feature in academic publishing than "normal", typical periods of time when a wider range of stories might arise. Of course, a research bid sampling an "ordinary" period of time might appear less easy to sell than capturing an important democratic moment (e.g. election) or focused issue or period of time (e.g. year-long study of cancer in the news). But, at the same time, previous academic research suggests that media audiences tend to be influenced more cumulatively than instantly, with people's understanding of the world being cultivated over many months, even years (Lewis 1991; Philo and Berry 2011).

What this suggests, ironically enough, is that empirically scholars make sense of *extraordinary* news ahead of the ordinary – the central critique journalism scholars make of practitioners regarding the selection of news e.g. "if it bleeds, it leads". This is not to imply that the everyday character and nature of news have not been empirically studied or debated at length. It is that relative to atypical moments in journalism, there is arguably less empirical research into news when nothing necessarily major or significant has occurred. Needless to say, "everyday news" does not exclude extraordinary moments. After all, at any one time wars or conflicts are typically ongoing in several regions around the world. But the attempt in this chapter is to explore *news agendas generally* when the sample under analysis is not deliberately constructed by one dominant theme such as war, crime, terrorism, health, elections, education etc. The focus, in other words, is on how news topics are routinely balanced on different media systems.

Before turning to how scholars have made sense of *news agendas generally*, it is important to reinforce how the democratic value of news is interpreted in this chapter. While distinctions between soft/hard, tabloid/broadsheet and light/serious news are made throughout this chapter and book, these labels should not be interpreted alone as wholesale evaluations of their democratic quality. Categories of stories have been grouped together to identify broad themes and dominant trends which do not always capture the nuance of every news report. Indeed, as Reinemann *et al.* (2011: 3) have pointed out in a review of hard/soft news empirical studies, "there actually is no consensus in the academic literature on the definition of hard and soft news". In an analysis of 24 studies they found that hard and soft news distinctions were defined by topic, production, focus, style and reception. However, they identified that 83 per cent of studies used the "topic dimension" as characteristics of hard and soft news (Reinemann *et al.* 2011: 6). Although not all the studies drawn on in this chapter used this interpretation, most did use the topic as a way of interpreting hard or soft news categories. In light of Reinemann *et al.*'s (2011) review of academic literature, the chapter interprets hard and soft news by their conceptual redefinition:

> The more a news item is politically relevant, the more it reports in a thematic way, focuses on the societal consequences of events, is impersonal and unemotional in its style, the more it can be regarded as hard news. The more a news item is not politically relevant, the more it reports in an episodic way, focuses on individual consequences of events, is personal and emotional in style, the more it can be regarded as soft news. (Reinemann *et al.* 2011: 13)

The democratic value of news, in other words, is more likely to be enhanced when hard news is given precedence over soft news (see Chapter 2), even if these are not precise categories and can somewhat overlap.

The balance of "soft" and "hard" news on competing media systems: longitudinal trends in an era of deregulation and commercialization

In *News as Entertainment: The Rise of Global Infotainment*, Thussu (2007) chronicled the implications of privatization, liberalization and deregulation on the standard of journalism around the world. He concluded that "In a market-driven, 24/7 broadcasting ecology, television news is veering towards infotainment – soft news, lifestyle and consumer journalism are preeminent, a conduit for the corporate colonization of consciousness" (Thussu 2007: 11). Even in countries heavily censored or influenced by tight state propaganda, Thussu (2007: 76–8) has pointed out that traces of infotainment have suffused their news values in recent years, such as Russia and China. Likewise, according to Thussu (2007: 32–6 and 38–42), public service broadcasters have not escaped commercial influence, changing their programming to remain competitive in the 1980s and 1990s. But while there is evidence to support a shift towards more infotainment in news programming generally, robust longitudinal data sets *charting the changing content* of public and market-driven news over an extended period are not in ready supply. This section draws on longitudinal studies of news carried out in a number of different countries, all of which have been subject to wider changes in their broadcast ecologies making it possible to explore prevailing trends in journalism in the context of ongoing privatization, liberalization and deregulation.

Barnett *et al.*'s longitudinal study of all UK terrestrial channels' early evening and nightly news bulletins from 1975–99 (Barnett *et al.* 2000) quantified stories routinely featured, their length and order in the agenda (they split news categories into broadsheet and tabloid – defined in Table 3.1).[9] By analyzing news over a long period of time, Barnett *et al.* (2000) were able to identify by the incidence of stories and the time spent on them where news agendas across television news channels had changed. The 1975–99 study provided some clear-cut findings across broadcasters operating under different media systems (see Tables 3.2, 3.3 and 3.4).

At first glance, what stands out in Tables 3.2, 3.3 and 3.4 is a broad decline in broadsheet stories across UK television news, with the exception of Channel 4. Comparatively speaking, however, it is the main commercial broadcaster in the UK, ITV News, which has reduced the time allotted to

Table 3.1 Classification of story topics into broadsheet and tabloid categories

Broadsheet	*Tabloid*
Politics/economic policy	Crime
Business/industry/finance	Consumer
Social affairs	Tragedy
Legal	Weather (general)
Foreign relations/diplomacy	Sport
European Union issues	Royalty
Unrest/civil disobedience	Showbiz/entertainment
War	Human-interest/animal stories
Northern Ireland	Humour/quirky stories
Health	Expeditions/adventure
Education	Other
Employment/industrial relations	
Environment/ecology/planning	
Natural disasters	
Science/technology	
Transport	
Religion	
Culture/media/arts	
Moral/ethical issues	
Military/national security	

(adapted from Barnett *et al.* 2000)

Table 3.2 Percentage of broadsheet news from 1975–1999 on nightly UK TV news bulletins

	1975	*1980*	*1985*	*1990*	*1995*	*1999*	*Difference over time*
BBC 6 pm	59.5	49.8	45.2	59.8	60.7	44.6	–14.9
ITV early evening	59.5	49.8	44.3	55.8	51.4	43	–16.5
BBC 9 pm	59.7	39.2	44.6	56	56.3	43	–16.7
ITV late evening	55.5	46.9	45	53.3	48.3	29.8	–25.7
Channel 4 7 pm	–	–	49	54.8	54.8	51.9	+2.9

Table 3.3 Percentage of tabloid news from 1975–1999 on nightly UK TV news bulletins

	1975	*1980*	*1985*	*1990*	*1995*	*1999*	*Difference over time*
BBC 6 pm	18.4	18.8	25.9	6.5	17	28.9	+10.5
ITV early evening	15.4	22.6	32.2	18.7	29.5	33	+17.6
BBC 9 pm	16.2	17.1	22.6	4.9	13.2	13.3	–2.9
ITV late evening	14.8	18.9	24.9	10.9	26.1	42.1	+27.3
Channel 4 7 pm	–	–	11.1	5.1	4.8	10.6	–0.5

Table 3.4 Percentage of foreign news from 1975–1999 on nightly UK TV news bulletins

	1975	*1980*	*1985*	*1990*	*1995*	*1999*	*Difference over time*
BBC 6 pm	21.7	31.2	28.9	33.7	21.6	26.5	+4.8
ITV early evening	24.2	28.5	23.5	25.6	19	25.6	+1.4
BBC 9 pm	24	43.6	32.9	39.2	29.7	42.8	+18.8
ITV late evening	29.4	34.7	28.9	35.9	25.6	28	–1.4
Channel 4 7 pm	–	–	39.4	40.7	39.3	37.5	–1.9

(all tables adapted from Barnett *et al.* 2000)

broadsheet stories by over a quarter between 1975 and 1999 in its late evening bulletin. Likewise, both ITV's early evening and late evening bulletins increased their tabloid coverage by a considerable margin. The arrival of Five, a commercial channel launched in the late 1990s, had, by 2000, exacerbated the tabloid turn of UK television news. The time Five afforded to broadsheet news was 30.8 per cent, compared to 23.6 per cent on foreign news – leaving 45.6 per cent – the largest across the five channels in 1999 – dedicated to tabloid news coverage. While the BBC's early evening bulletin adopted a more downmarket agenda between 1975–1999, in its flagship evening show it marginally decreased its tabloid coverage. The BBC also

Table 3.5 Percentage of news topics on UK early and late evening TV news bulletins

Story subjects	*BBC1 early*	*ITV early*	*BBC1 late*	*ITV late*	*Channel 4*	*Five early*
International news	27.4	22.8	35	24.8	48.3	17.6
Politics	14.7	8.9	16.6	13	22.2	12.1
Social/economic	13.3	10.1	13	8.8	10.1	8.2
Sport	13	20.3	12.9	17.8	5.8	20.2
Crime	10.1	13.1	7.6	8.4	9	11.7
Entertainment/human interest	8.4	5.3	1.2	11.1	5	21.3

(Adapted from Hargreaves and Thomas 2002)

spent far more time on foreign news, a trend that has increased on both its public service evening bulletins.

Using a similar code frame, the disparity between commercial and public service broadcasters was reinforced in another UK content analysis study a few years into the new millennium (Hargreaves and Thomas 2002). Table 3.5 shows a more detailed picture of the divergence in story subject between bulletins and channels. Channel 4 was the most committed to political and international news. While the BBC bulletins similarly devoted a relatively high proportion to these serious genres, the late-night bulletin, in particular, is by far the least tabloid (e.g. entertainment/human interest). By contrast, Five spent more time on entertainment/human-interest coverage than political news and paid more attention to sport than international reporting. ITV, meanwhile, prioritized sport over more serious topics (in the late-night edition), and tended to favour lighter stories compared to the BBC or Channel 4. At the same time, however, both ITV and Five did place some importance on covering international affairs and continued to report political stories and social/economic affairs. This commercial commitment to harder news topics is not always present in other countries, such as the US, where television news coverage of international news in particular has declined in recent decades.

According to a 1998 report from the Pew Research Center Project for Excellence in Journalism exploring the changing definition of news from 1977–1997 on US television networks, print (*New York* and *Los Angeles Times*) and magazines (the cover stories in *Time* and *Newsweek*), foreign affairs is, across the board, a far less prominent part of the news agenda than in the UK (see Table 3.6). The Pew Center report observed that the nature of news had also changed. In US television network coverage, "the percentage of 'straight news' stories that simply described events dropped, and the percentage of stories that emphasized a distinct narrative theme from the journalist framing the event increased" (Pew Research Center Project for Excellence in Journalism 1998). The dominant narratives that emerged included scandals

Table 3.6 Percentage of news topics covered on US network, print and news magazines from 1977–1997

	1977	*1987*	*1997*
Government	34.3	31.5	21.2
Military	1.4	1.3	1.7
Domestic affairs	8.4	7.7	9.3
Foreign affairs	22.2	21.8	16.7
Total traditional	**66.3**	**62.3**	**48.9**
Entertainment/celebrity	2.0	2.8	3.7
Lifestyle	2.7	2.9	4.2
Celebrity crime	0.4	1.1	3.2
Total feature	**5.1**	**6.8**	**11.1**
Personal health	0.7	0.6	3.5
Crime	8.4	6.1	11.4
Business/commerce	6.6	8.8	6.8
Science	2.7	4.6	5.9
Religion	0.5	3.1	3.7
Disaster – natural/manmade	8	3.7	3
Other	1.7	3.7	3

(Adapted from Pew Research Center Project for Excellence in Journalism 1998)

– "up from just one-half of one percent in 1977 to 17% in 1987 and 15% in 1997" – and human interest and quality-of-life stories, which doubled over the twenty-year period (to 16 per cent). Examining local and national TV and print media, Patterson (2000) found a similar trend in his sample of US media, whereby journalism had downgraded the significance of policy-orientated news. The study showed that "News stories that have no clear connection to policy issues have increased from less than 35 per cent of all stories in 1980 to roughly 50 per cent today [2000]" (Patterson 2000: 3).

A 1972–1987 content analysis study identified a relatively less marked shift in soft television news coverage. Scott and Gobetz's (1992: 411–12) detailed quantitative analysis of the three US networks news coverage concluded that: "In the early 1970s average seconds per broadcast devoted to soft news for all three networks ranged from 59 seconds to 73 seconds, compared with nearly 90 seconds in 1987." While they conceded that there was an upward trend in soft news coverage, they interpreted these data without raising the same concerns as the UK and US studies previously cited. They pointed out that "given a newshole of about 23 minutes, it could be argued that the amount of soft news per broadcast is small by comparison to coverage of hard news" (Scott and Gobetz 1992: 411).

To account for the more striking shift in soft news and conventions post-1990, many broad trends in society need to be understood beyond those directly related to the journalism industry. Wider social, political and economic values, right around the world, impact on what journalism is produced and which topics are pursued. As the Pew Research Center Project for Excellence in Journalism (1998) put it,

> The news media are clearly now covering more of the society, moving away from institutional coverage of buildings and trying to make the news more relevant to audiences. With the end of the Cold War and other social and economic changes, the relevance of many traditional stories change, naturally moving the press in other directions.

It should be acknowledged, then, that the wider environment has, for better or worse, changed journalism. Put another way, shifting values in society are not divorced from shifting news values since they help shape what is culturally produced by journalists.

But beyond changing values in society, many scholars have interpreted a retreat from hard news topics in the context of enhanced deregulation and commercialization of the media industries throughout the 1980s and 1990s (Caldwell 1995; Hallin 1994; McChesney 2000). As previous chapters have explored, this period of time witnessed the advent of cable and satellite technology, as many governments (most notably in Western Europe) deregulated media markets to allow commercial vehicles to develop and, in some cases, challenge the hegemony once enjoyed by many state broadcasters. While the US has always had a market-driven media system, its relatively minimal public interest regulatory requirements were weakened further in the 1980s as deregulation was notched up a gear to stimulate competition and enhance journalistic autonomy and freedom from legislators (Cushion 2012). In doing so, by the mid-1990s, according to Hallin (1994: 117), US commercial television news had

> come to resemble more closely the pace of the rest of commercial television, with 10 second soundbites and tightly packaged stories. The agenda of news has changed, with fewer traditional political stories and more stories that 'tug at the heart strings'. And the pressure is far greater today for the stories to have high 'production values', both narrative and visual: drama, emotion and good video. (Hallin 1994: 117)

After the 1996 Telecommunications Act, the entire infrastructure of US communications was further deregulated (Barkin 2003). The Act had many consequences for the media industry – on radio news, for example, as significant layers of ownership laws were relaxed (explored later in the chapter) – but the impact of media deregulation was not isolated to the US. In the UK, the 1990 Broadcasting Act arguably triggered a downmarket swing in news values. The Barnett *et al.* (2000) study concluded this to be most prominent in commercial news programming: "there has undoubtedly been a shift in most news bulletins towards a more tabloid domestic agenda ... . This shift has been particularly apparent over the last 10 years in the two ITN bulletins" (Barnett *et al.* 2000: 12). On the basis of a detailed content analysis, Harrison (2000) suggested that even the BBC had changed the character of its journalism, although its soft news coverage was not as pervasive as that of commercial broadcasters. She observed that in the 1980s into the 1990s:

> The BBC ... introduced a variety of entertainment format changes (such as a new studio set, and other devices such as graphics to help tell and sell the story), and will continue to do so; but the content of BBC news (especially the nine o'clock news and BBC2's *Newsnight*) in the main still avoids an excessive coverage of human interest or people-centred stories, although this may be changing. In contrast, ITN's Channel 3 news programmes, GMTV News, Channel 4's Big Breakfast News and Yorkshire Tyne-Tees Television's Calendar News programmes all show a strong commitment to a high percentage of human interest coverage. (Harrison 2000: 207)

While the deregulation and liberalization of media markets in recent decades have often been pejoratively linked to the increased commercialization of news, competition alone should not be assumed to automatically diminish the quality of journalism. ITN's arrival in 1955 broke the BBC's state monopoly of journalism and, in doing so, several media historians have credited the commercial broadcaster with diversifying the public broadcaster's news agenda and style of presentation, making the BBC less elitist and delivering stories more in tune with the concerns and anxieties of ordinary viewers (Crisell 1997; Cushion 2012; Williams 1998).

In other parts of the world where a more commercialized broadcast ecology has also been pursued, longitudinal trends have revealed connections between deregulation and a shift towards "lighter" news values. Television and radio in New Zealand was dominated by a state-run broadcaster (TVNZ) funded by a licence fee and advertising until 1988. It was then restructured and required to operate at a profit. Soon after the broadcasting spectrum was opened up to encourage commercial competition and foreign ownership was welcomed, transforming the wider broadcast ecology in New Zealand. In the context of these developments, Comrie's (1999) study aimed to explore whether TVNZ had changed the nature and diversity of its coverage after this period of deregulation. Comrie explored whether journalism had editorially changed by examining the actors used to inform news reports and the length of time they appeared on screen (see Table 3.7).

A post-deregulation trend emerged in the declining use of official sources (e.g. national and local government, or nongovernmental organizations) – from 80.5 per cent to 71.5 per cent – representing, according to Comrie (1999), a commercial trend in downgrading the importance of public figures

Table 3.7 Average length (in seconds) and percentage of time spent on sources in TVNZ from 1985–1996

Source	*1985*	*1987*	*1989*	*1990*	*1996*
Elected politician	23.2	15.1	13.2	10.7	10.1
	24.9	23.7	22	24.9	18.1
Organization official	19.9	14.8	11.6	9.3	9.2
	26.3	21.5	23.8	17.1	23.3
Celebrity	20.2	12.2	10.3	9.4	8.6
	16.4	14.5	12.6	14.3	17.2
Participant	16.3	14.8	8.2	8.6	7.6
	12.1	16.5	12.8	13.8	11.5
Government official	16.6	12.4	11.7	9.5	9.9
	11.9	10.7	14.8	13.2	9.3
Victim	16.8	12	8.8	9.3	8.1
	4.2	5.8	4.2	10.1	3.7
Non-affiliated citizen	7.3	9.3	8	4.7	5.2
	2.4	1.5	4.7	4.5	10.8
Eyewitness	15	14.3	17	8.2	11
	0.2	3.3.	4.4	1.2	0.7
Affiliated citizen	13	10.9	8.3	6.2	6.8
	1.6	2.5	0.7	0.9	5.5
Combined sources					
All government sources	36.8	34.4	36.8	38.1	27.4
All official sources	63.1	55.9	60.6	55.2	50.7
Enterprise sources	20.3	26.3	22.3	29.4	31.5
Celebrities and victims	20.6	20.3	16.8	24.4	20.9
Average sound bite length	18.5	13.7	10.9	9	8.6

(Adapted from Comrie 1999)

(use of elected politicians, for example, decreased by a third from 1987 to 1996). While the study expected TVNZ to source celebrities and victims since this would signal, it was argued, "a move towards popularizing the news", there was no significant shift in coverage. However, when the length of time apportioned to sources was investigated, celebrities did appear more prominent (for victims this was less clear since their rise in 1990 was reversed in 1996). When sources were combined, recourse to government and other officials had decreased whereas use of actors from less formal backgrounds had increased (see Table 3.7).

Of course, the reduction of soundbites does not automatically reflect a diminished quality of news. As Fehrman (2011) has pointed out, a reduction in the space dedicated to elected representatives could represent "the rise of a more sophisticated and independent style of journalism … . Letting politicians ramble doesn't necessarily produce a better or more informative

Table 3.8 Percentage of tabloid and sports news compared with political news on TV1 from 1985–2003

	1985	*1987*	*1989*	*1990*	*1996*	*2000*	*2003*
Political news	32.9	36.2	27.1	26.5	26.6	20.9	21
Tabloid	15.8	21.8	27.6	27.3	25	26.1	26.2
Tabloid and sport combined	42.4	46	46.3	51.1	51.9	57.4	58.7

(Adapted from Comrie and Fountaine 2005)

political discourse". The use of soundbites in election news will be returned to in Chapter 4.

Another longitudinal study explored New Zealand's changing news agenda over a longer post-deregulatory period. From 1985 to 2003, a content analysis examined the proportion of time spent on political news compared to tabloid coverage (crime, accidents, disasters, human interest and public moral problems), and then combined these tabloid stories with sport reporting (see Table 3.8). The proportion of time spent on political news reduced from a third of all coverage to just a fifth compared to a corresponding rise in tabloid-type stories. Once again, a tabloid turn in news coverage coincided with a period of deregulation and increased commercial competition among broadcasters.

Indeed, many scholars appear to hold deregulation responsible for the changing nature of journalism beyond the countries previously explored. In Australia, for example, reflecting on the state of current affairs programming, Turner (2005: 17) has observed that:

> the effect of deregulation on television's responsibility for informing the public by no longer requiring the media to properly resource the reporting of social and political issues; and the responses of those in charge of television news and current affairs to these changes and pressures, are interrelated contingencies that have produced the current situation: where current affairs must now be considered an endangered format.

The Indian news market, likewise, changed throughout the 1990s as it was privatized and expanded its television news landscape. Rao has observed that "since liberalization and privatization began in the early 1990s, Indian media have adapted global news formats and made news more entertainment driven, as critics charge, by infusing soft-news stories about celebrities and cricket" (Rao 2009: 486). Needless to say, interpreting the role deregulation has had in reshaping national news agendas varies significantly from one country to the next, since not all countries have been subjected to the same levels of deregulation and privatization.

Of course, market power alone cannot fully account for characterizing changing news agendas in recent decades. In Djerf-Pierre's (2001) longitudinal study of Swedish television news, a phase in popularization – of hard to soft news – since 1986, was not only explained by the rise in deregulation and commercialization. For the wider professional cultures journalists routinely work in contributed to, in Djerf-Pierre's (2001: 256) own words, "specific practices of news selection and modes of representation, connected to systems of journalistic ideals and norms". As Chapter 2 explored, journalism cultures play an important role in shaping everyday news agendas and must be acknowledged, in particular, when making sense of journalism cross-nationally. But irrespective of *how* news has been reshaped, it remains the case that journalism *has* empirically changed in recent decades across both public and market-driven news media.

Contemporary news values: which stories typically make and shape agendas on public and market-driven media systems?

The focus now turns to making sense of contemporary news agendas, asking whether continued trends in privatization, liberalization and deregulation have encouraged news outlets to adopt downmarket news values and conventions in the previous decade or whether public service and market-driven media have resisted commercial temptation and maintained a commitment to hard news.

A content analysis study of nine countries painted a comprehensive picture of the type of journalism routinely pursued on public service and market-driven television news (Curran *et al.* 2012).[10] The selected countries, overall, reflected a mix of different broadcast ecologies – Australia, Canada, Greece, India, Italy, Japan, Korea, Norway and the UK[11] – operating under different social, political and economic cultures that shape what kind of journalism is routinely produced. The study broadly examined the same period of news coverage cross-nationally, comparing the main public service television and the most watched commercial news evening bulletins. Table 3.9 shows the balance between hard and soft news cross-nationally and across each media system.

With the exception of Italy and Greece, every public television news bulletin had a higher proportion of hard than soft news. While just over half of Canadian public service television was hard news, the other seven countries devoted 60.6–66.1 per cent of their journalism to more serious topics. The remaining nation – Greece – had a considerably "harder" news agenda (72.5 per cent overall). By contrast, four commercial television bulletins dedicated less than half of their coverage to hard news, three had between 53.2–59.1 per cent while Norway had 64.4 per cent. Greece, once again, had a considerably harder news agenda than other commercial broadcasters (85.8 per cent). Put simply, public service news bulletins around the world were more likely to cover hard news stories than their commercial rivals.

Table 3.9 Percentage of hard and soft news stories on public service and commercial TV news bulletins across nine countries

Country	*Hard news stories*		*Soft news stories*	
	Public service outlets	*Commercial outlets*	*Public service outlets*	*Commercial outlets*
Australia	62.6	48.4	37.4	51.6
Canada	53.4	56.4	46.6	43.6
Greece	72.5	85.8	27.5	14.2
India	63.3	49.6	36.7	50.4
Italy	46.2	59.1	53.8	40.9
Japan	60.6	53.2	39.4	46.8
Korea	63.7	49.9	36.3	50.1
Norway	66.1	64.4	33.9	35.6
UK	61.5	48.4	38.5	51.6

(Adapted from Curran *et al.* 2012)

Table 3.10 Percentage of public service and commercial news bulletins including policy or personalized information across nine countries

Country	*Policy*		*Personalization*	
	Public service outlets	*Commercial outlets*	*Public service outlets*	*Commercial outlets*
Australia	36.2	27	24.5	33.3
Canada	26	25.7	28.8	27.7
Greece	62.2	72.9	0.9	5.5
India	43.5	10.1	1	17.1
Italy	18.4	13.2	62.2	49.8
Japan	18.2	21.5	14.1	28
Korea	11.4	10.1	1.1	–
Norway	7.3	34.8	5.5	17
UK	29	17	17.9	25

(Adapted from Curran *et al.* 2012)

Beyond hard and soft news distinctions, Curran *et al.*'s 2012 study also explored the type of journalism pursued across the nine nations. They asked whether a news story contained any policy information and if a story was personalized, focusing on one or more individuals as opposed to addressing a general issue (see Table 3.10).

In each country, what stands out, above all, is the diversity of journalism pursued cross-nationally with varying levels of policy and personalization. But while acknowledging that journalists have different professional codes, conventions and practices cross-nationally (see Chapter 2), a pattern remains that broadly distinguishes public from market-driven television news.

Of the nine countries, six public service broadcasters had comparatively higher levels of policy-orientated news than commercial outlets. While Greece had a low level of policy across both media systems, perhaps surprisingly Norway's NHK had just over 7 per cent of policy-related news, three times less than its commercial rival. By contrast, six commercially driven news bulletins had higher levels of personalized news (although in Korea this type of journalism is almost nonexistent). In both Italian public and commercial journalism, more than half of all news was personalized. This suggests a cultural or professionalized trend, rather than one defined by media ownership and is consistent with previous interpretations of Italian journalism where more sensationalist or human interest stories shape news values (Hibberd 2008). But, overall, the nine-nation empirical study of television news content demonstrated that public service television journalism by and large had a more serious news agenda addressing harder news topics (in politics, business and public affairs), containing more policy information and less personalized coverage than commercial broadcasters.

Cottle and Rai (2006) have sought to unpack the discursive structure of television news coverage across several countries by moving beyond an interpretation of which stories are routinely chosen to understand *how* journalism is communicated. They systematically explored television news (both public and commercial) content across four nations (the UK, Australia, India and South Africa) and identified a complex "communicative architecture" (Cottle and Rai 2006: 163) underlying the production and presentation of television news. Cottle and Rai's content analysis developed eleven communicative frames, which they split into three themes. When news is analytical, it can either, according to their framework, deliver a relatively limited reporting frame or a more in-depth reportage frame. In news stories about a conflict, their framework suggested that communication can be differentiated by dominant, contest, contention, exposé/investigative and campaigning frames. Finally, when a story is more consensually driven, with no apparent conflict or opposing view self-evident, communication can be distinguished by community service, collective interests, cultural recognition and mythical tales (see Cottle and Rai 2006 for more detailed interpretation of frames).

Cottle and Rai's (2006) central argument related to the range and diversity of television's communicative complexity irrespective of media systems. However, a close reading of related articles comparing public and market-driven news within national contexts reveals (Cottle and Matthews 2011; Cottle and Rai 2007, 2008a, 2008b, 2008c), once again, a distinctiveness in how journalism is reported across media systems (see Table 3.11).

In three of the four countries, the commercial broadcaster delivered the most basic communicative frame of reporting. According to Cottle and Rai (2006: 172), this communicative approach provides "at best thin accounts of

Table 3.11 Percentage of frames shaping how news is communicated across commercial and public service news media in the UK, Australia, India and South Africa

	UK		*Australia*		*India*		*South Africa*	
	BBC	*ITV*	*ABC*	*Channel 7*	*Doorshian News*	*NDTV x24*	*SABC 3*	*eTV*
Reporting	33.8	65.4	48.4	60.1	63.3	64.2	54.7	50.8
Reportage	5.1	0.5	0.8	–	–	0.7	–	1
Dominant	7.0	18	11	13.1	20.8	20.2	6.8	3.1
Contest	0.7	1.6	12.3	4.8	5.8	2.3	6.8	5.7
Contention	41.2	1.1	9.1	2.7	3.3	4.6	18.2	19.7
Exposé/investigation	0.7	0.5	–	0.3	–	–	–	–
Campaigning	0.7	1.6	0.8	–	–	–	–	1
Community service	–	–	4.4	1	1.7	0.3	0.7	1.6
Collective interests	5.1	6.6	13.1	13.7	4.2	7.5	8.8	13
Cultural recognition	0.7	–	1.2	–	0.8	–	0.7	1
Mythic tales	4.4	4.9	1.2	4.1	–	0.3	3.4	3.1

(Adapted from Cottle and Matthews 2011; Cottle and Rai 2007, 2008a, 2008b, 2008c)

events, which are often presented as occurrences without context, background or competing definitions and accounts". Reportage, by contrast, attempts to communicate more "background, context and analysis" (Cottle and Rai 2006: 179). Only the BBC, a well-funded public broadcaster, conveyed a meaningful level of communicative depth (see Table 3.11).

In coverage where news is driven by some form of conflict, there are differences in how far the diversity of viewpoints can shape a story. While a dominant frame primarily relates to one powerful source, a contention frame draws on a wider range of viewpoints to generate more pluralism, adding more complexity to a story or issue. In the UK and Australia, public television news bulletins pursued more contention than dominance frames, suggesting more depth in their journalism. In India much less contentious frames were evident, but NDTV x24 – the commercial broadcaster – did contain marginally more than the public broadcaster. Meanwhile South African journalism had a relatively higher cross-national contention frame (about a fifth for each) although, once again, the commercial broadcaster had slightly more.

Finally, in stories where little conflict within a story is evident – what the authors label "consensual frames" – there are fewer notable differences between media systems and cross-nationally. Where a minor difference in communicative frames does exist between media systems is in the reporting of collective interests, which feature more heavily on commercial bulletins in each country. According to Cottle and Rai (2006: 177), this frame embodies "values and ideals of presumed shared interest and collective relevance and appreciation". It is perhaps surprising that commercial broadcasters appeared to reflect the nation more regularly, since traditionally many public broadcasters have been identified as shaping national identities (see Chapter 1). Instead, they convey cultural recognition – deployed to display and endorse views of multicultural difference – more often than their commercial counterparts.

Overall, then, Cottle and Rai's (2006) study found that the nature of conflict frames on television news reflected the different media systems, with UK and Australian public television news bulletins containing more pluralism when explaining a news story, issue or event. While there were minor exceptions to this cross-nationally (especially in India and South Africa) and within media systems, the frames identified suggested that public service media tended to convey more communicative complexity when telling viewers what was happening in the world.

Smaller-scale, cross-national studies have also shown important if sometimes subtle differences in how news is routinely communicated across public and market-driven media. Dimitrova and Strömbäck (2010) examined a large sample of US (ABC World News and NBC Nightly News, both commercial) and Swedish television news (Rapport and Aktuellt, public service shows, and TV4's Nyheterna), in order to explore the nature of political journalism across media systems. They found that, while politician soundbites were far shorter in US (on average, just 3.7 seconds) than Swedish television news (9.7 seconds), the latter featured more politicians as on-screen sources. Dimitrova and Strömbäck (2010: 496) also examined the conventions and practices of routine television journalism, including the use of a stand-up news reporter, an anchor interviewing journalists live on location or an anchor interviewing a journalist or commentator in a news studio. They found that US television news was approximately four times more likely to use these elements than Swedish bulletins (61.4 per cent of stories compared to just 15.8 per cent respectively).

The study also explored how television news is repeatedly framed, drawing on Iyengar's (1991) landmark study to compare relative levels of episodic and thematic framing. Episodic framing is defined as "a style of TV reporting that provides news coverage devoid of context, like a 'fleeting parade of events'" (Dimitrova and Strömbäck 2010: 493). Thematic framing, by contrast, "is less personalized, offers more background to news stories and shows relationships between actors" (Dimitrova and Strömbäck 2010: 493). They also included a responsibility frame, asking whether a news story dealing with "particular problems or information" offered "possible solutions to [those] problems" (Dimitrova and Strömbäck 2010: 493). Whereas 34.2 per cent of Swedish television coverage was thematically framed, just 7.8 per cent was in the US. Episodic framing, by contrast, was overwhelmingly present in the US and in just under two-thirds of Swedish television news coverage. In addition, the responsibility frame was rarely part of routine US journalism (3.2 per cent), but was close to ten times more common on Swedish television news (29.9 per cent).

All of this, according to Dimitrova and Strömbäck (2010), represented significant differences in news cultures cross-nationally, making generalized claims about *the nature of television journalism empirically questionable.* They suggested that political and media cultures might account for why journalism is made and shaped in conflicting ways, reinforcing Hallin and Mancini's (2004) framework for understanding why journalism is comparatively different cross-nationally. But Dimitrova and Strömbäck (2010: 498) also concluded that "commercialism might be contributing to the differences in television news format and framing between Sweden and the US". They interpreted shorter soundbites, less direct political sourcing, a low level of responsibility framing and higher volume of episodic framing as trends that adversely impact on the quality of journalism and the democratic value of news.

However, it should not always be assumed that a high volume of serious news content automatically translates to a journalism upholding democratic values of transparency and accountability. Bek (2004) carried out a content analysis of TV news bulletins on five commercial stations (Star TV, ATV, Show TV and Channel D) and one public service channel (TRT-1) in Turkey, exploring the actors sourced, themes addressed and type of language used. While the study found TRT-1 provided a distinctive service compared to commercial channels, its political coverage was rigidly formal, anchored in elite discourse, what Bek called "a forum for parliamentary protocol" (Bek 2004: 377). In sources routinely drawn upon to inform a news story, Bek found TRT-1 was heavily shaped by politicians whereas commercial channels featured more celebrities and citizens (see Table 3.12).

Table 3.12 Number of actors sourced in the news in Turkish news bulletins over one week

Actors	*Star TV*	*ATV*	*Channel D*	*Show TV*	*TRT-1*
Politicians (Turkish)	34	34	22	12	114
Foreign politicians	–	–	8	16	11
Experts	4	13	9	14	2
Celebrities	17	33	17	59	1
Private citizens	28	32	65	39	2
Military	3	4	2	1	10
Police	–	2	–	1	4
NGO/civil society organizations/ associations	–	4	6	–	7
Journalists	–	–	4	6	–
Other	18	22	13	7	3
Total	104	144	146	155	154

(Adapted from Bek 2004)

On the face of it, TRT-1's commitment to the political world could be commended. But Bek (2004: 378) argued that many of "the reports are quite bland accounts of cabinet meetings ... . TRT just reports that such and such politicians met, in a formulaic way". Thus, while the public service broadcaster was found to be unrelentingly serious, defining itself in contrast to the populist coverage of the commercial bulletins, it was in a way that did not necessarily enhance an understanding of what was happening in the political world.

In the US, where commercial network and cable news bulletins overwhelmingly dominate, PBS has similarly received criticism for being establishment-led. Scott *et al.* (2010) examined every on-air source on PBS *NewsHour*. In doing so, the study identified that PBS *News Hour* featured a high volume of governmental (42 per cent), journalistic (19.2 per cent), academic (13.7 per cent) think tank (4.3 per cent) and corporate sources (4.2 per cent). On key issues, such as coverage of the war in Iraq (see Chapter 5), governmental sources increased substantially (61.3 per cent). In routine coverage, by contrast, just 3.5 per cent of sources were from grassroots organizations. All of which, they concluded, suggested that PBS *NewsHour* lacked diversity in interpreting everyday news, drawing primarily on a narrow group of elites to shape how news is interpreted. While distinctive from commercial journalism (which one study showed relied less on governmental sources – see Jones 2008), it perhaps suggests that some public broadcasters can deliver a top-down view of the world, turning primarily to elites to explain what is happening in the world.

Beyond conventional news bulletins, there is evidence that more hybrid forms of television journalism on public and market-driven news media pursue contrasting ways of conveying news, analysis and discussion on topical issues. Stevenson (2010) carried out a systematic content analysis of political talk shows in New Zealand. The analysis broke down aspects of the show meriting the definition of "quality discourse", such as focusing on hard news, delivering a diversity of views, fostering reasoned deliberation and developing a more analytical approach to journalism. The way in which each programme – *Eye to Eye*, *Agenda*, *Campbell Live* and *Breakfast* – featured these elements was then measured and evaluated. Stevenson (2010: 870) pointed out that quality discourse was present across the board but there were important distinctions, with market-driven programming more "explanatory, citizen orientated, and not altogether devoid of argumentation and critical analysis" than in public service shows.

Nevertheless, public service programming, overall, was interpreted as supplying a more democratically healthy form of political talk. The evidence concluded that "(non-market) public service television generally provides higher levels of discourse quality in terms of argumentation, institutional political focus and diversity, and critical orientation than market political talk television" (Stevenson 2010: 870). Once again, while there may be some interpretation about what quality means and delivers, the study suggested that public service media provided an approach distinctive from market-driven journalism.

A "window on the world"? Comparing local, national and international news on different media systems

The focus in this section moves from examining which stories routinely make up the news agenda to the location of stories being reported by comparing local, national and international news agendas between media systems. As Chapters 1 and 2 explored, the broad level of local and international news provision in national contexts can often be an imposed public service requirement. Commercial broadcasters, by contrast, may have some or no commitment to cover their immediate locale or regions around the world. At the same time, the geography of news agendas is shaped by the size and scope of a country, and whether a news service is local, national or international. In other words, when interpreting the geographic breadth of news agendas, the wider cultural, economic and political contexts shape what journalism is produced cross-nationally on different media systems.

It has been observed that local news has been subject to much less scholarly attention than national or international journalism (Aldridge 2007; Franklin 2006). Of course, this differs from one country to the next. While the US has a population five times larger than the UK, its geographical space is larger still (Michigan is roughly the size of England). In this context it is perhaps no surprise why local news in the US is the most popular source of television news and is at the forefront of attempts to hyperlocalize journalism (Pew Research Center Project for Excellence in Journalism 2011). However, the larger European countries, such as Spain and Germany, have developed more regional post-war broadcasting ecologies to reflect the wider geography and cultural differences within nation states.

Nonetheless, within a European context, studies into national and international news have tended to overshadow attention towards more localized journalism. In the US, a more robust supply of empirical studies about local journalism content has developed in the context of public and market-driven news media. Several studies into television and radio content have been carried out to explore whether levels of localism have increased or diminished since stations have been bought up by larger non-local companies. Yan and Napoli (2006) compared 285 US public and commercial broadcast television stations, and found a stark difference in the level of local public affairs programming over a two-week content analysis. They found that 59 per cent had some local affairs programming on commercial television while 90 per cent did so on public broadcasters. Put another way, they concluded that:

> On average, a commercial station aired about 45 minutes of local public affairs programming ... less than half an hour per week ... less than one complete programme a week suggests that the amount of time that commercial stations devote to this type of programming is insufficient ... [public stations] ... broadcast about 3.5 hours of said programming per

> week. It would seem, then, that the commercial imperatives of ad-supported broadcast television inhibit the production of local public affairs programming and that these results suggest that commercial broadcasters are ceding public affairs programming to their noncommercial counterparts. (Yan and Napoli 2006: 807)

However, the commitment towards local television news can differ across commercial broadcasters. Scott *et al.* (2008) compared local news coverage (10 pm newscast) in three network-affiliated stations – representing two larger, multistate media chains (KJRH and KTUL) and one small intrastate-owned channel – in the market of Tulsa, Oklahoma, over approximately five weeks. They concluded that the smaller media group showed "more local news, more locally produced video, more use of on-air reporters, and fewer news promotions than the larger chain-based broadcast groups investigated, suggesting a deeper commitment to local news quality" (Scott *et al.* 2008: 84). They thus argued that "stricter ownership limits would enhance the quality of local television news" (Scott *et al.* 2008: 84).

However, advocating tighter ownership laws challenges the premise behind the FCC's relaxation of ownership rules in recent decades. By allowing many more companies to own one or more groups, the FCC argued that the quality of local affairs news could be enhanced with broadcasters able to pool resources and share the costs of producing localized journalism. Yan and Park (2009) examined whether coverage of local public affairs had increased after their station had become duopoly-owned (a company owning more than one station) by comparing coverage with non-duopoly owners. They discovered that, while there was an increase in local public affairs programming between 1997 and 2003, it was present on both ownership types. They concluded that "joint ownership did not induce the minor stations to provide more local news, contrary to the assumption behind the relaxation of the duopoly rules" (Yan and Park 2009: 396). From another perspective, Schejter and Obar (2009: 577) examined coverage of the FCC's decision to relax media ownership rules across eight network-affiliated local news stations likely to benefit from the ruling and found that the news was framed as "unimportant" or coverage asserted that "media consolidation is not a problem". The lack of critical coverage, in their view, meant that the "stations failed to serve the public interest under the current ownership rules" or warn viewers that "media consolidation is dangerous to the healthy function of our communities" (Schejter and Obar 2009: 590).

As regulatory controls have been weakened in recent decades, studies have found a concentration of media ownership among television stations has led to non-local conglomerates decreasing the volume and nature of local affairs news and public affairs programming. Hood's (2007) observational analysis of local radio stations showed journalists lacked attention to detail when working at a distance from their designated locales, and they often produced more regional or national reporting. Likewise, Sanders's (2008: 173) content analysis of radio morning programming in the Salt Lake City market identified that "locally owned stations program more news for their communities than the large corporate station owners". In this context, corporate ownership is viewed as diminishing the commitment towards and quality of local news journalism.

In the UK the arrival of ITV – the first commercial channel operating under public service obligations – in the 1950s has been widely credited with enhancing journalism's commitment to local communities, addressing the ordinary concerns of local citizens in a refreshing alternative to the stuffy and serious news supplied by the BBC's more nationally orientated public service approach (Tait 2006). However, since the advent of the multi-channel television age in the 1990s, public service responsibilities have (since the 1990 Broadcasting Act and subsequent pieces of legislation) been lightened to compensate commercial stations for having to operate in a far more competitive advertising market (Cushion 2012). Most recently, ITN – which supplies local and regional news for ITV – has decreased its range of bulletins covering the UK from 17 to 9 (Fitzsimmons 2009). The BBC, by contrast, has maintained its regional and local provision, currently operating 18 bulletins around the UK (Cushion 2012).

In national UK television news, content analyses have shown that the public service broadcaster, the BBC, delivers a greater breadth and depth of news about the nations and regions across the UK compared to commercial journalism (see Table 3.13). In recent years, there have been concerns that UK national broadcasters are not reflecting all four nations or the political powers that now divide the UK after key areas of policy responsibilities were devolved to Scotland, Wales and Northern Ireland in 1999. A review, commissioned by the BBC Trust, identified a deficit in the reporting of the nations and in the accuracy of politics (Cushion *et al.* 2010, 2012).

Table 3.13 Percentage of reporters on location across TV news bulletins in 2007 and 2009

	England		*Scotland*		*Wales*		*Northern Ireland*	
	2007	*2009*	*2007*	*2009*	*2007*	*2009*	*2007*	*2009*
BBC 1pm news	91.5	86.0	3.7	4.7	3.7	4.7	1.2	4.7
BBC 6 pm news	88.8	84.5	4.1	6.9	4.1	6.0	3.1	2.6
BBC 10 pm news	91.5	83.6	4.3	9.6	–	2.7	4.3	4.1
BBC News	91.4	84.1	5.4	9.3	–	3.7	3.2	2.8
ITV 10 pm	95.2	92.2	1.6	3.3	1.6	3.3	1.6	1.1
Channel 4 news	96.2	98.7	3.8	–	–	1.3	–	–
Sky News	91.7	98.3	3.6	1.7	1.2	–	3.6	–

(Adapted from Cushion *et al.* 2012)

Table 3.13 shows how, across most bulletins, the BBC not only consistently reflected the whole of the UK more than their commercial counterparts but that coverage was improved *after* the BBC Trust's intervention. BBC journalism, in addition, delivered more accuracy and balanced coverage of the nations, fine-tuning how it communicated the world of devolved politics. By contrast, all the commercial broadcasters increased their coverage of England and did little to address inaccuracies in reporting devolved policy (Cushion *et al.* 2012). Moreover, the study found that the least regulated channel operating under minimal public service requirements – Sky News – provided the least coverage of the UK (carrying no stories covering Wales or Northern Ireland) nor did it enhance the accuracy in reporting devolved politics after the BBC Trust's first review (Cushion *et al.* 2012). Within England, however, the BBC and other commercial broadcasters continued to focus upon London or the southeast. This is understandable, since London is the home to the main political institutions and is where broadcasters are primarily located. Responding to criticism that it is too London-centric, in recent years the BBC has moved many of its services further to the north of England (primarily to Salford, just outside Manchester).

The decline in regional news and dominance of capital cities is apparent in news coverage elsewhere. Since broadcasting in New Zealand was heavily deregulated in the late 1980s, TVNZ cut much of its regional news programming in Auckland and Wellington (Comrie 1996). However, in 2003 the public charter for broadcasting promised a greater commitment to regional affairs. Fountaine *et al.* (2005) carried out a content analysis of TVNZ's *One News* and TV3's *Three News* – a commercial rival – 6 pm bulletins to explore whether the public broadcaster's ambitions to improve localized coverage had materialized (see Table 3.14).

Unlike the UK, where London dominates domestic news coverage, it was not the capital – Wellington – that received most media attention but Auckland (where both channels are based), the most populous city in New

Table 3.14 Percentage of regional and international TV news stories in 2000 and 2003 in New Zealand

Origin	*TVNZ* One News *2000*	*TV3* Three News *2000*	*TVNZ* One News *2003*	*TV3* Three News *2003*
Auckland	18.9	23.8	23.1	22.3
Wellington	18.1	15	14.2	15
Christchurch	7.5	6.8	5.3	6.8
Dunedin	3.1	1.9	1.6	0.5
Other North Island	10.7	9.8	13.4	9.1
Other South Island	5.6	6.8	6	6.3
Offshore islands	0.4	–	0.8	0.5
International	35.8	35.9	35.7	39.5

(Adapted in Fountaine *et al.* 2005)

Zealand. But while Christchurch is the second most populous, it is Wellington that receives greater coverage, primarily because New Zealand's Parliament is based there. With the exception of increased coverage of Auckland on TVNZ *One News*, there has been little enhanced coverage of New Zealand beyond the major urban areas or to the south of the country. While TVNZ *One News* has since received funding to help fulfil its public service obligations, at this point in time it was operating commercially and, compared to TV3 *Three News*, showed little difference in the supply of regional news.

But what also stands out in New Zealand television news coverage is the high proportion of international coverage (35.7 per on TVNZ *One News* and 39.5 per cent on TV3 *Three News* in 2003) relative to other countries. In bigger countries, where national priorities may supersede what is happening elsewhere in the world, international news occupies a less pivotal role in routine agendas (outside of atypical moments of war, famine and human disaster). For news media to routinely cover international affairs (beyond relying on news agencies or external news gatherers) it can, of course, be a resource-heavy genre. Funding an infrastructure of reporters and flying out equipment to remote regions around the world is a costly business and, while public service media have varying levels of obligations to cover international affairs, many commercial stations do not.

The commitment towards international news was demonstrated in Curran *et al.*'s (2012) content analysis study of nine countries drawn on previously in the chapter, since they examined the balance of domestic, international or mixed domestic/international stories across public and commercially driven television news bulletins (see Table 3.15).

Table 3.15 Percentage of domestic and international news on public service and commercial news bulletins across nine countries

	Domestic		*International*		*Mixed*	
	Public service outlets	*Commercial outlets*	*Public service outlets*	*Commercial outlets*	*Public service outlets*	*Commercial outlets*
Australia	43.2	48.1	9.3	4.4	47.5	47.5
Canada	40.4	38.1	23.6	29.7	36	32.2
Greece	41.9	53.3	31.1	16.1	27	3
India	68.1	69	11.6	7	20.3	24
Italy	62.2	60.9	14.8	19.6	23	19.6
Japan	61.8	51.1	6.5	10.8	31.8	38.2
Korea	81.7	66.8	10	21.1	8.2	12.1
Norway	50.4	57.8	30.7	24.4	19	17.8
UK	47.9	57.2	20.7	15	31.4	27.8

(Adapted from Curran *et al.* 2012)

In five out of nine countries, public service television news bulletins carried a higher proportion of international news than commercial outlets. While, in several countries, a considerable level of news mixed domestic and international affairs, in the UK and Norway – where two well-funded and robustly policed public media organizations exist (see Chapter 1) – international coverage ranged between 20.7 and 30.7 per cent respectively. Commercial television news bulletins, by contrast, tended to have a higher domestic agenda (again five out of nine), with some countries pursuing a higher volume of news dedicated to national concerns in both media systems (between 68.1–69 per cent in India and 66.8–81.7 per cent in Korea).

While it might be expected that international news content is higher in smaller states (in geography or population size) – New Zealand being the operative example – Table 3.15 suggests that this is not the rule of thumb (large states like Canada and the UK have a healthy supply of foreign news reporting). Kolmer and Semetko's (2010) study of international news in the US and Germany – two large nations – suggested that differences in the volume of international news reporting related to the dominant type of media system operating in each country. In a detailed longitudinal content analysis of German TV news bulletins, they found that foreign news had increased in recent years – peaking at 50 per cent of all news in 2004 – on public broadcasters. But, correspondingly, commercial channels remained above 40 per cent between 2001 and 2007. Kolmer and Semetko (2010) argued that international news remained highly valued in Germany largely because ARD and ZDF have strict public service obligations to carry foreign coverage. In fact, they have suggested that public service media

> may even have initially raised the bar for private channels in Germany which continue to devote a comparatively large share of the programs to foreign news, even though the channels are not subsidized nor bound by the same rules. (Kolmer and Semetko 2010: 712)

In the US, by contrast, their content analysis found the US commercial network evening bulletins – ABC, CBS and NBC – had a combined average of 22.9 per cent of foreign news coverage. With no public service obligations, the US has, over the course of the last few decades, shown little foreign news except during key moments in wars and conflict (like the Iraq war during 2003–4 – see Pew Research Center Project for Excellence in Journalism 2011).

Indeed, when evaluating foreign news, it is important to establish which parts of the world are being reported and why. As Beer (2010) has argued, the value of news alone should not be interpreted as reporting what is foreign but in how domestic/national journalism is understood in a wider global framework. So, for example, Beer's content analysis of media coverage from three regions around the world showed not just that Africa has a relatively low visibility in Western news media but that coverage is often pessimistically framed, with Africa depicted as the "Dark Continent" (Beer 2010: 598). Kolmer and Semetko's (2010) content analysis compared which regions of the world were covered by different national television news stations and found that geography (proximity to other countries) and national interest impacted on the nature of international news routinely pursued. For Germany (13.4 per cent), the UK (21.8 per cent) and – most notably the US (40.5 per cent) – the Middle East was high on the agenda primarily because the latter two countries were engaged in military conflicts in Afghanistan and Iraq.

US scholars, however, have raised concerns about the lack of sustained coverage of international affairs when immediate national interests are not relevant and drawn attention to the poor public understanding of foreign affairs in the country (Hamilton 2010). This was particularly the case in a post-9/11 environment, when Americans were making sense of why the terrorist atrocities had taken place (see Zelizer and Allan 2002/2011). But while international news increased in the aftermath of 9/11, it was only temporary. For several years later a content analysis identified that in a presidential election year – 2008 – network television news coverage contained a limited supply of foreign affairs. PBS's *NewsHour*, by contrast, continued to report international events beyond the election or the Middle East (Pew Research Center Project for Excellence in Journalism 2009). The 2009 State of US News Media report stated:

> Besides Iraq, the war in Afghanistan, the cyclone in Myanmar, the turmoil inside Pakistan, the elections in Zimbabwe and the Israeli–Palestinian conflict all made the *NewsHour*'s top-10 roster of stories in 2008. With the exception of Iraq and Afghanistan, none of them were on that list on the commercial networks' nightly programs. (Pew Research Center Project for Excellence in Journalism 2009)

This indicates that the public broadcaster played a distinctive role in supplying US audiences with international news, which commercial media have increasingly marginalized since 2001.

The democratic promise of the Internet: have public or market-driven media systems internationalized their news agendas or embraced citizen journalism in the online era?

Beyond conventional television and radio bulletins, new technologies have evolved in recent years with the potential to enhance the diversity of broadcasters' news agendas. Despite being relatively well-worn phrases within the industry, evidence about whether bottom-up, citizen or hyperlocal journalism are changing the content of news remains relatively thin on the ground. Many public service broadcasters have been at the forefront of experiments with ways of integrating UGC (user-generated content) with routine news practices and conventions (Allan and Thorsen 2011; Flew 2011; Harrison 2010; Lee-Wright 2008; Williams *et al.* 2011) and there have been recent attempts to develop hyperlocal initiatives (Berkey-Gerard 2011). However, while there have been many accounts of UGC online policy strategies or impressionistic observations about citizen journalism, empirical studies examining whether UGC actually shapes, in practice, commercial and public service journalism have been in short supply. Thus any conclusions drawn from what follows are necessarily tentative.

There has been some empirical analysis of the use of UGC in recent production studies of BBC journalism (Harrison 2010; Williams *et al.* 2011). While Harrison (2010: 255) found a well-intentioned journalistic desire to let citizens shape the news, "UGC actually reinforces a tendency toward soft journalism and human interest, as exemplified by the rise of stories centered on crime, calamities and accidents." These topics can be captured by eye-witness accounts via handheld mobile phones as opposed to less visually orientated news about politics, business or social policy. According to Harrison (2010: 255), overreliance on UGC may begin to chip away at the "architecture of public service news". Likewise, Williams *et al.*'s (2011) ethnographic study of BBC journalism suggested that, far from triggering any radical bottom-up, citizen movement to reshape day-to-day news agendas, UGC had done little to dislodge old-age journalistic practices and conventions.

Since the use of UGC continues to develop fluidly among large corporations – many of which now routinely integrate social media like Facebook and Twitter into online news items – journalism could potentially still change. However, while social media have been increasingly used in contemporary journalism, initial studies have suggested progress could be slower in larger, more corporate news environments. Lasorsa *et al.*'s (2011: 13) comprehensive analysis of how US journalists use Twitter – examining more than 22,000 tweets – concluded that:

> Those working for major national newspapers, broadcasting networks and cable news channels generally appear to be changing less then their counterparts at other news media, suggesting perhaps that those vested the most in current professional conventions may be the least willing or able to change.

Nonetheless, at this stage in the lifecycle of social media it is difficult to assess any fixed pattern of usage, let alone one that can be meaningfully compared across public and market-driven news media.

Since television and radio bulletins face considerable time constraints – especially on commercial broadcasters who tend to interrupt their journalism with adverts – online news is often seen as an antidote to the short and snappy world of broadcasting. So, for example, an analysis of the commercial broadcaster CNN's iReport.com project has suggested that it provides much more space and interactivity for the empowerment of citizens than most UGC platforms. While citizens are "encouraged to see … their values as not differing from the news values of the corporate media … this process is not uncontested. There is a perpetual process of negotiation and renegotiation" (Kperogi 2011: 324). Citizens, in other words, have more autonomy to shape their own contributions, even if the vast majority of their input is consigned to the website as opposed to being aired to far larger television news audiences.

But beyond citizen journalism, the online world is sometimes set up to be ready-equipped to supply a more diverse news agenda from around the world. With a growing online presence of public and market-driven news media, trends are appearing but, once again, caution must be exercised since relatively few comparative studies systematically compare cross-national online media systems. Recent accounts of journalism produced by new media have suggested that traditional news media have transferred their offline dominance to the online world, reproducing much of their content online without any meaningful editorial changes (see Fenton 2010). This is certainly the case in the US where, as the US State of News Media 2011 Pew report pointed out succinctly,

> Of the top 25 news sites for 2010 measured by Nielsen, only seven sites are online-only operations (meaning they do not have any traditional media as part of their organizations). The remaining 18 are all tied to traditional media properties. (Pew Research Center Project for Excellence in Journalism 2011)

As a result, empirical studies of commercial online news content have broadly remained constant. Wu (2007) found the international coverage of CNN and the *New York Times* to be proportionately higher in online editions (cnn.com and www.nytimes.com) but the scope of foreign news was broadly similar. He concluded that:

> the overall picture of the world presented by the websites reflects their traditional media counterparts well. This discovery could be a great disappointment for those who ideally envisioned the web as a truly global medium that can break away from the structural, systematic barriers to deliver more – and more diverse – information to people around the world. Ironically, the power of news agencies, the old guard of international news flow, seems to have resurged with the help of the Internet. (Wu 2007: 549)

On a more global level, Himelboim (2010) examined the use of external hyperlinks in foreign news across 73 countries, sampling a range of online news media within each nation including, when present, public service media. Overall, their use was remarkably low – just 6 per cent – contained one or more external hyperlink. While this was primarily explained by commercial considerations – since many online sources would not want to encourage users to go elsewhere – Himelboim (2010) does draw attention to the conflicting level of hyperlinks in the US and UK. Acknowledging the geography and history that binds the UK to many other foreign countries, it was also stated that:

> One explanation as to why the United Kingdom sent a large number of links is the important place the BBC has in the British news industry. As a public broadcaster, the BBC is service-driven and less concerned about the potential financial drop-offs associated with providing "ways out" to other Web sites via external hyperlinks. (Himelboim 2010: 385)

This was reinforced by specific revised BBC guidelines in September 2010 where an internal editorial policy document stated "links [are] essential to online journalism", with the aim "to double outbound links from 10m a month to 20m by 2013" (cited from Halliday 2010). In addition, editorial guidelines for more transparently sourcing the material used to shape an individual story or ways to encourage users to search for further analysis and context were recommended (Halliday 2010).

A comparative study of foreign news stories across 28 online news media in 15 countries suggested that the BBC was not alone in supplying external hyperlinks to enhance its journalism. Chang *et al.* (2009) found no state news media reports contained a hyperlink whereas 2.7 per cent of private outlets did. Public service broadcasters, by contrast, were nine times more likely to feature a hyperlink (24.4 per cent of stories) suggesting that media ownership shaped the depth of online news reporting cross-nationally. Chang *et al.* (2009: 156) concluded that public service media more effectively serve users than commercial outlets since

> market–media relationship produces economic restraints that compel the logic of the market to override public interest in the open global network by denying the users of news media websites the opportunity to jump from country to country.

While the use of external hyperlinks gives one dimension of online news coverage, it is of course only one measure of what remains, after all, a fluid form of journalism that has yet to develop the distinct characteristics long established by conventional forms of broadcasting.

Conclusions

The longitudinal trends in this section all point to an enhanced tabloid agenda across news media *generally*, displacing more serious news topics in politics and public affairs. Many scholars have suggested that changing news agendas and values have been shaped by wider forces in privatization and deregulation in recent decades. While the influence of professional codes and cultures should not be overlooked in understanding these changes (since coverage remains nationally idiosyncratic – see Chapters 1 and 2), it does suggest that the increasingly market-driven news media landscape has had a broader impact on the routine nature of journalism's news values, practices and conventions.

But while public service media have adopted some of these prevailing trends in journalism in recent decades, the longitudinal data sets drawn upon suggest that many have remained relatively distinctive from commercial outlets. Since public service media have not been directly impacted by deregulation, many have not been subject to the same degree of commercial pressure to report soft news or relay international news from costly regions around the world. When public service journalism has faced more direct impact – in New Zealand, for example, where a public service broadcaster was asked to operate as a commercial one in the late 1980s – longitudinal trends have shown that deregulatory shifts have coincided with political coverage being downsized in favour of sport and tabloid topics.

In contemporary coverage, a nine-country comparative cross-national study similarly demonstrated that public service broadcasters were broadly distinctive from their commercial counterparts. It found that public service television journalism, around the world, tended to have a more serious news agenda, supplied more policy information and contained less personalized coverage than commercial broadcasters. Smaller studies drawn on in the chapter reinforced this macro picture, with fully fledged commercial US networks – ABC, NBC and CBS – all featuring shorter soundbites, less direct political sourcing, a lower level of responsibility framing and higher volume of episodic framing than Swedish public service journalism, which has itself been accused of commercializing its content. Underlying *how* journalism is communicated, another cross-national study found that public service broadcasters conveyed more communicative complexity than commercial outlets when informing television viewers about world events. While there were minor exceptions to this cross-nationally and within media systems, well-funded public media – in the UK and Australia – provided far more pluralism in explaining a news story, issue or event.

This pluralism was extended to coverage of local or international affairs, consistent with the mission statements of many public service broadcasters to reflect the diversity of the regions within a nation and beyond it (see Chapter 1). In the UK, for example, a deficit identified in BBC news coverage of the nations and regions by the BBC Trust led to modest improvements, which enhanced the geographic spread of routine journalism and sharpened up the accuracy of devolution reporting. In the US, by contrast, local television and radio stations have had to fulfil fewer FCC public interest obligations to produce localized news in recent decades. While the FCC's relaxation of ownership rules was designed to strengthen local journalism by allowing stations to join forces and share costs, studies – pre- and post-deregulation – have suggested that this free-market approach has not enhanced local content.

There was a less clear-cut pattern of balancing international and domestic news reporting in the nine-country study of public and market-driven television news bulletins. The size of a country (smaller nations tend to have a higher international agenda) clearly shaped the balance of domestic and foreign news coverage. But even in relatively large geographic or well-populated countries, many public service broadcasters have been committed to delivering an international agenda. In Germany, for example, the well-resourced public broadcaster, ZDF, has been steadfast in its priority towards foreign news coverage over the last decade and this commitment has had a knock-on effect, arguably raising the standard and volume of international news on commercial outlets. Apart from during times of conflict and war involving US troops, studies have shown US commercial broadcasters to convey a rather narrow view of the world limited to a select few countries. PBS, by contrast, supplied a far more internationally rich diet of foreign news stories than the US network bulletins.

But public service broadcasters are not without fault nor have many escaped criticism. Studies have shown public broadcasters tended to deliver a top-down view, turning primarily to elites to explain world events as opposed to a wider constituency of actors that could add greater breadth and depth to the interpretation of politics and public affairs. Public media can thus sometimes construct a limited understanding of the world, drawing heavily on elite perspectives that represent a select few occupations or people from privileged backgrounds. Assessment of the democratic value of news, in this context, cannot rely entirely on *what* news is addressed but in *how* news informs people about the world or engages them in public affairs (addressed in Chapter 7). While the Internet continues to hold democratic promise in respect of engaging or diversifying news agendas, early studies have suggested some of its conventions – the integration of UGC for example – have encouraged softer news agendas on public media, making use of exclusive footage or instant reaction as opposed to anything revolutionary in recalibrating day-to-day norms in the production of journalism. But public compared to commercial media have sought to enrich their international online news stories by making available a greater number of external hyperlinks, encouraging users to explore journalism beyond what they can offer, from more countries around the world.

Taken together, the evidence amassed in this chapter has shown that viewers tuning into, or surfing the websites of, public and commercial news will most likely encounter different agendas and approaches to how news is communicated in day-to-day coverage. Overall, public service media tended to pursue more serious news than their commercial counterparts, delivering more analytical journalism and covering more local and international affairs. Put simply, public service media reflects a more diverse and in-depth "window on the world" than commercial journalism.

The next chapter explores an atypical period – elections – to ascertain whether journalism on different media systems remains distinctive at a critical moment in any democracy.

Chapter 4

Making sense of elections

The journalistic conventions and practices of campaign reporting

Introduction

Elections represent a key moment in which to assess the health of news media, an event widely seen as the "hallmark of a democratic political system" (Negrine 1989: 179). The role of news media at elections is considered critical to the development of people's understanding of election issues, their level of interest and engagement in politics (Norris 2000). Unsurprisingly, then, a great deal of attention has been paid to how the media cover elections, particularly in whether reporting is biased, encouraging audiences to vote for one party over another. Indeed, some of the early "media effects" studies in the US developed as a result of inquiries into elections (Katz and Warshel 2001), since scholars were preoccupied with understanding to what extent news impacted on the "people's choice" at election time (e.g. Lazarsfeld *et al.* 1948).

As television began establishing itself as the medium of choice in the 1960s, scholars began to explore TV's role in visually transforming election campaigns (Edelman 1964; Rosenbaum 1997), epitomized by the televised US presidential debate of 1960 that played to the telegenic strengths of John F. Kennedy (Coleman 2000). At the turn of the millennium, the Internet has become the new medium on the block and, over the last decade or so, studies have meticulously examined how election campaigns have been fought using a range of new media. In a bid to address voters more directly, politicians in particular, are beginning to take advantage of new communication technologies that can bypass mass media and construct niche messages for key voting demographics.

Under PR management, today many politicians remain largely "on message", sticking closely to pre-prepared party scripts and participating in strategically designed campaign events. At the same time, in recent years many political parties in Western countries have converged towards the "centre ground" of politics, with old-fashioned "left" or "right" categories less able to convey their ideological credentials. In this context, without easily discernible policy differences, *the election campaign itself* has become a more newsworthy topic. Many journalistic accounts of elections now centre on de-spinning campaign tactics, and interpreting the meaning behind political party speeches and statements. Meanwhile, attention has turned to party leaders, their speeches to large jeering crowds or to them meeting and greeting "ordinary" voters on the "campaign trail".

This has reinforced a wider trend in political reporting – a more human-interest, candidate-centred agenda – leading to a personalization of election coverage, focusing on the characteristics of individual candidates. Also, in a similar vein, coverage has undergone a "presidentialization", in which the leaders of political parties dominate media attention, marginalizing other key political actors (most unusually in parliamentary systems where parties, in theory, if not in practice, are supposed to play a more collective decision-making role). Paradoxically, however, politicians' voices have been downgraded and those of journalists enhanced, as the visual has taken precedence over the aural, delivering highly staged managed spectacles or "live" campaigning images.

Running parallel to these trends – or, arguably, to counter some of these news conventions – political parties have become increasingly sophisticated campaigners, using spin doctors to articulate short and snappy soundbites or to visually choreograph public appearances and press conferences. Consequently, scholars have shown that the tone of election coverage has changed, since news media increasingly report on hostile campaign advertising, something that political parties see as an effective tool to use against their opponents (Kaid 2006). Hence, studies have repeatedly revealed a media fascination with the tactics and strategies of spin doctors, increasingly pushing more substantive issues or policies to the sidelines. Put another way, academic literature about media coverage of elections has characterized them as sporting contests – a game to be won or lost, with heroes and villains – as opposed to reporting the campaign to fulfil a more critical public sphere role, where issues are debated and policy deliberated at length.

Tracing these developments over successive recent elections, empirical studies have increasingly found that policy issues have been less prioritized in news media coverage of elections than what is often labelled *the process of politics* or the *strategic game frame of politics*. This broadly refers to the reporting of political personalities (primarily the leaders of parties or quirky/outspoken politicians), the squabbling within and across parties (in "attack ads" or campaign speeches) and the *horse-race* elements of campaigning (opinion polls, focus groups, apathetic citizens etc.) (Bennett 2007; Cappella and Jamieson 1997; Cushion *et al.* 2006; Cushion *et al.* 2009a; Deacon *et al.* 2001; Farnsworth and Lichter 2007; Franklin 2004; Patterson 2000; Thomas *et al.* 2004a, 2004b). Whether the *process of politics* or the *strategic game frame*, both concepts share many characteristics and have been widely adopted in international political communication scholarship. However, their use and applicability can vary from one empirical study to the next. So, for example, in respect of the *strategic game frame*, Aalberg *et al.* (2011) conducted a review of academic literature employing this term and identified that while "most scholars investigating the framing of politics as a strategic game make references to the same scholarly work, how this framing has been operationalized in quantitative content analyses differs significantly" (Aalberg *et al.* 2011: 7). They suggested that "This makes it very difficult to make comparisons across studies, which decreases research cumulativity and hampers research into the antecedents and effects of this – or these – framing of politics" (Aalberg *et al.* 2011: 10).

Since the evidence amassed throughout the book depends on *existing* empirical news studies, it has not been possible in this chapter to reinterpret the categories employed by scholars to classify the characteristics of election reporting. Nonetheless, for the sake of what Aalberg *et al.* call "conceptual clarity" (2011: 11–12), where possible this chapter will try and distinguish the "game frame" from the "strategy frame", using the following proposed redefinitions:

- The *game frame* refers to news stories that portray politics as a game and are centered around: who is winning or losing elections, in the battle for public opinion, in legislative debates or in politics in general; expressions of public opinion (polls, vox pops); approval or disapproval from interest groups or particular constituencies or publics; or that speculate about electoral or policy outcomes or potential coalitions.
- The *strategy frame* refers to news stories that are centered around interpretations of candidates' or parties' motives for actions and positions; their strategies and tactics for achieving political or policy goals; how they campaign; and choices regarding leadership and integrity, including news coverage of press behavior. (Aalberg 2011: 11; *original emphasis*)

The academic literature features debates about whether the process of politics, the strategic frame or game frame enhances or diminishes citizen understanding of the relative strengths and weakness of politicians or whether such coverage engages people in the campaign and motivates them to vote in an election (De Vreese and Elenbaas 2002; Grabe and Bucy 2009; Irwin and Van Holsteyn 2008; Iyengar *et al.* 2004; Norris 2000; Street 2011). Since a voluminous literature traces all of these prevailing trends and their effects, the purpose of this chapter is not to go over already well-charted territory. The aim instead is to explore how far public and market-driven media have adapted many of these conventions, from one country to the next, to ascertain whether patterns in the nature of election coverage are evident across media systems. For what is widely accepted is that these election news conventions tend to reflect the incursion of commercial values, a shift – for better or worse – from the more serious, issue-based agendas historically pursued when state or public broadcasters were the more dominant media system. While there is some evidence that voter attention or election interest could be heightened by game-frame features (Iyengar *et al.* 2004), Aalberg *et al.* (2011: 12) reviewed the impact this coverage had on audiences and concluded it had "strong negative effects on the public". As a consequence, in assessing the many empirical studies drawn upon in this chapter, *news of democratic value will be interpreted as election news containing policy information likely to help citizens make an informed decision about the relative merits of a political party or a particular politician if they decide to cast their vote on election day.*

To understand patterns in international political communications, collaborations have grown between countries in recent decades, allowing scholars to identify the differences and continuities in election coverage around the world (De Vreese *et al.* 2006; Esser 2008; Katz and Warshel 2001). Strömbäck and Kaid's (2008) edited book, *The Handbook of Election News Coverage around the World*, is the most sustained attempt to explore how elections have been reported from one country to the next. Some 22 different countries were explored, primarily from a national perspective, examining campaign and media regulation during election periods, the influence of advertising, of party political campaigning, the use and impact of campaign sources by voters and, most relevant for this chapter, the volume and nature of election news coverage. Summarizing the book, overall, Kaid and Strömbäck (2008: 428) concluded that:

> One difference between the United States news media coverage and that of many other countries is the significant role played by public television systems. In the United States, public television has very low viewership and thus plays a, relatively speaking, minor role in the news coverage of elections. Outside the United States public broadcasting has retained significance even where private commercial broadcasting has gained strong footholds ... the effects of public broadcasting dominance are not the same in every country, and it is important to recognize the difference between public service broadcasting in solid democracies and in weaker transforming democracies.

If the influence of public media on audiences is left aside for a moment – since it is addressed more carefully in Chapter 7 – what Kaid and Strömbäck (2008) imply is that public and commercial services are distinctly different in the way they report elections cross-nationally. To interpret election coverage from one country to the next, Kaid and Strömbäck (2008) included a cross-national table about the characteristics of election coverage cross-nationally (see Table 4.1). This demonstrates which medium is dominant in each nation, if regulation of election coverage is present, and how election coverage is primarily framed.[12]

Table 4.1 Cross-national characteristics of dominant medium, regulatory culture and nature of news coverage at election time

Country	*Dominant medium*	*Regulation of election coverage*	*Dominant frame in election coverage*
Australia	TV	Yes	Horse race
Brazil	TV	Yes	Horse race/strategy
Britain	TV	Requires accuracy and balance	Strategy
Bulgaria	TV	Requires equal treatment of candidates and parties	Mixture of issue and game frame
Canada	TV	Must be fair and equitable	Horse race
France	TV	Extreme balance requirements monitoring	Strategy
Germany	TV	No appearance in entertainment shows	High percentage of strategy/game/horse race
Greece	TV	Yes, time allocated among parties	Candidate image given more prominence than issues
Hungary	TV	Equal footing in the news	Not available
India	TV	Yes	Not available
Israel	TV	Prohibit election propaganda during last 60 days, except for time given party spots	Balance issue and game frames; game frame usually dominant
Italy	TV	Must have balanced coverage	Not available
Japan	TV	Directives call for impartiality; no side taking	Issues in newspapers; game frame and negativity in TV
Mexico	TV	No	Candidates; not game frame or issues
Netherlands	TV	No	Substantive issues
Poland	TV	No	Horse race (polls)
Russia	TV	Yes	Not available
Serbia	TV	Requires objective, fair, equal	Not available
South Africa	Radio	Yes, required to give equal treatment to parties	Emphasis on polls and horse race
Spain	TV	Neutral coverage and reporting; proportional according to previous vote totals	Mixed
Sweden	TV	Should be impartial on TV, but no detailed regulations	Issues more than game frame in newspapers and public TV but game frame more in commercial TV and tabloids
United States	TV	No	Horse race

(Adapted from Kaid and Strömbäck 2008)

While Table 4.1 provides a useful overview of the regulatory environments policing coverage at election times in some of the most advanced democracies, elsewhere in the world there are many countries where heavy-handed governments censor, apply pressure or entirely control the flow of political news over the campaign period. Where regulation is not present in Western democracies, such as the US, bias is a more central issue. While accusations of "liberal" bias are a mainstay in US broadcasting, party bias has been detected from both sides of the political compass on the commercial television networks and, of course, some of the partisan cable news channels (Farnsworth and Lichter 2011). Even with regulation, bias can appear. Smaller political parties, for example, have long complained of being squeezed out as broadcasters conform to impartiality guidelines, meaning it is primarily mainstream party voices which are balanced over the campaign period. Nonetheless, in most advanced democracies, a professional code of journalistic practice or legally imposed regulation prevents outright propaganda in repressively governed states (see Chapters 1 and 2).

According to Strömbäck and van Aelst (2010: 41–2),

> Despite the major importance of the news media's election news coverage, there are still only a few cross-national studies on how the media cover elections ... more cross-national research on election news is needed for a better understanding of the antecedents of the media's framing of election news.

It is in this spirit that this chapter closely examines the nature of news coverage, drawing on contemporary studies into the fluctuations and patterns of election reporting cross-nationally. While it does not offer any new empirical light on comparative election coverage, it does bring together the latest research and develops a sustained understanding of how different media systems report elections.

The contemporary nature of election coverage: comparing how politics is framed on competing media systems

In recent years many scholars around the world have made sense of their national political communication systems by comparing how far they have "Americanized" coverage, adopting a more "horse race", candidate-focused, negative, opinionated or media-centric approach to election coverage (e.g. both game and strategic frames). After all, it is in the US where commercial values have most infused the form and style of election coverage and, since media systems are generally predicted to be heading in a commercial direction (Hallin and Mancini 2004), past and present trends in US election journalism are helpful to refer to when predicting what will happen in the future elsewhere.

Table 4.2 Amount of election news on US television networks from 1998–2004

	1998	*1992*	*1996*	*2000*	*2004*
No. of stories	589	728	483	462	504
Stories per day (average)	10.5	11.5	7.7	7.3	9.0
Total time (minutes)	1,116	1,402	788	805	1,070

(Adapted from Farnsworth and Lichter 2008: 44)

Of course, historical trends in US election journalism are well rehearsed. The commitment towards election coverage on US network television news between 1988–2004 has changed over successive campaigns (see Table 4.2). While the disparity in the volume of coverage between elections could be explained by a closely run presidential campaign that generated enhanced voter interest, the contest in 2000 arguably fell into this category but coverage did not significantly shift (even if much of the voting drama came after polling day). According to Farnsworth and Lichter (2008: 44), the marginally higher volume of election coverage in 2004 might have been journalists' response to criticisms of a shortfall in campaign news in the previous election.

Hallin's (1992) analysis of network television coverage of presidential elections from 1968 to 1988 established that the average time allocated to politicians' quotes on screen – soundbites – had reduced from 43 to just 9 seconds. But, while politicians have been heard less, journalists have inflated the prominence of their own voices. Steele and Barnhurst's (1996) study of presidential election network news bulletins from 1968 to 1998 established

> that when journalists spoke at the end of a report, they gave factual information much less often, by a factor of ten (from 24.6 to 2.4 percent). Making judgments about the elections' events grew to almost ninety percent of these final remarks. (Steele and Barnhurst 1996: 22)

Between 1968 and 1992, journalists themselves have been more regularly pictured in election coverage, exacerbating a trend of image bite news, where the visual replaces the aural, acting as a backdrop for reporters to make sense of the electoral drama and razzmatazz (Barnhurst and Steele 1997). And throughout the 1990s into the new millennium, images have increasingly shaped how US networks report presidential campaigns, visually framing an understanding of candidates and policies (Grabe and Bucy 2009). When politicians are heard more directly, studies of US television news have increasingly noted enhanced negativity in the tone of election coverage (Kaid 2006). The reporting of attack ads, campaign tactics and wider electoral processes have become more central to campaign coverage in successive presidential elections, with journalists more actively interpreting the "spin" behind party

Table 4.3 Percentage of stories related to the 2008 presidential election on the morning and evening US network bulletins over the year

	Network morning	*Network evening*
Political horse race	70	59
Stories about advertising, electoral calendar, endorsements and treatment by the press	10	11
Policy	11	15
Personal	5	7
Other	2	5
Public record	1	2

(adapted from Pew Research Center Project for Excellence in Journalism 2009)

Table 4.4 Percentage of election stories in the 2008 presidential campaign on US network TV news bulletins

Types of stories	*Per cent*
Policy debates	31
Strategy/tactics	31
Horse race	24
Campaign conduct	10
GOP VP choice	7
Debates	7
Personal background	6
Friends/family	6
Professional background	4
Election process	3

(Adapted from Pew Research Center Project for Excellence in Journalism 2009)

political messages and evaluating the momentum ahead of election day (Farnsworth and Lichter 2007).

Against this backdrop, the 2008 US presidential election exhibited many of these longitudinal trends, reinforcing the retreat from substantive issues to news about candidates, campaign and non-policy stories. Table 4.3 shows the balance of campaign stories on network television news on the morning and evening bulletins over the course of the election year, demonstrating the low overall volume of news about policy-related issues.

A more detailed breakdown of stories over the campaign period showed that, while policy news scored higher on the US networks during the election (primarily due to the global financial crisis), more than two-thirds of coverage did not concern substantive policy issues (see Table 4.4). Dedicated cable television news channels have also had an impact on the overall nature of election journalism in the US. Sotirovic and McLeod's (2008: 28–9) analysis revealed that:

> election coverage of 2004 ... saw clear splintering of the traditional journalistic professional model of journalism, with its emphasis on objectivity, toward more opinionated stands led by the Fox News cable channel. About 82% of Fox election stories included journalistic opinions, compared to about 44% in other network news, 13% in large newspapers, 7% on CNN, and only 3% on PBS. PBS seems to represent one of the last bastions of traditional news values in American media.

While this marks PBS as distinctive from its commercial counterparts, four years later another study suggested its coverage was not entirely divorced from the prevailing trends of network and cable journalism. PBS's *NewsHour* devoted more of its editorial agenda to presidential coverage than the networks (32 per cent as opposed to 27 per cent). These election stories contained marginally less horse-race (e.g. game-frame) coverage compared to the networks (54 per cent as opposed to 59 per cent) and more policy-related stories (19 per cent as opposed to 15 per cent) (all figures from Pew Research Center Project for Excellence in Journalism 2009). But while there were differences between PBS and commercial news media, the qualitative differences in the nature of PBS election news should not be overstated. Kerbel *et al.*'s (2000: 28) study of PBS and ABC news during the 1996 election concluded that, while more substantive issues were tackled on PBS, at the same time it invited viewers "to experience the election as they would if they were watching commercial television, as a political contest told by elite observers of the process rather than a battle of ideas involving politically viable candidates". Despite not being governed by the same degree of market-led imperatives, it would appear that the journalistic national culture within the US inhibits how far PBS departs from long-established election conventions and practices.

Beyond the US, what remains less well known is whether cross-nationally other public service media have been able to resist many of these commercial conventions and practices, and report elections differently from the US. Brants and Praag (2006) have compared the prevailing trends in US election coverage with the reporting of elections in the Netherlands since the 1980s. They compared election television news on the public television news bulletin, NOS-Journaal, with RTL-nieuws, a commercial station launched in 1989 (see Table 4.5). Coverage was categorized into substantive election policies, hoopla reporting (classified as news about the campaign or party activity e.g. the strategy frame) and horse-race coverage (e.g. the game frame), the proportion of which was split into opinion polls and reflections (related to electoral process stories such as potential coalition building).

Before the commercial channel was launched in the Netherlands, the content analysis study established that over half of all election coverage on Nos-Journaal was substantive in the 1986 election. In campaign coverage, 30 per cent of news featured on-screen politicians, with soundbites lasting, on average, 29 seconds (Brants and Praag 2006: 35). However, overall election

Table 4.5 Percentage of election type stories on public and commercial nightly TV news bulletins (with horse-race category broken down) from 1986 to 2003 in the Netherlands

					Per cent of horse-race stories	
		Substantive	*Hoopla*	*Horse race*	*Opinion polls*	*Reflections*
1986	Nos-Journaal	51	32	18	–	–
1989	Nos-Journaal	41	27	31	–	–
1994	Nos-Journaal	35	37	29	10	19
	RTL-nieuws	28	42	30	3	27
1998	Nos-Journaal	52	15	33	13	20
	RTL-nieuws	53	23	24	18	6
2002	Nos-Journaal	50	29	21	3	18
	RTL-nieuws	34	29	38	22	16
2003	Nos-Journaal	45	11	43	11	32
	RTL-nieuws	26	28	44	25	19

(Adapted from Brants and Praag 2006)

coverage immediately declined on the public broadcaster on the launch of RTL-nieuws, to just over a third of all election coverage in 1994. Since then substantive election stories have remained prominent, whereas on RTL-nieuws policy-orientated news declined to just over a quarter of coverage with more horse-race reporting evident. In interpreting the overall pattern of coverage from the 1980s to 2000s, Brants and Praag (2006) believed that the reporting of elections remained distinct from that of the US because of the presence of a public service infrastructure and the more unique political culture of the Netherlands. Based on these longitudinal trends, they argued that "the continuation of a strong influence of public broadcasting values on the quality, styles, and of the political culture of non-adversariality that comes with consensus democracy ... puts a break on negative and cynical reporting" (Brants and Praag 2006: 39).

Strömbäck and van Aelst (2010) carried out a detailed framing analysis of election coverage in Belgium and Sweden, two countries with well-funded public service broadcasters (see Chapter 1). Their analysis, above all, asked whether media systems within each nation had begun to prioritize more strategic game aspects (they did not distinguish between these frames) of the campaign (candidates fighting, advertising, polling etc.), rather than concentrating on the issues and policies of competing political parties. Table 4.6 shows that both Belgian and Swedish public service programming aired more issue-based news than their commercial rivals, who spent over a half (Het Nieuws) and close to two-thirds (TV4 Nyheterna) of their agendas reporting game-type news during the election campaign period. Strömbäck and van Aelst (2010: 51) also identified that public service television news contained

Table 4.6 Percentage of TV news metaframe stories (issue or game) in the 2006 Swedish and 2007 Belgian elections

Media system	*Country and television show*	*Issue*	*Game*
	Belgium		
Public TV	Het Journaal	70	30
Commercial	Het Nieuws	49	51
	Sweden		
Public TV	Rapport	66	34
	Aktuellt	55	45
Commercial	TV4 Nyheterna	37	63

(Adapted from Strömbäck and van Aelst 2010)

more substantive coverage of policies during the campaign than either the tabloid or the quality newspapers in both countries.

In coverage overall, the study compared the presence of a game metaframe in every election story and concluded that, while public service television news remained distinct, the difference was less striking. For one strategic frame – about horse-race, governing, political strategy or news management – was present in 40 per cent of election news on Het Journaal, 28 per cent in Rapport and 46 per cent in Aktuellt. On the commercial stations, by contrast, 45 per cent of stories had a strategic frame on Het Nieuws and 52 per cent on TV4 Nyheterna.

Strömbäck and van Aelst (2010: 53) also compared how far election news was personalized, where stories "focused on politicians as individuals or on human interest elements". On Het Journaal 18 per cent of election coverage had at least one personalized subframe within a news item compared to 51 per cent on Rapport and 26 per cent on Aktuellt. For the commercial broadcasters, personalized coverage amounted to 44 per cent on Het Nieuws and 52 per cent on TV4 Nyheterna. Overall, then, while the pattern is not entirely uniform – and Strömbäck and van Aelst (2010) point out that nationally unique characteristics inform election coverage – in both countries a pattern remained evident across media type. Public service television news bulletins covered more issue-based stories than commercial outlets over the election campaign, with less emphasis on game-type coverage and personalized reporting.

In an analysis of news coverage of UK and US elections throughout the 1980s, Semetko *et al.* (1991: 142) pointed out that "British election coverage on television is almost comprehensively different from campaign news on U.S. television ... it is more ample, more varied, more substantive, more party orientated, less free with unidirectional comment, and more respectful." Subsequent election studies in the 1990s and 2000s suggested these differences were less striking. While BBC television news bulletins reported more election news than its main commercial rival – ITV – in the 2001 election, overall coverage on both stations had declined steadily since 1992. Scammell and Semetko (2008: 84) observed that, over this time period, "not only were there fewer stories, they were shorter. In total on both channels [BBC and ITV] there was about 40% less time for the election in 2001 (about 8.5 hours) compared to 1997 (about 15 hours)". Moreover, a number of empirical studies conducted on both channels during the 1992, 1997, 2001 and 2005 general elections have revealed an enhanced focus on stories about the process of politics, relegating issue-based political news (see Norris *et al.* 1999; Deacon *et al.* 2001; Deacon *et al.* 2006). However, these longitudinal trends do not convey the distinct democratic value of the BBC's election news coverage. During the 2010 UK general election, the BBC 10 pm news contained the greatest number of policy-related stories of all the late evening UK television news bulletins (see Table 4.7). Five and Sky News bulletins, by contrast, featured the most election news stories with no reference to policy issues.

However, public service broadcasters do not uniformly follow a higher issue- driven agenda than their commercial competitors. Tworzecki and Semetko (2010) compared the Polish evening news bulletins of TVP's Wiadomeośći, the public broadcaster, and TVN's Fakty, the commercial equivalent and found striking differences during the 2005 general election. They concluded that:

> it is clear that Fakty (the news program on the private channel) featured nearly twice the amount of policy-orientated coverage when compared to Wiadomeośći, its public channel counterpart. Furthermore, the public channel had nearly twice the amount of news coverage that featured strategy or conflict frames, and nearly twice the amount of both humor and disdaining comments, compared to news on the private channel. (Tworzecki and Semetko 2010: 165–6)

Table 4.7 Percentage of election news relating to the level of policy on national nightly UK TV news bulletins[13]

Level of policy	*BBC1 10 pm news*	*ITV 10.30pm news*	*Channel 4 7 pm*	*Five 7 pm*	*Sky News 9 pm*
Entirely about policy issues	20.4	7.4	17.2	7.4	14.9
Significantly about policy issues	20.4	17.5	12.9	11.1	13.4
Limited reference to policy issues	28.1	38.1	34.4	30.9	19.4
No reference to policy issues	31.1	37	35.4	50.6	52.2

However, while the Polish commercial broadcaster bucked the trend cross-nationally – reporting more policy-orientated news than its public competitor – proportionally speaking, election coverage on both media systems contained a far higher agenda of stories related to policy than most other commercialized countries (39 per cent), most notably the US.

Esser's (2008) comparative analysis of US, UK, German and French elections throughout the 2000s illustrated some of the differences and similarities across national cultures and media systems. The study examined, in detail, the overall volume of election coverage, the average story time, length and nature of soundbites and image bites, and the relative time granted to candidates and journalists. Esser (2008) established that all public service television news bulletins spent more time covering the elections than commercial outlets (see Tables 4.8 and 4.9). In the early 2000s, politicians' soundbites

Table 4.8 Number and length of election news items in national TV bulletins during US, UK, German and French elections in the 2000s

	US 2000		*UK 2001*		*Germany 2002*		*France 2000*
	ABC	*NBC*	*BBC1*	*ITV*	*ARD*	*RTL*	*Not coded*
No. of election stories	75	56	147	87	54	30	–
Mean story length (secs)	118	138	138	114	178	107	–
Cumulative story length (mins)	148	118	338	165	161	53	–
Total length of election news (mins)	266		503		214		–

(Adapted from Esser 2008)

Table 4.9 Number and length of election news items in national TV news bulletins during US, UK, German and French elections in the 2000s

	US 2004		*UK 2005*		*Germany 2005*		*France 2007*	
	ABC	*NBC*	*BBC1*	*ITV*	*ARD*	*RTL*	*TF1*	*F2*
No. of election stories	120	94	141	171	59	36	103	135
Mean story length (secs)	99	126	149	122	137	103	113	113
Cumulative story length (mins)	199	197	351	344	132	62	193	255
Total length of election news (mins)	396		695		194		448	

(Adapted from Esser 2008)

Table 4.10 Average length of politician soundbite in national TV news bulletins during US, UK, German and French elections in the 2000s

	US 2000		*UK 2001*		*Germany 2002*		*France 2000*
	ABC	*NBC*	*BBC1*	*ITV*	*ARD*	*RTL*	*Not coded*
Average length of soundbite for political candidates (secs)	8.8	12.7	12.3	10.3	15.3	9.3	–

(Adapted from Esser 2008)

Table 4.11 Average length of politician soundbite in national TV news bulletins during US, UK, German and French elections in the 2000s

	US 2004		*UK 2005*		*Germany 2005*		*France 2007*	
	ABC	*NBC*	*BBC1*	*ITV*	*ARD*	*RTL*	*TF1*	*F2*
Average length of soundbite for political candidates (secs)	9.5	7.9	16.8	17	10.8	11.9	10.9	12.6

(Adapted from Esser 2008)

were notably longer on public service channels, although in the subsequent election the pattern changed somewhat. While the UK's average political soundbite in 2005 was broadly similar (17 seconds), on ITV it was marginally longer (11.9 seconds) than on the BBC bulletins (10.8 seconds). In the French 2007 election TFI – the commercial broadcaster – featured marginally longer soundbites than F2 (12.6 as opposed to 10.9 seconds) (see Tables 4.10 and 4.11). Comparatively speaking, however, even the French and British public broadcasters' lower volume of soundbites remained, on average, longer than on US television news bulletins of ABC and NBC (9.5 and 7.9 seconds respectively). However, the content of soundbites – whether it was about policy-substance or campaigning, attacking or defending another political candidate – indicated that cross-nationally trends were broadly similar (although soundbites on public service television bulletins were marginally more about policy issues, particularly in France – see Esser 2008: 416).

Esser's analysis (2008) also explored the degree to which journalists' own voices shaped every election news item (Tables 4.12 and 4.13). To what extent, in other words, do news media mediate the reporting of elections? With the exception of France, the study revealed that journalists on public service stations spent far more time speaking in routine election items than

Table 4.12 Average length of time journalist seen speaking in national TV news bulletins during US, UK, German and French elections in the 2000s

	US 2000		*UK 2001*		*Germany 2002*		*France 2000*
	ABC	*NBC*	*BBC1*	*ITV*	*ARD*	*RTL*	*Not coded*
Average length of time journalist seen speaking (secs)	36.8	42.9	43.3	34.1	71.6	41.0	–

(Adapted from Esser 2008)

Table 4.13 Average length of time journalist seen speaking in national TV news bulletins during US, UK, German and French elections in the 2000s

	US 2004		*UK 2005*		*Germany 2005*		*France 2007*	
	ABC	*NBC*	*BBC1*	*ITV*	*ARD*	*RTL*	*TF1*	*F2*
Average length of time journalist seen speaking (secs)	27.4	36.9	56.0	46.1	49.6	36.6	22.4	25.6

(Adapted from Esser 2008)

commercial broadcasters. While some scholars have argued this could represent an increasingly opinion-driven approach to journalism, Esser (2008: 414–15) suggested it can lead to a more informative delivery of political news. He pointed out that "a more journalist-centered narrative does not necessarily mean more cynicism. It can – for example, in the case of BBC1 – also mean in-depth reports to prepare citizens for better informed voting decisions and a more meaningful participation in the political process".

Esser (2008) also examined the use of image bites – "voiceless visuals of candidates" – which have become most prevalent on US television journalism (Bucy and Grabe 2009) and discovered that commercial bulletins contained many more of them than public service stations (see Table 4.15). Cross-nationally, the use of image bites varied, however, with candidates interpreted differently after visuals had been edited (see Esser 2008: 420–2). It was concluded that "the heavy reliance on visual-driven reporting constitutes a transnational trend in Western election news coverage, but it is more pronounced on commercial than public stations" (Esser 2008: 419).

Overall, while Esser's (2008) conclusions centred on the differences in national journalistic cultures as opposed to comparative media systems, his detailed cross-national analysis of sound and image bites showed some clear and, in some cases, striking differences across public and commercial broadcasters.

Table 4.14 Average length of image bites in national TV news bulletins during US, UK, German and French elections in the 2000s

	US 2000		*UK 2001*		*Germany 2002*		*France 2000*
	ABC	*NBC*	*BBC1*	*ITV*	*ARD*	*RTL*	*Not coded*
Candidates seen but not heard as % of average story length	16	19	10	16	7	17	–

(Adapted from Esser 2008)

Table 4.15 Average length of image bites in national TV news bulletins during US, UK, German and French elections in the 2000s

	US 2004		*UK 2005*		*Germany 2005*		*France 2007*	
	ABC	*NBC*	*BBC1*	*ITV*	*ARD*	*RTL*	*TF1*	*F2*
Candidates seen but not heard as % of average story length	13	15	10	12	9	16	11	12

(Adapted from Esser 2008)

In Strömbäck and Dimitrova's (2011) analysis of US and Swedish elections, they too emphasized the importance of national journalistic cultures when exploring the mediatization of news (e.g. the strategy frame). They found that the use of the strategic game was far greater on US commercial television stations compared to Sweden. Indeed, the Swedish public service channels featured the least amount of news related to game-type coverage (reinforcing studies already explored in this chapter). However, in other respects the differences between commercial and public service broadcasters were less apparent. Soundbites, the presence and interpretation of journalists, and the editing of image bites were, broadly speaking, similar within a Swedish context. In interpreting their study, overall, it was argued that "the effects of media commercialism may be moderated by national journalism cultures and national political news or political communication cultures" (Strömbäck and Dimitrova 2011: 44).

The role of national journalistic cultures and political structures (see Chapter 2) in shaping election coverage will be returned to in the chapter conclusion, which will analyze and interpret the prevailing comparative trends of election coverage across media systems cross-nationally. The next section explores how broadcasters have adapted their journalism to suit online platforms but it begins with an analysis of the way media systems have reported televised leaders' debates during election campaigns in recent years.

Old politics, new media: exploring the differences in public and market-driven reporting of the televised leaders' debates and elections online

So far the chapter has examined well-established trends in news coverage of elections. But, over the last decade or so, the Internet has increasingly shaped election contests, changing the way that campaigns have been conventionally waged since the 1960s. While much academic literature about elections has focused on the ability of politicians and political parties to harness new communication technologies to communicate with voters online, less attention has been paid to how broadcasters have shifted from "old" to "new" media to inform citizens beyond television or radio. This chapter unpacks the relatively scarce literature empirically exploring how commercial and public broadcasters have migrated online at election times.

Online media, of course, have not only impacted on the nature of election broadcast journalism. For, despite the rise of "new" media platforms, "old" media like television have remained central to election campaigns, reinforcing the influence and power it exerts at critical democratic moments (Cushion 2012; Gurevitch *et al.* 2009). This is not just because television has continued to be the most consumed media at election times. Televised leaders' debates have become stalwarts of election campaigns in many countries. Since the first US presidential leaders' debate in 1960, in advanced democracies such as Australia, Canada, France, Germany, the Netherlands, New Zealand and, most recently, the UK, candidates' performance in these staged televised events has had a wider impact on the nature of media coverage such as in the build-up to live debate appearances or in the subsequent reaction to them.

For the most part, academic literature concerning these debates has been primarily concerned with media effects, with studies assessing whether they have swayed viewers into voting – or not – for a particular candidate. But the extent to which the anticipation of leaders' debates have shaped election coverage before broadcast or in the "post-match" analysis has also been a focal point in scholarly research, since voters tend to form opinions not just when they watch it live, as it happens (Benoit and Currie 2001). In this context, the presence of the "spin room" – a space where journalists and political advisors debate the relative merits of each candidate's performance straight after it has finished – has been considered pivotal to how each leader is framed in subsequent media coverage. In doing so, from as far back as the classic Nixon vs Kennedy 1960 debate, empirical studies have shown media coverage to focus primarily on the character of candidates – their style, mannerisms, gesticulations, speech and tone, and marginalizing policy disagreements.

Summarizing research in Canada, Gidengil (2008) has suggested "Metaphors of warfare, violence, and stereotypically masculine sports like professional ice hockey and boxing dominated television news coverage of the 1993, 1997 and 2000 televised party leaders' debates". Likewise, in Australia, Tiffen (2008: 121) has observed that:

> after televised debates the press typically focus on whether there was a knockout blow and any indicators of 'who won' more than an examination of what was said. Such framing, signaling momentum and naming winners, means policy differences often come pre-interpreted.

Meanwhile, in the Netherlands, de Vreese (2008: 155) has pointed out that "television debates have gained in importance and have also become the focus of news coverage of the elections ... . In 2002, 2003, and 2006 the debates were important events in the campaign and generated much subsequent coverage". There is evidence in other countries too that debates have gradually enhanced both the game and strategic frames in subsequent coverage (Lawson 2008; Strömbäck 2008).

However, only a limited set of media content analyses have systematically compared how different media systems have reported post-election debate news. Since Germany introduced a live televised debate in 2002 between the two main leaders, studies have shown an increase in the use of visual imagery in media coverage, together with more strategy framing, marking a significant shift in how elections have historically been reported (Esser and Hemmer 2008; Reinemann and Wilke 2007). Schulz and Zeh's (2007) analysis of the 1990, 1994, 1998, 2002 and 2005 general election television news coverage established that the volume of visual images and the original voice of the main candidates increased on the nightly public news bulletins (ARD and ZDF) from approximately 40 per cent to over 60 per cent. The commercial bulletins (RTL and SAT1), by contrast, increased from over 30 per cent to over 80 per cent. Thus, while both public service television bulletins produced more personalized election reporting over the last two decades, they did not do so to the same degree as commercial outlets. In Greece, fascination with the televised leaders' debate has also shaped immediate television election coverage, but at a higher rate for commercial than public media. Demertzis and Pleios (2008: 203) identified that:

> In the 2004 national election, news about the single debate that took place between the leaders of five political parties (ND, PASOK, left coalition, Communist Party, and DIKKI) represented 19% of the first three news stories on all TV stations. The number of news stories about the debate in all commercial stations taken together was 182 (mean value 36.4) and 39 in the two public channels (mean value 19.5).

In New Zealand, where leaders' debates have become an established part of the election cycle too, the public service broadcaster has faced criticism for pursuing an explicitly commercial agenda. Atkinson, for example, suggested that New Zealand broadcasters in the run-up to the 2002 election were "recklessly indifferent to public service canons of fairness, impartiality and sobriety" (cited in Comrie and Fountaine 2005: 40). The device of the worm during the leaders' debate in 2005 – a controversial device measuring a small sample of voters' approval of particular candidates on an on-screen graph – was used more sparingly after a High Court ruled it could potentially bias election coverage. According to Comrie and Fountaine (2005: 40), "This new restraint meant television audiences heard more from all the leaders about themselves and their policies, but the lower key debates lacked the feisty appeal that had sparked newspaper headlines in previous elections".

In the UK, the first televised leaders' debates were not aired until the 2010 general election after several broadcasters ran campaigns promoting them (Boulton and Roberts 2011). The debates generated considerable publicity and content analysis studies have shown that they significantly impacted on the election news agenda. The first debate captured 59 per cent of all UK national broadcast and press election coverage on the day and the following two days, 45 per cent for the second debate and 35 per cent for the third one (Deacon and Wring 2011: 286). In another study, Coleman *et al.* (2011: 22) found public and commercial broadcasters more or less carried the same volume of election news about the debates (39 items on the late-night BBC and ITV bulletins). However, the detailed empirical study revealed that the way in which the BBC reported the debates, overall, was distinctive from the more commercially driven channels. On a five-point scale, Coleman *et al.* (2011) measured how far each election debate story contained substantive policy or game-type coverage (they did not distinguish between game and strategy frames) (see Table 4.16).

While BBC news outlets did pursue purely game election stories, most of the commercial broadcasters had a higher ratio of mainly game items. By contrast, with the exception of ITV *News at Ten*, the BBC news outlets – most strikingly the BBC 10 o'clock news – featured a greater number of purely substance stories about the leaders' debates.

More qualitatively, the study examined the use of "metaphorical language of sport ('the horse race' – 'own goal' – 'winners/losers', war ('battleground' – 'pincer movement' – 'all guns blazing') or the mysterious dark art of 'spin'" (Coleman *et al.* 2011: 24). It revealed that, while BBC outlets (38 per cent) used more sport and war references than the commercial stations (22 per cent) in coverage overall, they made fewer predictions about the so-called "winners" or "losers" of the debates (43 per cent compared to 68 per cent respectively). In addition, the BBC's 10 o'clock news included more substantial election television coverage, since it referred to more specific policies (20 per cent) than the commercial bulletins (13 per cent).

In making sense of the televised leaders' debates, criticism was launched at the instant, unrepresentative snap polls used to frame immediate post-match analysis (similar to New Zealand) (Chadwick 2011). The integration of social

Table 4.16 Percentage of level of game or substance election UK national news coverage of the leaders' debates

Media type	*BBC*			*ITV/Sky/Channel 4*			
Specific media	*BBC* News at Ten	Breakfast	Newsnight	*Channel 4 News*	Decision Time *Sky*	*GMTV*	*ITV* News at Ten
Game/scale substance (1–5 only)							
1 = Purely game	18	23	25	32	14	41	18
2 = Mainly game	13	21	16	32	38	22	21
3 = Some substance, some game	34	30	31	26	29	25	29
4 = Mainly substance	11	3	12	5	10	2	11
5 = Purely substance	24	23	16	5	10	11	21

(Adapted from Coleman *et al.* 2011)

media, such as Facebook and Twitter, was also called into question, as to whether it informed or confused viewers about the debates (Newman 2010). Broadcasters' live website blogs described what was happening in the debate and allowed simultaneous interaction with online users. With so much experimental online activity by UK news media outlets during the 2010 election, the evidence evaluating this material has primarily consisted of media commentaries or immediate post-election reports. Since these were often more impressionistic than evidence-based accounts, it is difficult to draw upon a reliable body of comparative analysis of public and market-driven online journalism. However, Newman's (2010: 15) in-depth review into the use of social media during the UK 2010 general election campaign observed that: "The process of monitoring and assessing activity in blogs and Twitter has become quite sophisticated at the BBC. Over the last four years, the user-generated hub has built up a considerable amount of expertise in social newsgathering." With the luxury of more production staff than most commercial media, the BBC had enough resources to experiment with its election online output.

Considering election news coverage cross-nationally, where Internet access is relatively widespread, such as in the UK, Australia and the US, audience studies have shown that voters have increasingly migrated online to find campaign news. There remain significant differences cross-nationally, of course, since Internet penetration levels can vary for a wide range of reasons (see Chapter 1). Broadcasters, in this context, have had to adapt their conventional coverage to websites, making use of interactive features and, more recently, integrating social media into their online news services.

Before exploring how broadcasters have responded to the challenges of online election journalism, it is advisable to identify any notable differences between online and offline news . However, as Karlsson and Strömbäck (2010: 6) have pointed out, "there are still rather few systematic studies on the content of online news". In addition, while they suggested that the interactivity and immediacy of online news have framed the design of many empirical studies, this "mainly focuses on the news site-level rather than news story-level of analysis" (Karlsson and Strömbäck 2010: 6). Methodologically, then, media scholars are grappling with how to research online news to take into account its fluidity (cf. Deuze 2006).

Making systematic sense of online election news agendas is therefore a difficult research endeavour. The Pew Research Center Project for Excellence in Journalism 2009 US *The State of the News Media* report, however, has comprehensively traced online election coverage and compared it to media coverage more generally. Over the course of 2008, Pew examined the five most popular news websites, AOL News, CNN.com, Google News, MSNBC.com and Yahoo News and established that election stories accounted for 25 per cent of the entire agenda of the year. By contrast, election news media more generally made up 36 per cent of coverage in 2008. When online election coverage was broken down and compared to the agenda of news media more generally, the nature of campaign reporting was broadly similar although a higher volume of political horse-race stories (e.g. game-frame coverage) was evident (Table 4.17).

The higher proportion of online horse-race stories can perhaps be explained by the greater emphasis this type of journalism places on breaking news, with the latest polls immediately uploaded and their significance debated. While online news media have the ability to instantly break stories, they also have the space to run more analysis and context than other fast-moving media such as rolling news channels (see Chapter 6).

Table 4.17 Percentage of the nature of election stories in US online and news media generally over 2008

Nature of election story	*Online*	*Media all over*
Political horse race	63	57
Other political	9	13
Policy	12	13
Personal	5	7
Public record	4	3
Other	7	6

(Adapted from Pew Research Center Project for Excellence in Journalism 2009, cited from PEJ, *A Year in the News*, 2008)

Since little empirical attention has been paid to online news agendas generally, understanding the differences between media systems at election time can be difficult. Nonetheless, several accounts of public service media in the digital era – see Chapter 1 – showed how many news outlets have transformed their conventional journalism online, pioneering innovative features that have now become well-established fixtures on news websites. But, as already pointed out in Chapter 1, the online expansion of public service media has been rigorously contested by commercial competitors, since most lack the resources to sustain the global infrastructure or depth of news websites such as the BBC's (Allan and Thorsen 2011). At election time, of course, news, analysis and context have to be repackaged to reflect the campaign and, moreover, complement existing online services. An analysis of online news about the UK's 2005 general election, in this respect, singled out the BBC's election news website for praise:

> The BBC, in line with its public service remit, offered a comprehensive and wide ranging web presence for the election. In addition to the large volume of news stories published each day, visitors could look up reference data on past results, details of candidates and see the projected impact of the polls on the composition of parliament. Feature coverage ranged from the very simple, how to physically cast a vote, to more complicated explorations of social and economic issues. (Downing and Davidson 2005)

According to Young (2011: 205),

> As with the BBC in the UK, in Australia the ABC was leading the way in online news. In 2007, the ABC website featured breaking news, interactive tools to follow the campaign, psephological information, maps, graphs and statistics, and ABC programs were streamed and downloadable via text, video and audio.

Meanwhile, SBS, Australia's multicultural public broadcaster, assisted a citizen journalism experiment, You Decide 2007, allowing members of the public to develop their own user-generated election content and produce "journalism as social networking" (see Flew and Wilson 2010: 131).

Attempts to develop a more grassroots, bottom-up, citizen-led approach to election journalism have been ongoing for many years. After the 2001 UK general election, which witnessed the lowest turnout for over 80 years, many broadcasters attempted to communicate more directly with voters and engage them in the political process (see Cushion *et al.* 2006). However, reflecting on coverage of the 2005 general election, Chris Shaw, senior programme controller of the commercial station, Five, suggested that "getting closer to the real people got out of hand". However, while there were many novel initiatives and specially developed programming, a systematic review of local newspaper coverage found citizens remained peripheral actors, there to help set the scene rather than play an active role in election debates, over the course of the election campaign. This is consistent with empirical studies that have explored routine television news coverage in other countries, where citizens tended to be portrayed as relatively passive players in politics, unable to dislodge the agenda of politicians or journalists (Brookes *et al.* 2004; Garcia-Blanco 2011; Garcia-Blanco and Cushion 2010; Lewis *et al.* 2005).

Regarding the same election, a systematic review of the BBC's online website reached a similar conclusion about the representation of ordinary citizens (Thorsen 2009). While there were several well-intentioned interactive web features, whether on the main election 2005 site, election monitor, UK voters' panel and Have Your Say sections, according to Thorsen (2009) these did not cast citizens in the most active light, failing to meaningfully kickstart a conversation between citizens, journalists and, importantly, elected representatives. He observed that "the BBC struggled to integrate the traditional journalism provision online with new content and innovations" (Thorsen 2009: 235).

Meaningfully comparing or forming any clear-cut conclusions about the relative merits of online election news between media systems has proven difficult in this section due to a lack of empirically informed studies. Before any firm conclusions can be drawn, further systematic research is needed into online news agendas as well as into how interactivity and immediacy can shape story selection and thus the quality of election coverage (Karlsson and Strömbäck 2010).

Beyond national news and presidential/prime ministerial campaigns: comparing coverage of "second order elections" on competing media systems

Most election studies relate to *national* presidential or prime ministerial campaigns. But there remain, of course, elections at different legislative levels, including regional and local, or at a supranational institution such as the European Union. Since these electoral contests tend to be interpreted as less politically significant than national elections, they have become known as "second order elections" (see De Vreese 2003). The term was coined to differentiate elections viewed as less important than prime ministerial or presidential national elections by voters, politicians and journalists. Of course, all-encompassing labels can crack over differences cross-nationally (such as attitudes towards the EU across Europe) or within nations (such as affinities to a state or regional institutions). But for the purpose of comparing different media systems, "second order elections" represent an important democratic moment, typically overshadowed by the hype or razzmatazz involved in increasingly expensive and long-running *national* election campaigns (Sussman 2005). After all, since the editorial missions of many public service media organizations are committed to enhancing democratic culture within nation states (see Chapter 1), informing voters about *all* their political institutions is fundamental to local or supranational democracies.

With the exception of the US, studies about the reporting of "second order elections" have tended to focus on national news media. Indeed, put another way, beyond the US, local/regional broadcast reporting of *any* elections has been relatively scarce (in the UK, there have been some systematic studies of local/regional press coverage of general elections however – see Cushion *et al.* 2006; Franklin 2004; Franklin and Cushion 2007; Franklin and Richardson 2002). Local/regional broadcast reporting of elections at a state/council/regionalized level has, in short, been little researched. It is thus difficult to establish how these elections have been routinely covered by different media systems cross-nationally.

Nevertheless, in this final section the reporting of "second order elections" by different media systems is longitudinally explored by drawing on (a limited set of) systematic national and more localized content studies across several elections at varying legislative levels. The focus, primarily, will be on the volume of election news as opposed to the nature of the coverage. As already explained in this chapter, the nature of election news can vary from game-centred coverage of candidates, including campaign tactics and horse-race polling, to more substantive issue- or policy-based political journalism. And, according to Schuck *et al.* (2010), "second order elections" can supply news frames distinct from national election campaigns such as in EU elections because clear-cut "winners" and "losers" are less immediately obvious (i.e. coalitions take time to form etc.). But, since there is a limited array of comparative studies upon which to draw, the main purpose here is to investigate the degree to which each media system is committed to reporting "second order elections".

A large-scale content analysis study of 26 nations' television news coverage of the 2009 EU election campaign shed considerable light on the depth to which both public and commercial television news reported the campaign three weeks prior to election day (see Table 4.18).

In making sense of the volume of EU campaign coverage overall, it is important not to overlook national characteristics. For, while many countries are supportive of EU institutions and have embraced a European identity, several remain Eurosceptic and, moreover, openly hostile to any pan-European institutions. This will clearly inform both the extent to which television news bulletins cover what is happening in the elections and the nature of campaign reporting. Put more bluntly, for many broadcasters "second order elections" represent a moment when commercial considerations and public service values collide, making the extent of different media systems' coverage all the more revealing. In addition to the contrasting news values cross-nationally, the overall frequency of EU news items was also strikingly different (Table 4.18), reflecting conflicting formats where reports may differ drastically in length. To draw fair comparative conclusions, the balance of public and commercial EU election coverage *within* nations is, above all, the most revealing.

Of the 26[14] countries examined, 21 public service television news bulletins reported the EU election campaign to a greater degree than their commercial counterparts (in Finland the same amount of news was covered). The four commercial broadcasters that reported greater EU campaign coverage than public service outlets – Slovenia, Poland, Bulgaria and Malta – supplied a relatively high level of campaign coverage (comparatively speaking) and, with the exception of Malta, the differences between media types were not hugely significant. Incidentally, in all these countries, according to the Eurobarometer, a majority of the population trusted the EU (2010).[15] In countries where distrust of the EU is more prevalent, public service broadcasters sustained more comprehensive coverage of the EU campaign (see Table 4.18 – in Austria, Germany, France and the UK). But overall there were some striking differences in the (again, relatively speaking) balance between public and commercial EU campaign coverage cross-nationally (see Table 4.18 – in Austria, Belgium, Czech Republic, Denmark, Estonia, Hungary, Romania and the Netherlands).

Longitudinal trends in the 1999 and 2004 EU elections were examined cross-nationally in comparative studies of 26 nations' television coverage. Put simply, De Vreese *et al.* (2006: 489) established that "EP [European Parliamentary] elections were consistently more visible on public broadcasting news programmes than on commercial television news." Moreover, as a proportion of all news over the campaign period, De Vreese *et al.* identified that election coverage increased far more on public broadcasters from 1999 to 2004 than commercial television news (see Table 4.19).

Since the many countries that make up the EU have different broadcast ecologies and funding structures (see Chapter 1), patterns remain within countries that should not be ignored. So, for example, public service television news bulletins in new member states appeared to have enhanced the overall level of EU election coverage after the millennium. Nonetheless, the general picture remains the same: in what have broadly been labelled "second order elections" most public television news reported more campaign news than commercial outlets. This is perhaps reflected most significantly in countries least engaged with the EU, where public media supplied coverage of the elections while market-driven media largely ignored them (De Vreese *et al.* 2006). More detailed cross-national content analyses could explore the hostility in coverage of the EU between different media systems.

If studies into EU election campaigns paint a useful macro national picture of how committed particular news media are to reporting "second order elections", local or regional news also has a vital role to play in covering more

Table 4.18 Number of 2009 EU election campaign news items across 26 European countries on public and commercial nightly TV news bulletins[16]

Country	*Public/state*	*No.*	*Commercial*	*No.*	*Public*	*No.*		*No.*
Austria	ZiB (ORF1)	45	Aktuell 19.20 (ATV)	12				
Belgium	Het Journaal (VRT)	21	VTM-Nieuws (VTM)	13	JT Meteo (La Une)	32	LE Journal (RTL-TV)	7
Bulgaria	BNT (Kanal 1)	33	bTV (bTV)	40				
Cyprus	RIK1	83	Ant1 (Antenna)	61				
Czech Republic	Udalosti (Ceska televise)	23	Televizninoviny (TV Nova)	4				
Denmark	TV-avisen (DR1)	26	Nyhederne (TV2)	12				
Estonia	Aktuaalne Kaamera (ETV)	21	Reporter (Kanal2)	8				
Finland	TV-uutiset ja sää (YLE TV1)	20	Kymmenen (MTV3)	20				
France	Le Journal (F2)	37	Le Journal (TF1)	29				
Germany	Tagesschau (ARD)	10	Aktuell (RTL)	8	Heute (ZDF)	14	SAT1	4
Greece	Net (bulletin at 9 pm)	148	Kentriko deltio (Mega)	134				
Hungary	Hirado (M2)	41	Esti Hirado (RTL-Klub)	16				
Ireland	Nine News (RTEI)	20	TV3 News (TV3)	10				
Italy	TG1 (RaiUno)	18	TG5 (Canale5)	16				
Latvia	Panorāmas (LTV)	19	T Ziņas (LNT)	11				
Lithuania	Panorama (LTV)	15	TV3 žinios (TV3)	8				
Malta	L-Ahbarijiet TVM (TVM)	56	One News (One TV)	150				
Netherlands	NOS Journaal	23	RTL Nieuws (RTL)	10				
Poland	Wiadomości (TVP1)	30	FAKTY (TVN)	35				
Portugal	Telejornal (RTP1)	87	Jornal Nacional (TVI)	57				
Romania	Telejurnal (TVR1)	21	Stirile (Pro TV)	4				
Slovakia	Spravy (STV1)	37	Televizne Noviny (TV Markiza)	21				
Slovenia	Dnevnik (TVS1)	32	24UR (POP TV)	47				
Spain	Telediario-2 (TVE1)	74	Telecinco (Tele5)	35			Noticias2 (Antena3)	51
Sweden	Rapport (TV2)	19	Nyheterna (TV4)	17				
UK	News at Ten (BBC)	14	News at 10 (ITV)	6				

Table 4.19 Percentage of election news as a proportion of all news over the campaign period in the 1999 and 2004 EU elections

	Public television news	*Commercial television news*
1999	6.3	4.9
2004	9.5	5.2

(Adapted from De Vreese *et al.* 2006: 489)

local democratic contests. At a micro level, local/regional elections rely almost exclusively on localized news media to report what is happening. However, as already pointed out, with the exception of the US, there has been little sustained attempt to longitudinally trace patterns in regional or local broadcast coverage of elections.

To explore localized coverage of "second order elections", a series of content analysis studies examining broadcast news coverage of Welsh electoral events can be drawn upon. Wales voted in a referendum for a new political institution in 1997 after the UK Parliament devolved some of its powers to the nations (including Scotland and Northern Ireland). Two years later Assembly elections took place and a new era of Welsh politics emerged. However, since many voters in Wales continued to rely on UK national news media, concerns have been raised about the extent to which both Welsh and UK broadcasters inform citizens about devolved politics (Barlow *et al.* 2005; Ferguson and Hargreaves 1999; Cushion *et al.* 2009a; Cushion *et al.* 2009b; Thomas *et al.* 2003; Thomas *et al.* 2004a; Williams 2000). In the very first Assembly election, for example, Ferguson and Hargreaves (1999) discovered almost no UK national broadcast coverage of the 1999 campaign.

In the 2003 Assembly election a media content analysis was employed to explore, in detail, commercial and public television and radio coverage of the campaign (Thomas *et al.* 2003). Once again, from a UK national perspective, there was minimal coverage of the election in Wales, although the BBC6 and 10 o'clock news bulletins were singled out for "some important contributions" (Thomas *et al.* 2003: 37). In Welsh television news, the two public broadcasters, BBC Wales and S4C (a Welsh-language channel), spent more time and reported more election news items than HTV, the then commercial station (see Table 4.20).

Overall, the BBC spent more than double the time on Assembly election news as its commercial competitor, typically running all its campaign news halfway through the bulletin, lasting between six to nine minutes. HTV, by contrast, afforded less space, on average, to election news but the prominence of its coverage was marginally higher than the BBC's. S4C, meanwhile, devoted the most time to the election, with the greatest number of lead stories and the longest average story length, and average bulletin space. For

Table 4.20 Percentage of campaign news in the 2003 Assembly elections on the early evening BBC, HTV and S4C bulletins

Bulletins	*Total time (in mins)*	*Total stories*	*Average story length (in mins)*	*Lead stories*	*2/3 Story*	*Average bulletin space (in mins)*
BBC 6.30pm	100.7	34	3.00	1	3	8.4
HTV 6pm	41.8	20	2.1	2	5	3.5
S4C 7.30pm	110.3	27	4.1	3	2	9.2

(Adapted from Thomas *et al.* 2003)

radio and online news media, a similar public service commitment to covering the Assembly election was evident. HTV's online website carried a total of nine stories overall and, in the words of the authors, "provided immediate and easily consumed nuggets of information rather than detailed news analysis" (Thomas *et al.* 2003: 64). BBC Wales Online featured 31 election news and comment stories, with "regularly updated and impressively supported … webcast audio and video reports … a mixture of interactive features and election information" (Thomas *et al.* 2003: 65). Finally, a comparative study of BBC Wales's 1 pm radio news bulletin and Real Radio – a commercial station – found more stories on the public broadcaster throughout the campaign (Thomas 2003 *et al.*, 2004).

A follow-up study was carried out to explore whether another "second order election" – the 2004 local council and European elections in Wales – would yield a similar commitment to campaign reporting across public and commercial television news bulletins. From a UK perspective, council and European elections arguably hold less significance than general and Assembly elections and could even be relegated to "third order" status. Once again, the BBC assigned approximately twice as much coverage as (the renamed commercial television broadcaster) ITV Wales (53 and 28 minutes respectively).[17] However, there were no lead stories on either channel, perhaps reinforcing its status as a "third order election".

Election stories were also broken down by whether the focus was on the local or European elections, or a mixture of both (Table 4.21). On both public and commercial news bulletins, the local council elections took precedence over the European elections. But what the authors also point towards is the high level of "general" election news, blurring together two separate and distinct elections. Proportionately speaking, this was far higher on ITV Wales, since well over half of all campaign coverage mixed local/European compared to a third on the BBC. BBC Wales, in other words, provided the most focused coverage, examining a particular election in more detail, whereas ITV Wales ran more mixed campaign news items. Moreover, both content analysis studies of broadcasters during elections shortly after devolution revealed the

Table 4.21 Percentage and volume of campaign Welsh broadcast television news in the 2004 local and European elections

	Local council	*Mixed*	*European*
BBC 6.30 pm	14 (36%)	13 (33%)	12 (31%)
ITV Wales 6 pm	5 (26%)	11 (58%)	3 (16%)

(Adapted from Thomas *et al.* 2004b)

extent to which Wales relied on the BBC to inform voters about what have become known as "second order elections".

There have, however, been no replicated election content studies of BBC Wales or its commercial competitor since 2004 to explore subsequent longitudinal trends.[18] ITV has faced serious funding issues in its regional budgets (including that for Wales) and its public service requirements to report local news have been relaxed in recent years (Cushion 2012). O'Malley (2011: 22) believes that "The retreat of ITV from its public service obligations has weakened the range, quality and depth of coverage in Wales by public service television." In this context, it is left to the BBC to supply the editorial content that the commercial broadcasters (despite some regulatory pressure to carry local news) have been increasingly downsizing in recent years.

In the US, where the market-driven landscape in local news is more widespread, there has been some research into whether corporate ownership shapes the quality of election news coverage beyond presidential elections. Dunaway (2008), for example, examined local television news coverage of the 2004 US Senate race in Colorado and a gubernatorial race in Washington to explore, above all, if issue-based election news featured more in the news bulletins of stations under corporate or private ownership or if competition had enhanced the level of election reporting overall. The study found television news under corporate ownership carried a lower level of issue-orientated election stories. In addition, news stations operating with less competition within a state market had a higher ratio of issue-based campaign coverage than broadcasters in more commercially competitive environments. From Dunaway's (2008: 1200) statistical model, it was concluded that "The probability that a local television station produces issue coverage decreases by 23% under corporate ownership as opposed to private ownership." Put simply, the study argued that the quality of election coverage (i.e. issue-based news) is likely to diminish when journalism is produced in a more corporate environment.

Conclusions

The chapter began by comparing whether broadcast news is subjected to the same level of regulation cross-nationally at election time. Since most advanced democracies impose some form of electoral obligations concerning balance or impartiality (Kaid and Strömbäck 2008: 424), questions about overt forms of media bias have not been central to election studies around the world (with some notable exceptions, of course, such as the US – see Farnsworth and Lichter 2011). Thus, the focus of the chapter was less about bias or balance and more about the information voters received during the campaign, comparing the volume and nature of election coverage cross-nationally between media systems. In respect of quantity, the longitudinal trends of election coverage showed that, in most countries, public service media tended to report more campaign-based news over the campaign period than their commercial counterparts. Beyond the volume of election news, many national studies explored how "Americanized" journalism had become. For past and present studies of US elections have established that commercial media have increasingly adopted game or strategy framing of politics over more substantial issue-based coverage, downsizing the time and space afforded to understanding party policy differences. This appears to be a deeply ingrained approach to covering elections in the US, with even PBS favouring horse-race conventions in the 2008 presidential election and reporting only marginally more policy than network television news or the cable news channels.

Cross-nationally, public service media have maintained a relatively more distinct approach to election coverage than that prevalent in the US. For a general picture of election studies would conclude that public service television news stations, for the most part, covered more issue-based stories than commercial outlets at election time, with less emphasis on game or strategy framing of politics, or the personalization of reporting. Even since televised leaders' debates have become the centre-point of many campaigns, public service media appeared less susceptible to privileging game over substance election stories. While systematic reviews of online news agendas are relatively scarce, within the commercial world of US media marginally more horse-race coverage was reported on the most popular news websites, since they can instantly break stories on the latest poll or election gossip. However, all broadcasters have been criticized for not providing meaningful online conduits for citizens at election time. But public service broadcasters in the UK and Australia have been singled out for harnessing the immediacy and interactivity inherent in new media to enhance election coverage.

Comparatively speaking, it is perhaps in "second order elections" where public service and commercial media diverge most strikingly in their commitment to reporting elections. Longitudinal studies of previous EU elections have found European public broadcasters, taken together, have reported more campaign television news than their commercial counterparts. In the 2009 elections, a study of 26 countries found 21 public news bulletins carried more election stories over the campaign period, notably in countries where the majority of the population is hostile to European political institutions. Public service media, in other words, appeared to feel more democratically obliged to cover elections to which much of the public are, at best, indifferent or, at worst, openly hostile. While it was difficult to draw cross-national patterns in local/regional broadcast coverage of "second order elections", several systematic content analysis studies in Wales found public service media more committed to covering the newly acquired National Assembly for Wales. With more coverage on television news, radio and online platforms, public service media outflanked their market-driven news competitor. While the commercial broadcaster had fewer resources available to cover the elections, it was also not as obliged to report the campaign after public service obligations were reduced. In an overwhelmingly market-driven environment, such as the US, commercial competition and corporate ownership appeared to work against improving the level of issue-based coverage of Senate and gubernatorial contests.

But while most of the findings in this chapter paint public service media in a good "democratic light", they do not entirely reflect the longer-term trends evident in election studies in previous decades. Most comparative studies have shown that the nature of public service election news coverage has begun to resemble that of their commercial competitors. Whether in response to their commercial rivals, because more countries participate in televised leaders' debates or to counter the increasingly sophisticated and tightly run campaigns of political parties, public media have increased their proportion of horse-race stories, of candidates and personalities, of game-like reporting and, in particular, have adopted a more meditative or interpretative role during the election period (e.g. the strategy frame). Indeed, according to Esser's (2008) cross-national study, journalists on public television news spent more time than their commercial counterparts de-spinning the campaign and interpreting the election for their viewers.

However, while shades of "Americanized" election coverage stand out in election coverage generally in many countries around the world, there was a degree of variation in how far broadcasters relegated policy-related news in favour of reporting campaign processes. It has been observed that national journalistic cultures can act as a buffer against commercial impact while political structures can shield broadcasters from pressure to incorporate game or strategy conventions into routine election coverage (Esser 2008; Strömbäck and Dimitrova 2011). But while the agency of journalists, political structures or newsroom cultures should not be marginalized when making sense of cross-national trends, the evidence in this chapter suggests that the presence of a well-resourced public service broadcaster and a robust regulatory framework plays an important role in maintaining high quality journalism. So, for example, in Norway, where NHK – the public broadcaster – has long maintained a central role in television culture and can be seen to have influenced the journalism of TV2, a commercial channel launched in 1992. Jenssen's study of the Norwegian election observed:

> Their [TV2] coverage of the 2001 election campaign was almost identical [with NHK] in terms of volume and format. With the benefit of hindsight, this could have been predicted. Many of the journalists in TV2 were recruited from the NRK, and the government made the owners accept many of the standards of public broadcasting. Perhaps even more important, some of the key figures in TV2 were personally committed to these ideals. (Jenssen 2008: 260–1)

In the same spirit, the reverse of Jenssen's analysis can also take place: public broadcasters can emulate how commercial channels cover the elections. And, as this chapter has shown, there is evidence to support the view that public service media have begun to adopt conventions and practices more attuned to the commercial world of journalism. What the studies drawn on in this chapter suggest overall, however, is that in countries where a strong infrastructure of public media has remained in place, many commercial outlets have resisted undergoing a full US-type transformation in election reporting. Public service media appear, in short, to be leading the way in election coverage while indirectly maintaining the standards of commercial campaign coverage.

The next chapter explores another critical moment for news media, the reporting of war and conflict. While many broadcasters aim to cover events impartially (see Chapter 1), this can be extremely difficult during times of war amid a sea of misinformation and propaganda.

Chapter 5

Between patriotism and independence

The politics of reporting wars and conflicts

Introduction

Since historians started analyzing the impact of military campaigns, the supply of information in moments of war and conflict has proved critical in understanding the relative success and failure of warfare (Allan and Zelizer 2005a; Bennett *et al.* 2007; Carruthers 2011; Knightley 2003; Taylor 1992; Zelizer and Allan 2002/2011). From posters encouraging military recruitment – "Your Country Needs You!" – to the highly sophisticated US PR campaign waged at the headquarters in Qatar during the Second Gulf War, the "information war" has only intensified since the advent of cable and satellite news channels and, most recently, the proliferation of online news and use of social media (see also Chapter 6). If we accept, writing about military campaigns stretching back to the 1850s, the acclaimed war journalist Philip Knightley's (2004) widely quoted maxim that the first casualty of war is the "truth", then the availability of more information sources means even closer attention needs to be paid towards how war is reported by competing media systems.

Since the media environment has grown more competitive in recent decades with a wider range of news sources participating in "information warfare", scholarship exploring the relationship between the state, media and citizens in times of war and conflict has grown exponentially (Allan and Zelizer 2005a; Bennett *et al.* 2007; Hoskins 2004; van der Veer and Shoma 2004; Matheson and Allan 2009). The arrival of a new academic journal in 2008, *Media, War & Conflict*, represented the demand for this growing body of scholarship. It has also been observed that media accounts of times of warfare are "extensive: shelves in second-hand bookshops groan under the weight of journalist memoirs" (Cottle 2006: 77).

Cottle's (2006: 80–85) summation of the "voluminous" literature on media coverage of conflicts provides a useful context to the broad conclusions of the relationship between reporting and conflict. He identifies six overlapping areas that inform coverage:

1 the ownership of media, notably the commercial interest of advertisers in the US media, most prominently Fox News;
2 sourcing elite voices, primarily Western military institutions like the US state department;
3 adhering to the sensitive demands of censorship and regulatory rules governing information;
4 being able to access information held by military powers such as loss of civilian lives;
5 sociological reasons that tie reporting to national interests, including the sense of nationalism and patriotism amongst journalists; and finally
6 media self-censorship, which relates to news media having to sanitize the brutality of war to avoid offending largely Western audiences.

For the purposes of this book, what is missing here is a more nuanced appreciation of the political economy approach that unpacks in detail the differences between how wars and conflicts are reported across differently funded media systems. So, for example, while the political economy argument might explain how commercial broadcasters adopt a patriotic stance to appeal to viewers (reflecting public anger/emotions), most public service media operate under strict impartiality guidelines *but also* with a strong duty to bind rather than divide the "nation" (see Chapter 1). In this respect, it might follow that public media provide a different type of journalism in moments when the state is actively engaged in warfare. This chapter will ask whether there are any notable differences in the nature of war reporting between media systems cross-nationally and explores the tone and style of language used to convey what is happening and why.

In evaluating war reporting, Allan and Zelizer (2005b: 4) have suggested that it can act as a "litmus test for journalism", a prism through which to evaluate whether news can remain impartial and authoritative, or fair and balanced at moments when there is intense lobbying from state and military actors, or when journalists' own set of national loyalties or emotional sympathies are potentially compromised. Consistent with their impartiality guidelines (see Chapter 1), many broadcasters follow strict guidelines when reporting war or conflict. So, for example, the BBC's editorial guidelines state:

> The BBC has a special responsibility to its UK and international audiences when reporting conflict including wars, acts and planned acts of terror, sieges and emergencies. Large numbers of people across the world access our services for accurate news and information. They also expect us to help them make sense of events by providing context and impartial analysis

> and by offering a wide range of views and opinions. At such times, when there may be conflicting information and opinions, and with reliable information hard to come by, we need to be scrupulous in applying our principles of accuracy and impartiality. (BBC editorial guidelines)[19]

Thus, *in assessing the democratic value of news throughout this chapter, the quality of war reporting will be interpreted by whether different media are able to remain objective, impartial and balanced at times when journalists could be susceptible to heightened political, social and cultural pressures and influences.*

On a global scale, many studies of war reporting have tended to conclude that journalism is largely shaped by Western political and military elites rather than a wider pool of sources including those possibly opposed to military action or emanating from countries in conflict with Western interests. This is by no means uniform, and becomes complicated when Western opinion is split, a point of time when elite consensus (Hallin 1986) is not shared. This has been exemplified in recent years with the mixed public reaction to the ongoing Israeli–Palestinian conflict (Gamson 2002) and, of course, the 2003 war in Iraq. It is the latter war that is the central focus of this chapter. This is a case of necessity rather than choice, since in order to comparatively explore war reporting cross-nationally a large body of empirical scholarship is needed on the *same war or conflict*. In this respect, while in recent years assessments of particular wars or conflicts, such as in Lebanon, Syria, Egypt, Tunisia or between Israel and Palestine (see Philo and Berry 2004 and 2011 for extensive research in the UK context) have been ongoing, there is a limited body of empirical studies available examining the *same sustained period of time from around the world*. The controversy in the run-up to the war in Iraq in the aftermath of the terrorist acts of 9/11 has attracted the most scholarly attention. Because this generated a great number of empirical studies of news coverage, the *immediate post-9/11 reaction and the war in Iraq make up the primary focus of this chapter*.

Needless to say, an analysis of the war in Iraq alone cannot deliver a complete picture of the nature of war journalism. While Western attention was firmly fixed on Iraq in 2002 and 2003, many other wars have not generated the same media attention nor attracted the attention of scholars. A systematic content analysis of journalism journal articles found that studies focused on just a select few wars with Western interests, leaving many areas of the world largely neglected (Cushion 2008). So, for example, many nations in Africa, such as the Congo, Sudan, Uganda, Angola, Sierra Leone and Liberia, have not been subject to sustained academic attention despite huge human rights violations and the loss of millions of lives in wars and conflicts. This chapter regrettably reinforces this neglect of particular wartorn counties, since it is to a great extent reliant on secondary analysis of *existing* scholarship.

Limitations also extend to the nature of war reporting examined. For while the Internet has impacted on the nature of war journalism over the last decade or so (see Hall 2001; Taylor 2000), as with other chapters in this book, only a limited bank of comparative data is available to meaningfully distinguish between the nature of new online reporting across media systems (thus, the empirical studies drawn on are almost exclusively based on large-scale television news studies). Since most news organizations have an online presence, its immediacy and interactivity have enabled journalists to develop new war-reporting conventions beyond the possibilities offered by real-time television news channels (see Cushion 2010a; Thussu 2002; Thussu and Freedman 2003). No longer reliant on big news organizations, new sources of information and opinions have challenged their monopoly, with instant news and weblogs documenting updates on the war and images of conflict and casualties (see Matheson and Allan 2009). In the most recent conflicts, social media such as Facebook and Twitter have emerged as significant information sources for citizens, but also journalists, in places experiencing civil unrest, like Iran, Tunisia, Libya, Bahrain and Syria.

But while several empirical studies have looked at online news coverage of the war in Iraq (Al-Saggaf 2006; Dimitrova *et al.* 2005; Fahmy and Al Emad 2011; Schwalbe 2006), taken together these do not generate sufficient cross-national comparative evidence between different media systems to merit sustained evaluation in the chapter overall. So, for example, Dimitrova *et al.* (2005) uncovered many differences in online news coverage between US media and many other countries around the world (Egypt, Turkey, the UK, China, Argentina, Spain, Russia, Italy, France, the United Arab Emirates, Japan, Costa Rica, Pakistan and Malaya) with non-US media framing the success of the war in Iraq far more critically than US online journalism. Their sample, however, mixed newspapers, television and radio news without any meaningful comparisons between the ownership of different media. Other studies, in addition, confined analysis primarily to online newspapers rather than broadcasters with a web presence (Dimitrova and Connolly-Ahern 2007; Dimitrova and Neznanski 2006).

With these limitations acknowledged, the chapter now turns to exploring the immediate reaction of news media on different media systems to 9/11 cross-nationally before unpacking, more substantially, studies that have empirically compared the extent and nature of Iraq war coverage.

Making sense of conflict and terrorism: the framing of post-9/11 and subsequent wars on public and market-driven media systems

Many scholars have examined, from a variety of perspectives, the post-9/11 information environment that led first to war in Afghanistan and then in Iraq. In the US it has been pointed out that a climate of anger was cultivated by politicians and opinion formers, as demands for instant revenge and immediate warfare became the dominant response to the terrorist atrocities of 9/11, retold on mainstream media with limited opposition. It has been observed that a shared sense of patriotism began shaping news coverage as journalists understandably became caught up in the nation's emotional desire to execute swift justice (Zelizer and Allan 2002/2011). In this context, fulfilling a watch-dog role on the state became a difficult job, since the "heroes" and "villains" were quickly established, symbolized by George Bush's good vs evil speech, which identified Al-Qaeda as the "bad guys" (and, more subtly, linked Iraq's president Saddam Hussein with their acts of terrorism). Within the US network television news industry, many senior journalists all but relinquished values of independence, making clear their commitment to support of government action. Days after 11 September 2001, Dan Rather, a long-standing news anchor on CBS News, put it bluntly on *The David Letterman Show*: "George Bush is the president, he makes the decisions and you know, as just one American wherever he wants me to line up, just tell me where." Less than a year later, Rather conceded "patriotism run amok" had prevented many US journalists from robustly scrutinizing government about international affairs (quoted in Engel 2002).

While a sweeping sense of patriotism tells part of the story about why US broadcasters failed to hold the government to account at a critical period in American democracy, it has also been observed that the commercial structure of news media prevented any sustained criticism of US government foreign policy. Days after 9/11 all the major networks reverted to a rolling news format, pushing back regular programming and, temporarily at least, suspending their advertising breaks. According to Friedman (2001), $400m of advertising revenue was lost in just four days and the editorial content was closely policed (scenes of the World Trade Center on NBC's *Law and Order*, for example, were discreetly edited out). Since the advent of television, it was estimated that this was the longest period of time without on-screen advertising. At the time, a media vice president was quoted as saying "the emotions are too raw to be commercialized" (quoted in Friedman 2001). Most famously, Bill Maher, host of *Politically Incorrect*, witnessed firsthand the cost of offending audience sensibilities, after he rebuked George Bush for his claim that terrorists were cowards by suggesting that the description better fit Americans, since it was they who were "lobbing cruise missiles from 2,000 miles away". Some advertisers immediately pulled their support for the show while several local affiliate ABC stations refused to broadcast it after the comments gained national attention.

With lost advertising revenue and a media environment largely unwilling to accept any criticism of US foreign policy, the reporting of 9/11 and the subsequent wars in Afghanistan and Iraq was clearly compromised not just by a culture of patriotism. The editorial content of US networks appeared to be policed by commercial forces with executives reluctant to offend advertisers and lose further revenue. It was, after all, Dan Rather who conceded retrospectively that fear of public backlash prevented many journalists from carrying out their fourth estate role in the aftermath of 9/11 and the run-up to the subsequent wars.

Many systematic studies of network television news have revealed that coverage of international affairs almost exclusively replicated the government line, promoting the idea that war was unavoidable (see Altheide 2006 for overview). So, for example, Edy and Meirick (2007) examined the nightly network television news bulletins from 15 October to 2 November 2001 and identified that, rather than 9/11 being framed as a crime committed against the US, it was twice as likely to be discussed in the context of *war*. In the aftermath of 9/11 a six-month study of network American television found that 92 per cent of stories about the war in Iraq emanated from the White House, Pentagon or state department (Tyndall cited in Boehlert 2009). Lule (2004: 188) examined NBC *Nightly News* from February 2003 to the run-up to the Iraq war in late March and discovered that, despite ongoing diplomatic efforts in this period, metaphors used by the broadcaster "displaced other possible tropes that might have better profited a nation considering war". In company with other television news stations, NBC carried on-screen banners such as "Countdown: Iraq", "Showdown: Iraq" or "Target: Iraq" (Lule 2004: 183). Needless to say, these captions imply war to be inevitable, mimicking the countdown often displayed when a "big" sports game is imminent. Throughout the war in Iraq, too (explored in detail in the next section), a FAIR report demonstrated that minimal airtime was granted to any oppositional voices on ABC *World News Tonight*, CBS *Evening News*, NBC *Nightly News*, CNN's *Wolf Blitzer Reports*, Fox's *Special Report with Brit Hume* and PBS's *NewsHour* with Jim Lehrer. Despite many large anti-war demonstrations across the US and the fact that over a quarter of the nation indicated their opposition to the war, anti-war sources in television news bulletins ranged "from 4 percent at NBC, 3 percent at CNN, ABC, PBS and Fox, and less than 1 percent – one out of 205 U.S. sources – at CBS" (Rendall and Broughel 2003). While previous chapters have found PBS tended not to conform to the dominant patterns of network coverage, in this period it would appear that even the public broadcaster was reluctant to give regular access to opponents of the Iraq war.

Comparing the largely commercial US news media reaction to 9/11 and the prelude to the wars in Afghanistan and Iraq with news media beyond America is problematic for several reasons. Since the terrorists' attacks took place on US soil and the wars were primarily waged by American forces, frames of coverage will inevitably vary cross-nationally. For international comparisons of the reaction to news media around the world have demonstrated how far the geo-politics of the reaction to 9/11 and the wars launched to defeat "terrorism" shaped the nature of coverage. So, for example, essays in *How the World's News Media Reacted to 9/11* indicated how patterns of media coverage were often explained by the political relationship each country had with America (Pludowski 2007). Likewise, in an edited book, *Leading to the 2003 Iraq War: The Global Media Debate*, many chapters showed how *national* political, economic and social circumstances helped navigate how each country made sense of the possibility of war in a post-9/11 environment (Nikolaev and Hakanen 2006). In both edited books almost all of the chapters centred on how newspapers framed the terrorist attacks or provided a more impressionistic than systematic analysis of comparative broadcast media. Ottosen and Figenschou (2007), however, compared coverage of the Norwegian public and commercial main television news bulletins the week after 9/11 and their framing analysis revealed some differences. TV2, the more commercial station, began reporting the terrorist atrocities of 9/11 an hour and a half before the public broadcaster and delivered more emotionally charged accounts of events. But beyond the first couple of days, both broadcasters broadly interpreted the causes and consequences of 9/11 in similar ways, drawing on the same set of actors and exploring events through either neutral or Norwegian perspectives (Ottosen and Figenschou 2007).

Clausen (2003) examined cross-national differences in the reaction to media coverage of the 9/11 one-year anniversary – the US commemoration event held in New York and reported around the world – on public and commercial television news bulletins in the US (PBS, CBS, NBC, ABC), Canada (CBC), Japan (NHK, Asahi, TBS, Fuji and NTV), Ireland (RTE), Denmark (TV2) and Saudi Arabia (Al-Jazeera). Once again, the central conclusions related to how a global television event (9/11) was (re)interpreted by national priorities and geo-political relationships with America – a process Clausen labels "domestication". On closer examination, however, important if subtle differences between media systems cross-nationally were evident. This suggested that "domestication" can be negotiated differently across media systems. According to Clausen, this was evident in how each type of broadcaster observed the two-minute remembrance silence:

> public service channels in all countries (the American PBS, the Japanese NHK and the Irish RTE) broadcasted the two minutes of silence in NY. This seemingly long 120-second sequence was not broadcast by any private stations, which shows a difference in priority and broadcast style between the public service and the commercial stations. The Japanese commercial stations that send commercial slots are particularly careful with their time – and make a special effort to keep up the pace and excitement. (Clausen 2003: 109)

Even within the US, Clausen's (2003) analysis revealed a subtle difference in journalistic interpretation between media systems. She observed that:

> PBS broadcasted events at length. For instance, President Bush's speech on Ellis Island was televised in full. PBS let the cameras roll without much commentary. CBS stood out with its several-minute closing speech

> about 'American virtues' made by CBS anchor Dan Rather. Significant for the NBC programmes was its description of the 'different ethics' of the country-side in relation to 9.11. In the NBC programme, ordinary people were chosen to express rural ethics … . ABC presented a feature on how thousands of people have visited the square. 'They have come to find a way to deal with their grief.' It was also stated that 'This was the day when the American people went back to business as usual.' (Clausen 2003: 109)

Perhaps the most striking cross-national observations were found in providing a Middle Eastern perspective to events since, at this point in time, America was engaged in the Afghanistan war. While PBS and other public broadcasters attempted to remain relatively "neutral" (Clausen 2003), commercial broadcasters either adopted a pro- (in the US) or anti-war (primarily in Japan) interpretation of events.

> The US public service station did not refer to Middle eastern political actors whatsoever. The three commercial stations, on the other hand, did make several references to the proclaimed US invasion of Iraq, which was the top item on the political agenda of the UN meeting in NY the following day … . The commercial US stations presented the invasion as inevitable, while stations outside the US, including Canada and Denmark, merely referred to it. The Irish station appealed to the US to let the issue be decided within the framework of the United Nations, while Al-Jazeera was the only station to present reactions from Arab countries … . CBC represented the Arab view through several interviews … . Many of the Arab interviewees were intellectuals who voiced critical opinions on the Bush Administration's foreign policy. (Clausen 2003: 112)

Consistent with its attempt to remain politically neutral and to avoid any potential controversy, the Japanese broadcaster, NHK, did not feature any Arab voices but its US focus was not viewed as pro-American or pro-war (Clausen 2003: 114–15). The commercial broadcasters were more critical of the ongoing war although TV Fuji presented an historical account of Arab extremism, it "did not take sides" (Clausen 2003: 112). Al-Jazeera, however, was the most explicitly critical and framed coverage from a Middle Eastern perspective. RTE, meanwhile, featured Arabs and emphasized the role of the UN in discussions about a potential war in Iraq. TV2, by contrast, featured Bin Laden and used "dry humour" to explore the relationship between him and George Bush (Clausen 2003: 112).

In coverage more generally, then, it was possible to detect a less overtly politicized interpretation of the anniversary on PBS compared to commercial networks. However, criticism was more explicit on public than commercial media beyond the US. It was found that:

> The political commentary of the US public service PBS was short and to the point in presenting the commemoration event without victim stories and on-location journalistic impressions. The three US commercial stations in this light made use of untold amounts of 'God bless America', 'God loves America' rhetoric along with extensive use of American symbols: the flag, military effects, national buildings, the national anthem and general statements about the nature of the American people ... . In contrast to the US commentary, most comments made by anchors and correspondents in the Canadian public service station CBC were understated or indirect. The Canadian channel took up the issue of US patriotism and commented that 'Patriotism has gone too far in the US' (Peter Mansfield, CBC). Pictures supported the statement. (Clausen 2003: 111)

Meanwhile, the public service media stations in Japan and Ireland were described as neutral and reserved. By contrast, all the commercial Japanese broadcasters criticized US involvement in the war in Afghanistan and, according to Clausen, on TBS this bordered on the sensationalist with the use of dramatic music and a punchier format.

Since these countries had no active military involvement in the war in Afghanistan (excluding the US, of course), nor were they likely to participate in an impending war in Iraq, these national media perhaps had more leeway to criticize the actions of a *foreign* government and *foreign* soldiers. In the UK, by contrast, journalists were afforded no such luxury with Tony Blair's New Labour government controversially agreeing to a US/UK military invasion of Iraq despite considerable public opposition to the war beforehand. The reason why the UK went to war – and why reluctant Labour MPs voted to commit troops in Iraq – was largely because the government produced a report that Weapons of Mass Destruction (WMD) were, in Tony Blair's words, a "real and immediate threat". However, this claim and the report used to sell the war ("Iraq's Weapons of Mass Destruction: The Assessment of the British Government") – later to be known as the "dodgy dossier" – began to be challenged just months after military action had taken place, most famously by a BBC journalist, Andrew Gilligan (also less colourfully reported by Gavin Hewitt and Susan Watson), who claimed the case for war had been "sexed up" by government ministers and PR operatives. This triggered widespread public debate not just about the reliability of the government's case for the war, but about the BBC's journalistic practices and editorial aims and, importantly for this chapter, the role of public service media and their independence from government. For while it has often been argued (in the US most prominently) that public media tend to fall under the spell of the ruling government of the day during times of war and conflict, contrary to this received wisdom, it was the BBC that most robustly challenged the legal basis of the UK's military involvement in Iraq.

According to Barnett (2005), the BBC's scrutiny of the dossier represented a much threatened form of news – investigative journalism, a vital function of the fourth estate. Moreover, he believes the public broadcaster's rigorous policing of impartiality and extensive journalistic resources exposed the government's case for war in a way its commercial rivals could not have done:

> ITN, after a series of cuts and redundancies, no longer has the resources to pursue difficult political stories with rigour and determination. And it is difficult to believe, given that Sky News is ultimately owned by Rupert Murdoch, that a story of such political sensitivity ["sexing up" evidence of WMD] would have been pursued within the News International stable with the same vigour. (Barnett 2005: 337)

In the aftermath of the war in Iraq, it could thus be argued that the BBC displayed its independence from the state and challenged any accusations that as a public broadcaster it was a "mouthpiece" for the state. With no similar public service presence, studies have shown that US news media did not generate sustained questioning of WMD or the intelligence that justified the war (although, in America, the pretext to the war was politically and legally different) (Haynes and Guardino 2010; see also Kellner 2004). A systematic content analysis of network commercial television news between 1 August 2002 and 19 March 2003 showed that "Bush Administration officials were the most frequently quoted sources, the voices of anti-war groups and opposition Democrats were barely audible, and the overall thrust of coverage favoured a pro-war perspective" (Haynes and Guardino 2010: 59). Longitudinal content analyses in 1998, 2002 and 2003 showed that the US public radio broadcaster, NPR, did not meaningfully depart from the commercial line which largely accepted the existence of WMD either (Moeller 2004).

The conventional wisdom in the UK was that the BBC was anti-war, distorting coverage of the buildup and military invasion of Iraq. However, the next section suggests that, during the most intense military action (in March/April 2003), the public broadcaster's journalism was broadly similar (use of sources, story focus etc.) to commercial stations' coverage of the war in Iraq. Moreover, cross-nationally there were some differences between media systems in many countries around the world, though none striking, since war coverage tended to be framed by *national* concerns and anxieties.

Reporting the war in Iraq: making sense of global news nationally on competing media systems

As the previous section illustrated, amid the dramatic and emotional events immediately after 9/11, many US journalists no longer claimed to be independent, choosing to sacrifice professional ideals of "objectivity" and "impartiality" (see Chapter 2) and more or less reinforce rather than question government decisions about future wars (most controversially) in Iraq but also beforehand in Afghanistan. Many scholars have explored the subservient role US journalists played in helping to cultivate an environment where war seemed either necessary or inevitable (see Bennett *et al.* 2007). But for our purposes, it is important to establish empirically the way that US commercial broadcasters covered the Iraq war in order to compare cross-nationally whether other media systems conformed to or deviated from the perspective of the US government. In addition, while US media have been roundly criticized for the way that they reported the war, a closer examination suggests some subtle differences across the commercial networks and public broadcast journalism.

Aday *et al.* (2005a) examined US television news coverage (including the network bulletins of ABC, NBC and CBS along with the rolling stations, CNN[20] and Fox News) of the war in Iraq (between 20 March and 20 April 2003) and, as a point of comparison, explored whether the tone, balance and agenda of reporting were different from the Arab 24-hour news station, Al-Jazeera, over the same period (a channel discussed in more depth towards the end of this chapter). Table 5.1 shows that while the dominant story frame revolved around what was happening on the battlefield (most notably on Fox News and CNN), the US networks and, to a lesser extent, Al-Jazeera, spent less time covering war from this perspective.

What also stands out in Table 5.1 was that US television coverage failed to report any opposition to the war, either among American citizens or the wider

Table 5.1 Story subject percentages in reporting of the war in Iraq on US TV news and Al-Jazeera

	ABC	*NBC*	*CBS*	*CNN*	*Fox News*	*Al-Jazeera*
Battle	29.5	26.4	29	35.5	41	23.7
Strategy	7.4	8.6	10.7	6.5	13.7	4.8
Diplomacy	1.8	5.1	2.3	0.3	6.2	12.8
Reconstruction	4.8	5.1	9.2	2.8	7.5	6.5
Saddam Hussein	1.8	4.1	3.1	6.1	8.1	2.4
Media	2.5	3	0.8	1.5	1.2	3.7
POW: coalition	4	5.6	5.3	9.5	1.2	0.9
POW: Iraqi	0.9	0.5	–	0.8	–	0.4
Casualties: coalition	7.5	5.1	6.1	4.7	1.2	4
Casualties: Iraqi	–	0.5	0.8	0.6	–	0.7
Casualties civilian	4.4	3.6	3.1	3.4	0.6	4.5
Protest	2.6	3	1.6	1.2	–	6.4
Public opinion	0.8	1.5	–	–	1.8	0.7
Humanitarian crisis/relief	2.2	4.6	5.3	0.3	2.5	2.2
Weapons of mass destruction	2.6	2	0.8	3.6	0.6	1.6
Other	27.6	22.7	22.2	23.6	16.1	24.8

(Adapted from Aday *et al.* 2005a)

Table 5.2 Tone of war reporting percentages on US TV news and Al-Jazeera

	Critical	*Neutral*	*Supportive*
ABC	2.2	95.6	2.2
NBC	1	94.4	4.6
CBS	–	95.5	4.5
CNN	3.9	91.6	4.5
Fox News	–	62.1	37.9
Al-Jazeera	10.6	89.2	0.2

(Adapted from Aday *et al.* 2005a)

international community. Al-Jazeera news reports, by contrast, featured 6.4 per cent discussing the protests and, further still, 12.8 per cent related to international diplomacy. Since Fox News coverage centred on the battle and strategy aspects of war, together with the highest proportion of stories including Saddam Hussein, casualties of war (either American/British or Iraqi) barely featured in its coverage. In other words, Fox News painted a highly sanitized picture of war, with limited oppositional voices or images of casualties.

While journalists can only strive to be objective, Aday *et al.* (2005a) attempted to measure, relatively speaking, whether during the Iraq war news was fair and balanced. They examined the tone of every Iraq war story and assessed whether it was critical of the coalition, supportive or neutral (see Table 5.2). With the exception of Fox News, all the US television news networks achieved a relatively high level of neutrality. Fox News, by contrast, contained no critical coverage of the coalition but 37.9 per cent of reporting was spent supporting its activities. Al-Jazeera had a degree of critical coverage (10.6 per cent) but it was relatively similar to the neutrality of CNN's coverage. How Al-Jazeera covered the war will be explored more qualitatively later in the chapter, since the station's non-Western perspective cut across media systems to produce a more human interest angle to the military conflict.

While the opening weeks of war coverage revolved around the battlefield (with the use of live reporting or embedded journalists explored in the next section), Aday *et al.* (2005b) found that on Fox News and CNN the focus on military conflict and strategy shifted once the statue of Saddam Hussein was toppled on 9 April 2003. Both channels adopted what they call a "victory frame" after this event, as celebratory scenes replaced the reporting of continued military conflict and casualties. The lack of scrutiny paid to "on the ground" fighting, in other words, meant the US administration's military and political strategy was not held to account.

Since the intense period of fighting, studies have shown that less attention was gradually paid to the ongoing wars in Iraq and Afghanistan. Aday (2010: 150) found that, throughout 2005, NBC and Fox News downplayed the significance of acts of violence and military and civilian deaths. Once again, this was particularly the case on Fox News, where Republican sources far outweighed oppositional voices and coverage of Iraq and Afghanistan continued to be supportive despite military and political setbacks (Aday 2010: 155). The Pew Research Center Project for Excellence in Journalism (2005) *The State of the News Media* report suggested that there was some variation between US commercial television and PBS's *NewsHour* coverage of Iraq over the course of 2005. It found that 84 per cent of stories were free of "overt journalist opinion" and that, "on PBS, not a single Iraq-related story included journalist opinion." The tone of PBS's Iraq coverage presented a more mixed picture than the evening and morning network news bulletins (see Table 5.3).

Table 5.3 suggests that PBS did not conform to the apparent neutrality evident in many of the commercial morning and evening bulletins, and adopted a stance where the tone did not explicitly shape war reporting. PBS drew on fewer sources overall but a quarter of its reports were informed by more than four sources (a higher proportion than on any of the networks – see Table 5.4). This suggests that PBS news contained more in-depth stories, drawing on a range of perspectives to interpret the ongoing military conflict and political situation.

While PBS news had some distinctive qualities, overall, empirical studies of US television news – in particular Fox News – showed that, while battlefield scenes of the war in Iraq initially dominated coverage, the reporting frame

Table 5.3 Tone of Iraq war coverage in 2005 on commercial network evening and morning bulletins and PBS *NewsHour* (%)

	Evening	*Morning*	*PBS*
Positive	16	31	16
Neutral	44	36	18
Negative	28	19	26
Multifaceted/NA	13	13	40

(Adapted from Pew Research Center Project for Excellence in Journalism 2005)

Table 5.4 Number of sources used in stories on the Iraq war over 2005 on commercial network evening and morning bulletins and PBS *NewsHour* (%)

	Evening	*Morning*	*PBS*
No sources	29	33	36
1 source	20	28	21
2–3 sources	36	26	20
4+ sources	14	12	23

(Adapted from Pew Research Center Project for Excellence in Journalism 2005)

shifted towards a more victorious and celebratory tone, reinforced by elite and mostly Republican sources. News about civilian or military casualties or, indeed, voices opposed to the war were far less prominent. All of which, scholars have pointed out, has raised considerable doubts about the independence of US news media at a critical democratic moment, when citizens needed to understand what was happening on the ground in Iraq as well as remain informed about wider diplomatic efforts to prevent ongoing conflict. But how does the US's largely commercial coverage of the war compare with that of other nations?

Kolmer and Semetko's (2009) analysis of television news between 20 March and 16 April 2003 in the UK, US, Czech Republic, South Africa, Qatar and Germany shed considerable light on how the reporting of the Iraq war differed cross-nationally. In the first two weeks of the conflict, they found that, although all countries led with news about the military involvement, media in many countries opposed to the war also discussed the wider political context. So, for example, while the US and UK featured 9 per cent and 8.6 per cent respectively of news dedicated to the politics behind the war, on Al-Jazeera 21.8 per cent of stories covered a broader perspective of the conflict, as did 18.7 per cent in South Africa and 14.5 per cent in Germany (Kolmer and Semetko 2009: 648). In all countries the actions of the coalition forces (primarily the US and UK) were the central actors shaping war coverage in its first two weeks (see Table 5.5). However, in Germany, the Czech Republic, South Africa and on Al-Jazeera reporting also featured voices beyond the allied forces, such as the United Nations or national governments (from 16.3 per cent to 21.6 per cent). In the UK and US, by contrast, third parties accounted for just over 1 per cent.

The study also found the US to be far more likely to depict the actions of the Allies in a positive light than any other country including the UK. US news media were also more likely to evaluate news about Iraqis in a negative fashion (see Tables 5.6 and 5.7). Overall, Kolmer and Semetko (2009: 654) concluded that "the reporting of the war was conditioned by the national political contexts in

Table 5.5 Cross-national percentage figures for news about the Allies, third parties, journalists and Iraq in the first two weeks of coverage of the Iraq war

	Allies	*Third parties*	*Journalists*	*Iraq*
US	68.5	2.9	1.3	27.3
UK	56.4	1.2	7	35.4
Germany	50.6	16.3	3.8	29.3
Czech Republic	44.6	17.4	–	38.1
South Africa	40.8	21.6	4.8	32.8
Al-Jazeera	59.6	10.5	0.9	29

(Adapted from Kolmer and Semetko 2009)

Table 5.6 Negative, positive or unclear evaluations of Iraq war coverage towards the Allies (%)

	US	*UK*	*Germany*	*Czech TV*	*South Africa*	*Al-Jazeera*
Negative	14.4	12.3	16.3	12	26.9	16.5
No clear rating	60.5	83.2	75.9	82.4	68.3	81.6
Positive	25.1	4.5	7.9	5.6	4.8	1.9

(Adapted from Kolmer and Semetko 2009)

Table 5.7 Negative, positive or unclear evaluations of Iraqis in coverage of the Iraq war (%)

	US	*UK*	*Germany*	*Czech TV*	*South Africa*	*Al-Jazeera*
Negative	55.2	19.6	23.8	24.5	36.7	10.1
No clear rating	35.5	76.8	71.9	71	60.5	86.4
Positive	9.3	3.6	4.3	4.5	2.8	3.6

(Adapted from Kolmer and Semetko 2009)

which it was produced. The cross-country comparisons raise serious questions about the credibility and impartiality of TV news in the reporting of the war."

However, while the study rightly points out that the political environment helped shape coverage of the war in Iraq, it also glosses over important differences *between national broadcasters* in how the military conflict was reported. For if content analyses and more discourse-based studies of Iraq war coverage are examined in more detail, some striking differences can be identified in how public and commercial broadcasters reported the military action and wider political discussions.

In the UK, where impartiality is closely scrutinized in times of war and conflict, during the military conflict in Iraq, the four main television broadcasters – the BBC, ITV, Channel 4 and Sky News – varied in the access and time they granted to different on-screen actors. So, for example, Lewis *et al.* (2006) found that the 6 pm BBC bulletin contained the most news from UK/US government or military sources during March/April 2003 and, of all the broadcasters, was the only one not to reference any Iraqi citizens (see Table 5.8). By contrast, the more commercial broadcasters drew on a wider array of sources beyond other news media to inform coverage.

Over a longer period of time, Robinson *et al.* (2010) likewise found a heavy reliance on elite or official US/UK sources on the BBC's 10 pm news bulletin (see Table 5.9). With the exception of Channel 4, the other commercial news bulletins showed a greater reliance on these sources – most notably Sky News, where over 70 per cent of story sources were from US/UK officials. Channel 4 was the least reliant on coalition related sources and, if all sources are taken in context, appeared to be the most likely to feature actors challenging or

Table 5.8 Percentage of on-screen sources on national UK TV news during the Iraq war

	BBC	*ITV*	*Channel 4*	*Sky News*
US/UK government/military	56	50	42	48
Official Iraqi sources	26	22	36	27
Other media	11	8	3	4
Iraqi citizens	–	11	5	8
Other (e.g. Red Cross)	7	8	15	13

(Adapted from Lewis *et al.* 2006)

Table 5.9 Percentage of on-screen sources on national UK TV news during the Iraq war

	BBC	*ITV*	*Channel 4*	*Sky News*
All coalition	56.9	59.1	52.5	70.3
Iraqi regime	4.3	3.7	4.4	5.2
Iraqi opposition	4.4	1.3	1.1	3.2
Anti-war	2.9	2.3	2.8	0.6
International leaders anti-war	0.7	–	0.2	–
Arab political	1.2	–	4.7	–
UN	–	–	1.2	0.5
Experts	4.5	9.7	14.9	1.2
Humanitarian	2.7	2.7	4.8	1.2
Religious	–	0.4	0.3	–
Iraqi civilians	5.1	7.3	4.2	9.6
Terror groups	–	–	–	–
Opinion/citizens	14.1	7.1	1.5	4
Media	1	5.2	3.2	3.7
All other actors	2.2	1.4	1.3	0.6

(Adpated from Robinson *et al.* 2010)

opposing US/UK military and political elites. This is discussed later in relation to embedded reporters.

Like the BBC, the SABC's reporting of the war in Iraq in South Africa was not as critical as some commercial broadcasters. A Media Tenor (2003) report found e-tv (a commercial outlet) four times more critical than SABC, who "remained clearly ambivalent in its evaluation of American military actions" (cited in Buchinger *et al.* 2004: 218). Moreover, e-tv drew on a wider range of political actors, such as the UN, to explore the political context of the war. In the overall war coverage in March and April 2003, while the proportion of stories devoted to US military actions on SABC was similar to the US and UK (53 per cent – see Kolmer and Semetko 2009), e-tv relied less heavily on the Allied forces (41 per cent). Perhaps reflecting a more timid approach to reporting the war in Iraq, SABC drew extensively on reports from international news stations to make coverage as impartial as possible. The Media Tenor report observed that the SABC opted "to balance in-house correspondents' material with ZDF, BBC, and other network materials to gain a well-balanced, total coverage" (Buchinger *et al.* 2004: 219 but drawing on Media Tenor data).

Nord and Strömbäck's (2006) analysis of Swedish news media coverage during the initial reporting of the 2001 terrorist attacks in the US, the war in Afghanistan later that year and the war in Iraq a year later found that there was little to distinguish the coverage of the commercial broadcaster TV4's Nyheterna from either of the two public service television news programmes, *Aktuellt* and *Rapport*. All broadcasters appeared to rely heavily on US sources to shape coverage and were, for the most part, not in a position to independently cover the immediacy of conflict, especially in the case of the Iraq war (Nord and Strömbäck 2006: 102). Thus, journalists across media systems shared a degree of speculation when reporting on each conflict. Put bluntly, they concluded that structural factors such as private vs public service ownership cannot explain the nature of war and conflicting reporting in Sweden, a country with a historically strong commitment to public service broadcasting (see Chapter 1).

Paz and Avilés (2009) examined Spanish television news coverage of the events leading up to the war in Iraq and the military action, and found all stations broadly replicated the government's interpretation, in turn shaped largely by US propaganda. Each broadcaster, it was argued, tended to rely on US footage of military action as opposed to offering alternative perspectives on public opposition to the war or to Iraqi sources. They established that the public broadcaster, TVE-1, was more likely to accept this official interpretation of events than the commercial broadcasters:

> When covering the invasion and occupation of Iraq, TVE-1 adopted a position most closely aligned with that of the Spanish government, followed by Antena 3. TVE-1 emphasized the purported necessity of intervening in Iraq, minimized the opposition to such policy by most European governments, highlighted Saddam Hussein's 'demonic' brutality, and devoted the least amount of air time to Spanish anti-war demonstrations. (Paz and Avilés 2009: 72)

However, Spanish commercial television news also uncritically accepted the views of official sources. So, for example, according to Paz and Avilés (2009: 72), "Antena 3's discourse largely reflected the official US position, both by its framing of reasons for the invasions and by its construction of Hussein as 'evil'." While Telecinco, another commercial station, did offer "the position furthest from that of the Spanish government" and attempted to engage with the "complexities and contradictions of the Iraq presidency", it relied also on "pro-government and official US perspectives" (Paz and Avilés 2009: 72).

The broad thrust of the comparative studies explored in this section suggests that public service broadcast coverage of the Iraq war was broadly similar to that of commercial television news. Of course, South African, Swedish, Spanish or UK public media do not represent all public service broadcasters. But in the absence of any other empirically driven comparative studies of Iraq war coverage identified, it could be tentatively concluded that, while the commercial broadcasters in the US were the most overwhelmingly pro-war, media systems elsewhere largely delivered a similar overall picture of the war and its wider context.

The previous two sections in this chapter have drawn attention to how the wider political environment can shape the nature of war coverage. But it is also important to recognize the changing structural issues that journalists face in contemporary military conflicts. The final section explores how new technologies can potentially impede the independence and impartiality of war journalists in military situations while also investigating how new alternative sources of news from the Middle East have challenged the hegemony once enjoyed by Western international news channels.

A threat to impartiality? How embedded journalists on different media systems reported the 2003 war in Iraq

Since CNN's live coverage of the First Gulf War, journalists have taken advantage of more sophisticated mobile digital and interactive technologies when reporting military action. These have enabled journalists and eyewitnesses to readily convey information and images to the public domain, whether through traditional mass media or more recently via social media such as Facebook and Twitter. New mobile filming equipment able to broadcast remotely has allowed war correspondents to become more easily embedded with soldiers involved in military action. While this vouchsafes firsthand perspectives of warfare on the "front line", questions have been raised about the impartiality of journalists reliant on military personnel for their safety in extreme conditions.

At the same time, where once Western news media tended to control the flow of information about war and conflict internationally, rolling news channels from around the world can now be viewed online or with satellite subscription. Since many recent disputes have revolved around the Middle East, channels such as Al-Jazeera, Al-Arabiya and the Abu Dhabi Channel have risen in prominence, often challenging the perspective of Western news outlets and thus pluralizing the global flow of information. This section explores the rise of new Middle Eastern channels and asks how far they have enhanced pluralism during the war in Iraq. First, however, it examines empirical studies into the role of embedded journalists and asks whether journalists can remain impartial whilst embedded with military forces.

Embedded reporters, of course, are not an entirely new phenomenon. Journalists and the military have colluded with one another for a long time. But the more pervasive use of embedded reports in 2003 raised significant questions from many countries about how fair and balanced they could be (Kolmer and Semetko 2009). For while such unprecedented access has allowed viewers to watch military action at the "front line", at the same time it has raised widespread concern about journalists' ability to report impartially while effectively under military control in an environment where they are likely to befriend members of the platoon in which they are placed. In this respect, studies in the US have compared embedded and unilateral reporters and found that the former tended to be used more in the war in Iraq than the latter (Aday *et al.* 2005a). In doing so, coverage of the battlefield or the coalition force's tactics was enhanced, since embedded reporters, primarily from the US, were in the thick of the military action. Unilaterals, by contrast, reported more news about Iraqi soldiers and civilian casualties from both sides (Aday *et al.* 2005a). Pfau *et al.* (2005) found embedded reporters on ABC, CBS, NBC and CNN delivered a far more positive portrayal of US/UK military forces than non-embedded journalists. A study of CNN's embedded reporters showed that they were more likely to refer to themselves or the soldiers than non-embedded reporters, potentially compromising standards of detached journalism (Fox and Park 2006). Overall, then, a number of studies from the US tend to confirm the impression that embedded reporters on commercial network and cable stations were less critical of Allied forces than other war correspondents.

In the UK, however, a detailed content analysis of television news coverage of the Iraq war revealed little to distinguish embedded news from other types of war reporting. Lewis *et al.* (2006: 116) found a broad similarity in the proportion of stories from embedded television reporters during the war in Iraq (on ITV and Channel 4 13 and 11 per cent respectively, on Sky News and the BBC 7 and 6 per cent respectively). To explore how cautious and careful embedded journalists' reports were compared to more general war coverage, they examined every reference to Weapons of Mass Destruction (WMD) which either implied or doubted that the Iraq government possessed this capability (this was before the widespread acceptance that were no WMD, after all) (see Table 5.10 and Table 5.11).

Table 5.10 References to claims about the WMD capability of Iraq on national UK TV news bulletins

	BBC	*ITV*	*Channel 4*	*Sky*
Implying capability	21	26	59	59
Doubting capability	6	4	9	2

(Adapted from Lewis *et al.* 2006)

Table 5.11 References to claims about the WMD capability of Iraq across news reports on national UK TV

	Implying capability	*Doubting capability*	*% of WMD references*	*% of total reports*
Embedded reporters	6	1	5	9
Baghdad reporters	5	–	4	6
Reports from briefings	10	1	8	4
Unilateral reporters	1	–	–	1
Available footage	23	6	21	15
Studio analysis	10	4	10	4
Interview with reporter	9	3	9	3
Interview with expert(s)	9	3	9	3
Anchor	27	4	23	48
Other	14	–	10	5

(Adapted from Lewis *et al.* 2006)

While the numbers are relatively small (N=127) when broken down by the type of news report (see Table 5.11), UK embedded reporters did not overwhelmingly succumb to any military pressure when compared to other types of reporters, most notably television news anchors. Table 5.10 also demonstrates that, in coverage of the war in Iraq more generally, the public broadcaster, the BBC, appeared less complicit in promulgating government claims that WMD represented a real and immediate threat. By contrast, Sky News by "a ratio of nearly 30 to 1, was both most likely to suggest the presence of WMD and least likely to cast doubt on Iraqi capability" (Lewis *et al.* 2006: 121).

Comparatively speaking, the BBC was identified as being broadly similar in its portrayal of the Iraqi people to other broadcasters (Lewis *et al.* 2006). However, Channel 4, once again, had the most balanced mix of reaction from Iraqi citizens. It made the most reference to Iraqi casualties whereas the BBC's coverage was almost identical to ITV's. Sky News appeared the most celebratory in its depiction of Iraqi citizens, e.g. showing them as welcoming liberation. If the BBC was not necessarily as distinct from the market-driven channels in its coverage of the war, it was far more balanced about military events than US network news bulletins and cable news channels. This was well put by Piazza and Haarman (2011) in a detailed discourse and narrative analysis of BBC and CBS news during the war in Iraq. They found that:

> the cultural value most invoked in CBS items is that of patriotism and for the BBC a sense of duty and emotional reserve. These features too can be linked to political, social and cultural circumstances. American coverage of the war in general was focussed to a large extent on the soldiers themselves, their personal feelings, their families at home. On the other hand, while Britain was obviously an essential partner in the military occupation,

> BBC national coverage focussed principally on the *events* of war, and very little on the *actors*. (Piazza and Haarman 2011: 1547; *original emphasis*)

In this respect, the underlying institutional values of each channel – the commitment to maintaining standards of impartiality on the BBC compared to the more consumer-orientated delivery of news on CBS – shaped the dominant narrative of each broadcaster.

Haarman and Lombardo's (2009) edited collection of essays in *Evaluation and Stance in War News: A Linguistic Analysis of American, British and Italian Television News Reporting of the 2003 Iraqi War* draws some distinct conclusions about cross-national differences in public and commercial coverage. Lombardo (2009: 69) examined news presenters in detail and observed that the US commercial station, CBS, appeared to adopt "an apparently 'objective' reporter voice style, at times he [male presenter] personalizes events and expresses an explicitly evaluative 'patriotic' stance". The news presenter on the BBC, meanwhile, represented "reporting typical of investigative journalism which tends to challenge official sources and construes events as problematic" (Lombardo 2009: 69). There is a similar attempt on Rai uno to be balanced in semantic terms, but unlike the BBC "Evaluation is more implicit than explicit" (Lombardo 2009: 70). However, the Italian news presenter on the commercial broadcaster, TG5 (Canale 5), did not conform to any journalistic displays of balance and was openly critical of the Allied forces.

In a close textual reading of embedded reporting on CBS and the BBC, Clark's (2009: 112) discourse analysis revealed that the "Explicit evaluation, predominantly unfavourable, is found more frequently in BBC [news] and is far more evident when considering the effects of the conflict on civilians." Haarman's (2009: 135–6) analysis of evaluative language in war reporting found that, whereas CBS did not "ever question the war effort *as such*, explicitly or implicitly", on the BBC "An implicit negative stance towards the war is instead a recurrent feature" (*original emphasis*). Since (unlike the US and UK) the Italians were not combatants, they were under less pressure editorially and could be more critical. But, according to Haarman (2009: 136), "The public broadcaster attempted to represent both the government and the people, who were to large extent anti-war. TG5 [the commercial broadcaster] tended to frame its coverage specifically for an audience of the latter." Indeed, with the exception of the US broadcaster which relied to a large degree on elite military sources, Piazza's (2009) detailed analysis during the war suggested that the European public broadcasters (BBC and Rai uno) tended to privilege establishment-type figures in their reporting, such as politicians.

As already pointed out in this chapter, the discourses journalists draw upon to explain the latest news in Iraq represent not only structural differences in ownership, but encompass wider dimensions including the demographic makeup of audiences, the political environment in which news was produced and conflicting journalistic cultures cross-nationally (Chapter 2). Drawing primarily on Western television news coverage (due to the availability of comparative empirical studies), while differences in the news agenda, balance and tone have been identified, there were also (across public and commercial broadcasters) broad similarities in the reliance on US officials and a focus on the war itself rather than its wider political context.

Beyond Western media, scholars have observed that a different approach to coverage of the Iraq war was available on Al-Jazeera, in particular, but also on other Middle Eastern news channels such as Al-Arabiya and the Abu Dhabi Channel. Studies have shown that these channels offered a less West-centric perspective of the war and conveyed the plight of ordinary Afghanistan and Iraqi citizens more explicitly when many other international news channels were preoccupied with US/UK military tactics (Samuel-Azran 2010; Miles 2005; Zayani 2005). Al-Jazeera defines itself as an independent broadcaster but is financially sustained by the Emir of Qtar. The channel's broadcasting roots and ethos lie in BBC-style public service journalism. In the wake of the BBC's closure of its Arabic-language service, Al-Jazeera was formed in 1996, employing many former BBC employees. Located in the heart of the Middle East, it had the resources to cover the war in Afghanistan when many other Western stations had not had time to set up an infrastructure of reporters to cover the military events live on location. Since then Al-Jazeera has gained journalistic currency and expanded its dedicated rolling news service right around the world on television and online platforms. The rise of Arab rolling news channels is seen to represent a more plural infrastructure of communications worldwide, challenging the hegemony of US/Western journalism (Samuel-Azran 2010; Zayani 2010).

At the same time, Al-Jazeera has been criticized (most controversially by US politicians) for being anti-Western/American, promoting the ideas of terrorists and sensationalizing the suffering of ordinary Middle Eastern casualties caught up in warfare. As Tables 5.1 and 5.2 showed (at the beginning of the chapter), Al-Jazeera's coverage of the war in Iraq was driven less by coverage of the US/UK military actions and more by the opposition to the war and the plight of ordinary citizens. Iskandar and El-Nawawy (2004: 323) have observed that, during the war in Iraq, "Al-Jazeera's on-the-ground, non-embedded correspondents did provide a corrective to the American official line that the military campaign was, barring occasional resistance, going according to plan."

Meanwhile, Zayani and Ayish (2006) examined how Al-Jazeera, Al-Arabiya and the Abu Dhabi Channel covered the fall of Baghdad on 9 April and the toppling of Saddam Hussein's statue. Unlike the celebratory "victory frame" Aday *et al.* (2005b) identified in US commercial television news, according to Zayani and Ayish's (2006: 494) visual and narrative analysis of the Arab news channels, "the coverage of the fall of the Iraqi capital amounts to a visually enhanced narrative about subduing Iraq rather than liberating it". In their view, cultural, political and historical considerations shaped this shared journalistic perspective. Since each channel has somewhat different ownership structures, the Arabs' alternative picture of the Iraq war shows how the wider political, economic and cultural environment in which journalism operates influences how the same event is framed and understood cross-nationally.

Conclusions

With the exception of the US, the thrust of the comparative studies explored in this chapter suggests that public service media coverage of the 2003 war in Iraq was broadly similar to that of commercial television news. Whereas previous chapters have found that in routine periods of news (Chapter 3) or during election times (Chapter 4) public media could generally be distinguished from their rivals, it would be harder to make this case during moments of war and conflict. In making sense of 9/11, in reporting the most intense phase of the war in Iraq or in providing a wider context to foreign policy decision-making a review of empirical content studies reveals that the most striking differences were cross-national rather than between media systems. Instead, the nature of Iraq war coverage was shaped most significantly by the geo-political environment of individual nation states, their level of involvement in a war, militarily or diplomatically, together with their past and present relationship with the US.

However, while events on the international stage were interpreted by distinct national frameworks of relevance, US official sources and images continued to influence how war and conflict were portrayed in most countries. Structurally, of course, most news media outlets remained largely reliant on larger Western news agencies for footage and for the latest updates, with US official sources seen as more reliable and authoritative than the fragmented voices emanating from the Middle East. Embedded reporters, in this sense, extended the US version of events and its military mission, further decontextualizing the wider diplomatic picture and alternative understandings of the war. Indeed, few Western media outlets, public or commercial, strayed too far from the "official" US line during the war in Iraq and, for the most part, reinforced rather than challenged the interpretation of Allied forces. It was left to Middle Eastern news channels to convey the Iraqi perspective and a human interest interpretation of the military conflict and to report news about civilian casualties. Overall, then, it could be concluded that, while commercial media in the US were the most overwhelmingly pro-war, systematic content analysis studies have shown media systems elsewhere (with the exception of the Middle Eastern news channels) largely delivered a similar overall picture of the war and its wider context.

The harshest criticism, however, has been launched at US commercial media. For on US network and cable news channels many studies found – and many journalists have since acknowledged – that none of the major broadcasters adequately scrutinized the government's response to 9/11, the existence of

WMD and the reasons for military action in Iraq. Haynes and Guardino's (2010: 80) systematic review of US network television during the war in Iraq put it simply: "[their] findings support the view that the media's performance did not live up to the democratic standards most journalists hold themselves to, much less than those expected by their critics". Fox News, in particular, rose in prominence during the war in Iraq because its patriotic mode of address appealed to viewers, tapping into the anger and emotions of many Americans post-9/11. Journalistically, however, its value diminished, with numerous systematic studies of Fox's coverage demonstrating an explicit pro-war bias, abandoning any conventional notion of balance or impartiality.

Of course, since the US military was leading the wars in Afghanistan and Iraq, without strict impartiality guidelines (see Chapter 1), America's dominant market-driven news media operating in a largely self-regulated environment were perhaps always going to be less balanced than those of other countries not actively engaged in war. The UK was the only other country to meaningfully commit military forces in Iraq and this action caused considerable controversy, since polls showed, before the war, the majority of its people to be opposed to warfare (Lewis 2004). Unlike in the US, however, the UK government faced considerable pressure and scrutiny on the issue of WMD just months after the war had begun, most notably when a BBC report accused it of "sexing up" the case for war. Of most significance for this chapter is that it fell to a public service broadcaster – the BBC – to most robustly challenge the government at a vulnerable political moment. This is significant because in many countries – most notably the US – arguments against the idea of a public broadcaster have often implied that it could not remain independent from the state in times of war. Critics have suggested that, when a state is actively engaged in conflict, publicly owned organizations would be pressured to conform to the government's version of events. While BBC coverage of the war was broadly similar to that on other commercial bulletins during the intense period of military action (March/April 2003), after this point in time it would be hard to characterize the public broadcaster's coverage as being entirely governed by the state, let alone suggest that it acted like a government propaganda machine.

Indeed, in the period of time under analysis in this chapter – the post- 9/11 environment to the aftermath of the war in Iraq and subsequent inquiries into BBC journalism – Wall and Bicket (2008a) have identified sustained US conservative attacks on the BBC for being too critical of the state and acting as a mouthpiece for the Iraqi government. They examined the reaction of bloggers, think tanks and journalists from print media in the US and identified three main criticisms. First, because the BBC reported multiple viewpoints on the war in Iraq, it was viewed as being biased, portraying anti-war voices or Iraqi propaganda too favourably. Second, after the BBC was criticized for its reporting of WMD, most notably in the Hutton Report, which questioned some of its journalists' ethics, critics claimed that BBC journalism should be discredited. Third, and most importantly for this chapter, the BBC's perceived bias or low-quality journalism was linked to its state ownership, a funding structure that afforded journalists too much editorial licence and power. Wall and Bicket (2008a: 133) observed that:

> The fact that US think tanks and news media condemned publicly funded media outfits or those with alternative funding structures is not surprising. What is striking, however, is that they have extended their critique beyond their own nation to Britain as well. As the BBC in particular becomes more visible in the USA, it serves as an example of high quality reporting funded by taxpayers. As such, it is a threat to arguments that privately funded media work best.

Five years after the start of the Iraq war, Carruthers (2008: 70) suggested that the US is seeing a "disappearing audience for war". While this might echo mummers of compassion fatigue (too much war coverage), it might just as plausibly be a symptom of "the flag waving, cheerleading and Scud-busting" (Carruthers 2008: 74) that distinguish highly commercial US institutions from public media such as the BBC and their more regulated practice of impartial reporting on world events.

Of course, the BBC impartiality rules should not be uncritically celebrated. Systematic studies of UK national television news of the ongoing conflict between Palestine and Israel, for example, have demonstrated that guidelines on impartiality do not always translate into fair and balanced reporting, since Israeli accounts routinely dominated coverage of the Middle East (see Barkho 2008; Philo and Berry 2011; Thomas 2011). Nevertheless, while BBC international news should not be unreservedly championed, the relative democratic value of its public service journalism appears to be spreading organically beyond national boundaries. For many US audiences are turning to the BBC as a "super-alternative" to mainstream commercial media with television channels and online news sources that are more globally accessible, offering alternative perspectives on domestic and international issues (Bicket and Wall 2009: 365).

The next chapter now turns to dedicated news channels – many of which have significant global reach – comparing their editorial aims and, more significantly, assessing the democratic value of rolling journalism operating under different media systems.

Adapting to the 24/7 environment of journalism

Chapter 6

The evolution and development of rolling news channels

Introduction

The democratic value of news has so far been explored by examining journalism at key democratic moments – at elections and in wartime – or during more routine periods of time. While rolling news coverage has been part of the analysis, this chapter is less interested in how a particular story or issue is addressed and more in the medium of 24-hour news journalism. Or, put another way, the aim is to not only look at what information is conveyed but how it is crafted and communicated to audiences in a 24/7 format and environment.

To understand the medium of 24-hour news, the chapter traces how dedicated rolling news channels emerged around the world, comparing their form, style and conventions, and, importantly, it asks how far the genre's historical development has been shaped by different media systems over previous decades. Public service media with an editorial mission to inform and educate have, in particular, been granted the journalistic licence to report news in more depth than breadth, to not just cover the world but uncover it in a continuous rolling format. After all, while broadcasters generally have historically complained that the brevity of news culture has – most notably on television – prevented journalists from exploring issues in more depth and greater context, the birth of always-on 24-hour news channels has, at least in theory, afforded reporters the time and space to explain world events to viewers.

But while 24-hour news channels held much democratic promise when they were first launched, many Western broadcasters fast became become associated with the speedy delivery of conjecture (Lewis 2010; Lewis *et al*. 2005; Marriott 2007). For many early accounts of the 24-hour news genre revealed how the rolling format was used to relay the latest breaking news or live footage (MacGregor 1997). The demands of what might be described as "fast news culture" are nothing new to the culture of journalism. Many of the classic ethnographies on news production (Gans 1979; Schlesinger 1987; Tuchman 1978) picture the struggle journalists face finding the time and space to report cogently when editors demand instant copy or immediate analysis. But rather than break with convention, since the first rolling news channel – CNN, a commercial broadcaster – burst onto the scene in 1980, it has injected immediacy and pace into television news journalism (Cushion 2010a). With a limited financial infrastructure, CNN's journalistic endeavours were constrained by its resources (Flournoy and Stewart 1997). While investigative journalism is a costly business and would be difficult to fund 24 hours a day, anchors recycling the day's news or using news agency footage with voiceovers has become the accepted norm of much rolling news journalism, since it is more affordable. Indeed, it is important to recognize the significant costs involved in producing continuous, rolling news 24 hours a day. While some public service media, particularly in parts of Europe (see Chapter 1), boast well-resourced newsrooms, many commercial stations are constrained by limited budgets and a poor infrastructure of journalists and editors when trying to produce high-quality rolling news. News channels, moreover, are not the most commercially lucrative operations and many have found it difficult to operate at a profit and ceased broadcasting (Cushion and Lewis 2010). Any understanding of the quality of journalism supplied by news channels must acknowledge the financial limitations impacting on the production of 24-hour news and whether this influences news selection and conventions.

CNN's influence on the 24-hour news genre has been long-lasting but, as cable and then satellite communications enabled channels to broadcast more cheaply and easily around the world, its influence began to diminish. The relatively short lifespan of 24-hour news channels can be characterized in three phases (see Cushion 2010a). With the arrival of CNN, the first stage represents the 24-hour news genre "coming of age", most strikingly on the international stage during its live and exclusive reporting of the First Gulf War (Livingston 1997; Robinson, 2002, 2005; Volkmer 1999). After CNN had captured the world's attention, and others witnessed the influence such a channel could potentially wield, the second phase of rolling news can be characterized as a race for transnational reach. In the late 1980s and 1990s more international channels were launched to challenge the hegemony of the US values CNN was seen to represent. As the global battle between international channels to influence world affairs has grown fiercer, the third and ongoing phase can be interpreted as the regionalization and commercialization of 24-hour news channels. For over the previous decade or so rolling news channels with a more localized remit were established and, in some regions around the world, commercial channels are involved in an intense competition for audiences.

This presents a broad trajectory of the history of the 24-hour news genre. But it is important not to generalize about the emergence of world 24-hour news channels since they did not evolve in a uniform manner (see Cushion and Lewis 2010). Australian television viewers, for example, have only had access to one commercial 24-hour news channel – Sky News, which launched in 1996 – on a pay subscription basis for well over a decade (Young 2010). The public service broadcaster, ABC, was long denied the opportunity to launch a rolling news channel after fierce lobbying by Rupert Murdoch's News Corporation, and Seven and Nine Networks (co-owners of Sky News Australia) argued that it would put the commercial broadcaster at a competitive disadvantage because it was state financed. ABC's 24-hour news channel was finally launched as a free-to-air service in July 2010. In the UK, the BBC 24-hour television news channel – then called News 24 – faced a similar battle after it launched a free-to-air service in 1997. The commercial broadcaster, Sky News, who had held a monopoly on 24-hour news since 1989, legally challenged BBC use of state funding to provide what the commercial station – BSkyB – already supplied. The European Commission rejected the Sky legal case in 1999 on the grounds that the BBC did not charge cable operators as BSkyB did and that state costs were justifiable and proportionate to the channel's costs (Meade 1999).

The battle for 24-hour news airwaves in the UK and Australia largely centred on whether the entrance of a public broadcaster would economically threaten the commercial market. But it is also important to evaluate whether public broadcasters have editorially enhanced the 24-hour news genre or simply replicated the services already supplied by commercial broadcasters. The aim of this chapter is to explore whether public service rolling news stations are distinct from commercially driven stations around the world. As rolling news stations have further proliferated over the last decade or so, it will also assess whether increased competition has compromised the quality of journalism, examining, in particular, if public service broadcasters – developed several years after commercial channels had already been established – have challenged conventional rolling news wisdom or reinforced the existing culture of 24-hour news journalism.

Despite 24-hour news channels' relatively short lifespan, in scholarly circles the medium can sometimes be viewed as somewhat dated, since online news and social media have now surpassed it, delivering more immediacy, choice and in-depth breaking stories (Cushion 2012). So, for example, BBC journalist Paul Mason predicted the imminent death of rolling news in 2006, arguing that:

> rolling news is no longer the future ... . As anyone who uses any half-decent news platform on the web understands, the internet is faster, delivers instant depth and unrivalled interactivity. Rolling news – and here I mean the concept of a separate channel and its traditional front-end studio format – is the genre of television least suited to survive the transition to the digital age. (Mason 2006)

In the digital age, social media such as Facebook and Twitter have been celebrated as *the* contemporary tools chosen to access immediate news. Passively watching television break news on air, in this respect, seems almost a quaint pastime, since the attentive news seeker might have already read it as a tweet or on a Facebook news feed. But while social media challenge existing journalism practice, it remains to be seen whether they will last the pace. Twitter, after all, was launched in 2006 and it is only in more recent years that it has become a familiar part of broadcast news, whether used for audience responses or by journalists to tweet their immediate analysis of a story.

Although more limited in scope and interactivity than social media, *examining 24-hour news as a medium for immediate news* allows its evolution to be carefully studied. For 24-hour news channels have a longer history than social media and a more reliable bank of empirical studies exists from which to draw conclusions about their relative democratic value between media systems – the purpose of this book – cross-nationally. While research on social media and journalism has become an increasingly fashionable topic to investigate in recent years (see Cushion 2012), their relative newness means they are often understood more theoretically rather than empirically. Moreover, in this context it would be difficult to build up a systematic picture of how tools such as Facebook and Twitter have been taken up by different media systems around the world. Since 24-hour news channels have been operating for several decades, it is possible to draw on a more reliable body of scholarship to compare empirical studies of rolling news cross-nationally.

Nevertheless, beyond studies of US cable news channels, empirical studies about 24-hour news content and their conventions remain in relatively short supply. When 24-hour international news channels first arrived, many scholars became fascinated with the theoretical arrival of a global public sphere. In more recent years, news channels in the Middle East have similarly attracted attention for challenging the information flow and hegemonic might of Western news organizations (Volkmer 1999). By contrast, since national rolling news channels are watched by just a minuscule share of the audience in some countries, such as the UK (Lewis *et al.* 2005), their significance has been subject to less academic scrutiny. But while 24-hour news channels have not necessarily had much of a direct impact on audiences, they have impacted more systemically on the wider culture of broadcast journalism (see Cushion 2012). For in the more conventional fixed-time television news bulletins – the most watched form of journalism in many democracies – recent years have seen an increased use of rolling news conventions such as live broadcasting, on-location reporting or news updates (Cushion 2012). News, in other words, that brings viewers up to speed on the latest events rather than putting an event into a larger context or exploring an issue in more depth (Lewis *et al.* 2005).

The purpose of this chapter is not to rehash the common critique levelled at 24-hour news journalism. Instead it is to compare rolling stations cross-nationally, beginning first with an empirical map of public and commercial 24-hour news stations around the world. Rolling news channels are then explored in more detail, comparing their form, style, conventions and, importantly, whether different media systems offer different understandings of the world.

The commercial dominance of rolling journalism: drawing an empirical map of commercial and public service 24-hour news channels

Rai and Cottle (2007) have comprehensively mapped the global rise of 24-hour news channels in recent years. In 2006 they identified more than 100 operating channels with varying audience reach – global, regional, national and subnational (Rai and Cottle 2007). Three years later they revisited the study and discovered rolling news channels had "continued to grow steadily ... and now cut across virtually every region of the globe, with many of them broadcasting in different languages" (Rai and Cottle 2010: 53). While their analysis primarily revolved around the regional spread of 24-hour news channels, most notably their enhanced regionalization (cf. Cushion 2010a), it can also be observed that most were commercial rather than public service operations. Drawing on Rai and Cottle's comprehensive list of 24-hour news stations across regions around the globe (2010: 55–64), Tables 6.1 and 6.2 split them into public and commercial broadcasters.

As Rai and Cottle's (2010) analysis was based on stations operating in September 2009, new channels have been launched since while some others have ceased broadcasting.[22] But even after acknowledging levels of operating stations will fluctuate from year to year, Tables 6.1 and 6.2 demonstrate that, for every public/state or not-for-profit 24-hour news channel, over two and a half more can be found broadcasting in the commercial sector. Put simply, commercial channels dominate the 24-hour news market in many regions around the world.

While CNN laid the generic foundations of 24-hour television news (Cushion 2010a), it took some time before a public service broadcaster established a dedicated rolling news channel. A BBC World news channel was launched in 1991 (known as BBC World News since 2008) and is today broadcast in more than 200 countries, with an estimated 74 million people tuning in each week. The BBC world channel, at this point in time, was not funded by the UK licence fee (in 2011 it became the BBC's responsibility as part of the Conservative-Liberal Democrats' coalition plan to cut public finances) generating income from subscriptions and advertising – but it still abides by the editorial values of the public broadcaster. Germany's international public service international news channel, Deutsche Welle (DW-TV) was launched in 1992, and broadcasts hourly news in English and German with scheduled current affairs programming in between. Whereas the BBC news infrastructure is shared along many platforms, DW-TV pays the public stations, ARD and ZDF, for material (Chalaby 2009: 181–182). It has not matched the international reach of Euronews, a pan-European news channel, launched a year later. It too was informed by a public service ethos and has benefited from EU financial aid. Underlying its editorial remit was a commitment to reinforcing a European political identity and presenting a challenge to CNN's grip on the flow of international news.

Into the 2000s, many of the biggest and most recognized public media organizations around the world have been much slower to take up dedicated international news channels. So, for example, France 24 was launched in 2006 and NHK in 2009 while other more government-controlled operations were established like CCTV International (now called CCTV News) in 2000 and Russia Today (now called RT) in 2005. In each case, however, there is limited evidence to suggest that they have matched the reach or stature of BBC World News, CNNI or Euronews. CCTV, according to Bakshi (2011: 147), has not "attracted a sizeable audience over the past ten years due to poor production values, staid news presentation, and viewer scepticism about the channel's objectivity". Kuhn (2010: 278), meanwhile, has suggested that despite France 24's influence in some regions, its more national agenda is unlikely to "pose a viable challenge to the dominant position of the three majors (CNNI, BBC World and Al-Jazeera) on the world stage, while in Europe Euronews has reached a level of popularity well ahead of the French transnational service".

Indeed, it is the Middle East channel, Al-Jazeera, funded by the Qatar government, that has had most success in dislodging the hegemony of Western news channels with the greatest global reach. Despite being launched in 1996, Al-Jazeera gained little international attention or subsequent global reach until it began reporting on the Afghanistan and Iraq wars at the turn of the century (see Chapter 5). Since then, its audiences have gradually spread beyond the Middle East and the broadcaster is today recognized as a real competitor to the globally established brands of CNNI and BBC World News. As the previous chapter noted, when Al-Jazeera was launched it was heavily influenced by the BBC's editorial brand of public service journalism. After the BBC's Arabic-language service was closed in the 1990s, many former BBC employees joined Al-Jazeera and, according to Zayani and Sahraoui (2007), brought with them the UK public broadcaster's institutional values (see Zayani and Sahraoui 2007 for analysis of Al-Jazeera's internal journalistic culture). Today it has forged its own identity with channels broadcasting in many languages and countries around the world. More recently, TeleSUR launched as a continuous rolling news channel in 2005 after Venezuela president, Hugo Chavez, invested more resources in the station to challenge the flow of American news into the country and wider region (see Painter 2008: 45–53). TeleSUR has gained publicity for representing an equivalent Al-Jazeera-type counterpoint to the American influence pervasive in the region although to what extent it can operate editorially without state interference remains open to question.

Table 6.1 Commercial 24-hour news channels around the world[21]

Name	*Ownership and language*	*Reach*
Global		
CNN & CNNI	Time Warner, various languages	Global
CNBC	NBC & Dow Jones, English	Global
Bloomberg TV	Michael Bloomberg, English	Global
Fox News	News Corporation, English	Global (except parts of Africa, Oceania and South Asia)
North America		
MSNBC	Microsoft & NBC, English	US
Headline News	Time Warner, English	US
CTV News Channel	Canada's Bell Globemedia Company, English	Canada
LCN	Canada's TVA Group, French	Canada
Local/city-based news channels	Various, English	Canada
LCN	Canada's TVA Group, French	Canada-Quebec
Local/city-based news channels	Various, English	US/Canada cities only
South America		
Todo Noticias	Argentina's Grupo Clarin, Spanish	South America, part of North America
Globovision	Venezuelan Private, CNN Affiliate, Spanish	Venezuela
Canal i	Private Venezuelan Network, Spanish	Venezuela
Globonews	Brazil's Globo Group, Portuguese	Brazil
Band News	Brazil's Banderantes Group, Portuguese	Brazil
Record News (terrestrial only)	Brazil's Rede Record, Portuguese	Brazil
CNN Chile	CNN & Chile's VTR Group, Spanish	Chile
Nuestra Tele Noticias	Colombia's RCN TV, Spanish	Colombia
Cable Noticias	Colombia's Global Media, Spanish	Colombia
Europe		
n-tv	Germany's Bertelsmann, CNN (minor), German	Germany
n24	Germany's SevenOne Media, German	Germany
CNN Plus	CNN & Spain's Sogecable, Spanish	Spain
SIC Noticias	Portugal's SIC Network, Portuguese	Portugal

TVI24	Portugal's Grupo Prisa, Portuguese	Portugal
TV2 Nyhetskanalen	Norway's Egmont, A-Pressen Groups, Norwegian	Norway
Antena 3	Romania's Intact Group, Romanian	Romania
N24	Romania's Central National Media, Romanian	Romania
Realitatea TV	Romania's Realitatea-Catavencu Group, Romanian	Romania
B92 Info	Serbia's B92 Trust & local businesses, Serbian	Serbia
TVN 24	Poland's ITI Media Group, Polish	Poland
Polsat News	Poland's Polsat Group, Polish	Poland
TA3	UK's Millennium Electronics, Slovak	Slovakia
La Chaine Info	France's TF1-Bouygues Group, French	France
BFM TV	France's Nextradio TV Group, French	France
CNN Turk	CNN & Turkey's Dogan Media Group, Turkish	Turkey some West Asia/Middle East/North Africa (Arabic speaking mainly) and Central Asia (mainly former Soviet states)
NTV	Turkey's NTV Media Group, Turkish	Turkey some West Asia/Middle East/North Africa (Arabic speaking mainly) and Central Asia (mainly former Soviet states)
West/Central Asia, Middle East		
Al Arabiya	Saudi MBC Group, Dubai-based, Arabic	West Asia/Middle East/North Africa (Arabic speaking mainly) and some Central Asia (mainly former Soviet states)
Africa		
eNews Channel	South Africa's etv Group, English	South Africa
South Asia		
Zee News	India's Essel Group, Hindi	South Asia, West Asia/Middle East/North Africa (Arabic speaking mainly) and some North America, Europe including Russia and rest of Africa
NDTV India	India's NDTV Group, Hindi	South Asia, West Asia/Middle East/North Africa (Arabic speaking mainly), some Europe including Russia and rest of Africa
NDTV 24x7	India's NDTV Group, English	South Asia, West Asia/Middle East/North Africa (Arabic speaking mainly), some Europe including Russia and rest of Africa

Table 6.1 *continued*

Name	*Ownership and language*	*Reach*
South Asia (*continued*)		
Sun News	Indian Sun Network, Tamil	South Asia, West Asia/Middle East/North Africa (Arabic speaking mainly), some North America and Central/East Asia
Asianet	India's Asianet Ltd, multiple regional channels, various languages	South Asia, West Asia/Middle East/North Africa (Arabic speaking mainly)
Indiavision	Private Indian Network, Malayalam	South Asia, West Asia/Middle East/North Africa (Arabic speaking mainly)
Gemini News	Indian Sun Network, Telugu	South Asia, West Asia/Middle East/North Africa (Arabic speaking mainly)
ETV Network	India's Eenadu Network, multiple regional channels, various languages	South Asia, West Asia/Middle East/North Africa (Arabic speaking mainly)
TV9	Private Indian Network, Telugu	South Asia, West Asia/Middle East/North Africa (Arabic speaking mainly)
ARY News	Pakistan's ARY Network, Urdu & English	South Asia, some Central Asia (mainly former Soviet States), West Asia/Middle East/North Africa (Arabic speaking mainly)
Star News	News Corporation, India-based, Hindi	South Asia, some Europe including Russia, West Asia/Middle East/North Africa (Arabic speaking mainly) and Central/East Asia
Aaj Tak	India Today Media Group, Hindi	India
Headlines Today	India Today Media Group, English	India
Sahara Samay	India's Sahara Group, Hindi	India
CNN-IBN	Time Warner & India's TV18 Group, English	India
Times Now	India's Times Group & Reuters, English	India
IBN7	India's TV18 Group, Hindi	India
Live India	India's SAB Network, Hindi	India
India TV	Private Indian Network, Hindi	India
Star Ananda	News Corporation & ABP, India-based, Bengali	India
Tara Newz	India's Tara Network, Bengali	India

People TV	India's Malayalam Comm. Ltd, Malayalam	India
Manorama News	India's Malayalam Manorama News Group, Malayalam	India
News One	Pakistan's Interflow Group, Urdu	Pakistan
Dawn News	Pakistan's Dawn Media Group, English	Pakistan
Geo News	Pakistan's Jang Group, Urdu	Pakistan
Express News	Pakistan's Daily Express Group, Urdu & English	Pakistan
Indus News	Pakistan's Indus Media Group, Urdu	Pakistan
Local/City-Based News channels	Various, various languages	Indian/Pakistani cities only
East Asia		
Phoenix News	HK's Phoenix Holdings, News Corporation (minor), Mandarin	Central/East Asia
CTI TV News	Taiwan's CTI Group, Mandarin	Taiwan
ETTV News & News S	Taiwan's Eastern Broadcasting Co., Mandarin	Taiwan
Era TV News	Taiwan's Era Multimedia Group, Mandarin	Taiwan
FTV News	Taiwan's Formosa Media Group, Mandarin	Taiwan
SET News	Taiwan's Sanlih Entertainment Group, Mandarin	Taiwan
TVBS Newsnet	HK's TVB Group, Mandarin	Taiwan
TVB News	HK's TVB Group, Cantonese	Hong Kong
TVBN2	HK's TVB Group, Cantonese	Hong Kong
TVB i news	HK's TVB Group, Cantonese	Hong Kong
News 1 & 2	HK's Wharf Holdings Ltd, Cantonese	Hong Kong
JNN News Bird	Affiliate of Japan's TBS & JNN Groups, Japanese	Japan
Asahi Newstar	Japan's Asahi Group (Sony, minor), Japanese	Japan
YTN	Korea State Electric Corp, CNN partner, Korean	Central/East Asia (Korea), some North America
ABS-CBN News Channel	Philippines' Lopez Family, Tagalog & English	Central/East Asia (Phil.), some North America and West Asia/Middle East/North Africa (Arabic speaking mainly)
Astro Awani	Malaysia's Astro Group, Malay	Malaysia
TNN 24	Thailand's True Visions Group, Thai	Thailand
Sky News Australia	BSkyB (News Corp.), Australia's 7 & 9 networks, English	Oceania

(Adapted from Rai and Cottle 2010)

Table 6.2 Public/state/not-for-profit 24-hour news channels around the world

	Ownership and language	*Reach*
Global		
BBC World News	UK public broadcaster – commercial, English	Global
North America		
C-SPAN 1, 2 & 3	US cable industry – nonprofit English	US
CPAC	Canadian cable industry – nonprofit, English	Canada
CBC Newsworld	Canada's public broadcaster, English	Canada
RDI	Canada's public broadcaster, French	Canada-Quebec
South America		
TeleSUR	Latin American governments, 51% Venezuela, Spanish	South America
Europe		
Euronews	European public broadcasters, various languages	Europe, some Central Asia (mainly former Soviet states)
France 24	France's public broadcaster, French, English, Arabic	Europe including Russia, some West Asia/Middle East/North Africa (Arabic speaking mainly), Central Asia (former Soviet states) and rest of Africa
Russia Today	Russian state-owned RIA-Novosti – nonprofit, English	Europe including Russia, some West Asia/Middle East/North Africa (Arabic speaking mainly) and Central Asia (former Soviet states)
Vesti	Russian state-owned VGTRK, Russian	Russia
BBC News	UK public broadcaster, English	UK
RAI News 24	Italy's public broadcaster, Italian	Italy
TVE 24 Horas	Spain's public broadcaster, Spanish	Spain some North America
3/24	Catalan public television, Catalan	Spain-Catalonia
RTP Noticias	Portugal's public broadcaster, Portuguese	Portugal
TV2 News	Denmark's public broadcaster, Danish	Denmark
CT24	Czech public broadcaster, Czech	Czech Republic
TVP Info	Poland's public broadcaster, Polish	Poland

West/Central Asia, Middle East		
Al-Jazeera	Qatar government-financed, Arabic	West Asia/Middle East/North Africa (Arabic speaking mainly), some North America, Europe including Russia, Central Asia (former Soviet states), South Asia, Oceania
Al-Jazeera International	Qatar government-financed, English	West Asia/Middle East/North africa (Arabic speaking mainly), rest of Africa, some North America, Europe including Russia, South Asia, Central/East Asia
Al Ekhbariya	Saudi Arabian state-run, Arabic	West Asia/Middle East/North Africa (Arabic speaking mainly), some Central Asia (formerly Soviet States)
Al Hurra	US-based, US government-funded, Arabic	West Asia/Middle East/North Africa (Arabic speaking mainly), some Central Asia (former Soviet states)
Al Alam	Iran state-run, Arabic	Mainly Iran/Iraq
Press TV	Iran state-run, English	West Asia/Middle East/North Africa (Arabic speaking mainly), some Europe including Russia and rest of Africa
PTV News	Pakistan's state broadcaster, Urdu & English	South Asia, some Central Asia (former Soviet states), West Asia/Middle East/North Africa (Arabic speaking mainly)
Doordarshan News (also terrestrial)	Indian public broadcaster, Hindi & English	India
East Asia		
CCTV-9 (International)	China's state broadcaster, English	Central/East Asia, some North America, Europe including Russia, Central Asia (former Soviet states), rest of Africa, South Asia
Channel News Asia	Singapore's MediaCorp (government-owned), English	Central/East Asia, some South Asia, West Asia/Middle East/North Africa (Arabic speaking mainly)
CCTV News	China's state broadcaster, Mandarin	China, some Central Asia (former Soviet states)
NHK World TV	Japan's public broadcaster, English	Central/East Asia (Japan), some North America, Europe including Russia
TV1	Malaysia's public broadcaster, Malay	Malaysia
A-PAC	Australian cable industry – nonprofit, English	Oceania
TVNZ 7	NZ public broadcaster, English, Maori	Oceania

(Adapted from Rai and Cottle 2010)

Despite the recent emergence of several well-respected public service media organizations and transnational state broadcasters around the world, it is in the commercial market where 24-hour news channels have bloomed and regionalized the genre (Cushion 2010a). As Rai and Cottle's (2010) empirical map of rolling news channels revealed (Tables 6.1 and 6.2), just a few genuinely global providers exist – CNN, Fox and BBC World News – with most being regional or national in reach. But while Rai and Cottle (2010) usefully mapped out the geographical terrain of rolling news channels around the world, they did not editorially evaluate 24-hour television nor did they assess the democratic value of news between media systems. It is a point, in another study, that Cottle and Rai (2008d: 177) partly concede: "it is time to engage much more closely and empirically with ... the communicative structures of global news channels". Since 24-hour news channels have become more localized, it is also imperative that we empirically scrutinize *all* rolling stations, large or small.

It is in this context that the rest of the chapter aims to investigate whether the ownership structures of 24-hour news channels have impacted on the type and nature of rolling news journalism, unpacking the agenda pursued, conventions employed and styles adopted. For while the 24-hour television news genre arrived in the commercial market more than 30 years ago, the following section demonstrates how the editorial direction of rolling news channels has varied according to the ownership structure, regulatory environment and journalistic culture in which they operate.

Global 24-hour news warfare: comparing the "windows on the world" of competing media systems

The three 24-hour news channels with the most global reach are, according to Rai and Cottle (2010), based in the US (CNN and Fox News) and the UK (BBC World News). While the two US channels are fully fledged commercial stations, BBC World News is a commercial subsidiary of the BBC. It is not directly funded by the licence fee, but sustained by advertising. While BBC World News' ownership model is commercial, its journalism is shaped by a public service ethos and it abides by the BBC's editorial framework of impartiality and accuracy. For that reason it will be referred to as a public service broadcaster. However, Cottle and Rai (2008d) have suggested CNNI (the international not domestic channel) has more in common editorially with the BBC than Fox News. In a systematic content analysis of routine rolling coverage they found that Fox News delivered the most "thin" updates about world affairs (70.2 per cent compared to CNNI's 55.2 per cent) and supplied the most dominant frames (14.2 per cent compared to CNNI's 11.8 per cent) – interpreted as stories "clearly dominated and defined by a single external news source" (Rai and Cottle 2008d: 168). By contrast, CNNI featured more in-depth stories (7.9 per cent) than Fox News (1.5 per cent). According to Rai and Cottle (2008d), these frames impacted on the quality of journalism. They suggested:

> The predominance of communicatively restricted frames, such as the reporting and dominance frames, can certainly be interpreted as likely vehicles for dominant messages, discourses or ideology, especially when deployed so heavily, as they are, by the highly partisan US channel Fox News (but noticeably less so by CNNI). (Rai and Cottle 2008d: 176)

While the differences are more minimal, the public broadcaster, BBC World News, contained more thin news stories (66.8 per cent) than CNNI but fewer than Fox News. However, it reported stories with less dominant frames (10.6 per cent) than the two commercial channels and featured the most in-depth coverage (9.9 per cent).

As discussed at the beginning of the chapter (also see Chapter 5), the arrival of Middle Eastern channels such as Al-Jazeera – a Qatari-financed and sponsored broadcaster – has been viewed as a powerful counter-hegemonic weight to Western information flows (Zayani 2010). So, for example, in the Israeli/Palestinian conflict, studies have systematically shown Western media tend to favour the former nation in military and diplomatic disputes (see, for example, Philo and Berry 2011). Ayish's (2010b: 227) framing analysis of the Gaza conflict on Al-Jazeera between Israel and Hamas during 2007–2009 found that the dominant source – almost doubling references to the Israeli government – constituted Palestinian civilians. While Ayish (2010b) argued that professional judgement was exercised by Al-Jazeera journalists, a degree of political sympathy also appeared to shape coverage of the ongoing dispute. He concluded that Al-Jazeera "demonstrated explicit moral support for Palestinians in Gaza as evident in the framing of issues, actors, salience, and treatment" (Ayish 2010b: 238).

Since Al-Jazeera established an English-language service in 2006, scholars have explored the channel's influence beyond Arab audiences to ascertain whether it has maintained its commitment to reporting international news from a Middle Eastern perspective (Figenschou 2010; El-Nawawy and Powers 2010). After all, while the channel enjoys relative financial security and claims to report without state interference, has its journalism reoriented itself editorially to capture the Western/English-speaking market? Figenschou (2010) carried out a content analysis of Al-Jazeera's English 6 pm *NewsHour* flagship programme during October–December 2007 and May–July 2008 to assess its geographic commitment to covering parts of the world typically marginalized in Western news media. Figenschou (2010: 91) found 61 per cent of all stories were from the south – Africa, Asia, and the Middle East – covering more of the developed world than developed. If coverage is broken down by region, the study demonstrated that often

Table 6.3 Percentage of regions around the world covered on Al-Jazeera English's 6 pm *NewsHour* in 2007 and 2008

Country	*Per cent*
Asia	20.8
Africa	10.1
Latin America	10
Middle East	19.6
Europe	23.6
North America	14.6
Oceania	0.2
International	1.1

(Adapted from Figenschou 2010)

Table 6.4 Percentage of story time devoted to regions around the world on Al-Jazeera English, BBC World News and CNNI

	Al-Jazeera English	*BBC World News*	*CNNI*
Africa	6	1	–
Asia	19	17	19
Latin America	14	10	9
Middle East	42	19	25
Developing countries total	**81**	**47**	**53**
Europe	17	44	23
US	1	1	20
Other industrialized countries	1	3	1
Industrialized countries total	**19**	**48**	**44**
Other	–	6	3

(Adapted from Painter 2008)

neglected areas of the globe – Africa and Latin America – as well as Asia and the Middle East were routinely part of Al-Jazeera's agenda (Table 6.3).

Further still, the analysis found that Al-Jazeera featured more in-depth reports (42 per cent packages/interviews and 24 per cent studio-based analysis) than the North (31 per cent and 22 per cent respectively). The North, moreover, included more brief news items (45 per cent) than the South (32 per cent). Finally, the geographic spread of resources was reflected in more journalists reporting on location from the South (45 per of all stories) compared to the North (27 per cent).

Painter's (2008) study of Al-Jazeera English identified an even higher focus on the developing world compared to BBC World News and CNNI (see Table 6.4). But most strikingly, while Al-Jazeera in recent years might have increased its reach to communicate more globally, editorially a significant portion of time – 42 per cent – was spent reporting news about the Middle East. While Al-Jazeera has received criticism (largely in Western countries) for its coverage of war and conflict – whether in Afghanistan, Iraq, Israel or Palestine – Painter (2008: 44) concluded that "there is little evidence to suggest that AJE [Al-Jazeera English] is following an overtly partisan agenda … . Most stories have some degree of balance". The role of Al-Jazeera as a state broadcaster but with public service motivations will be revisited at the end of the chapter.

Painter's study also extended to a Latin American news channel – TeleSUR – and found evidence of a more politically motivated framing of news. Applying the BBC's editorial impartiality guidelines, the study found that the state-owned channel was not explicitly biased but highly selective in its news stories and framing of political events. On the basis of a systematic content analysis, four conclusions were reached:

1 Telesur is not falsifying the news, but choosing news stories according to different editorial criteria to those of CNN for example.
2 There is strong evidence to suggest that Telesur selects information that puts its sponsoring governments in a favourable light, in particular Cuba and Bolivia, and puts President Bush in a bad light.
3 There is some evidence to suggest that Telesur is more pluralistic in its coverage of countries who are not sponsoring the channel, but this would have to be corroborated by more content analysis of countries like Colombia, Mexico and Peru whose governments are not supporters of President Chavez. (Painter 2008: 64)

Boyd-Barrett and Boyd-Barrett's (2010) content and framing analysis of TeleSUR and its commercial competitors in the Latin America region, CNNesp and NTN24, suggested that the state broadcaster had the strongest regional identity and distinctive non-Western perspective. So, for example, TeleSUR's news agenda was centred mostly on Latin America and had the least amount of coverage of North America (see Table 6.5).

Table 6.5 Percentage of stories devoted to regions around the world on CNNesp, NTN24 and TeleSUR

	CNNesp	*NTN24*	*TeleSUR*
Latin America	41	39	62
United States	41	29	8
Middle East	5	11	10
Europe	7	18	8
Other	6	3	12

(Adapted from Boyd-Barrett and Boyd-Barrett 2010)

Based on a detailed framing analysis, Boyd-Barrett and Boyd-Barrett (2010) drew a clear set of conclusions about how distinct coverage on the commercial channels was to that on the state broadcaster, TeleSUR. They wrote that:

> TeleSUR is the counter-hegemon, cutting news of hegemonic preoccupations down to size. It provides more breadth and depth on Latin America than its rivals. It exhibits commendable concern for the indigenous peoples and poor of Latin America ... . Yet TeleSUR's counter-hegemonic status also constrains. Any friend of the US is a likely enemy of Venezuela's government, which is also TeleSUR's major patron. (Boyd-Barrett and Boyd-Barrett 2010: 214)

What this suggests, overall, is that while TeleSUR has pluralized the information environment in Latin America, it does not operate independently of the government, as do many other public service broadcasters (see Chapter 1).

The pan-European channel, Euronews, also has a hybrid funding structure, and does not subscribe to the conventional rolling news format. Broadcast in five languages, the news channel was launched to convey a shared political, cultural and linguistic image of European nation states (González Martín, 1995). According to its own promotional material, Euronews "editorial policy prefigures that of a European public service" (Euronews 2008: 4). A systematic study of its routine schedule and content found Euronews to be distinct from many commercial 24-hour news channels (Garcia-Blanco and Cushion 2010). A two-week content analysis of Euronews evening bulletins revealed its

Table 6.6 Percentage of topics covered in Euronews evening bulletins

Topic	*Per cent*
Third state politics	21.1
Social protest	11.2
Natural catastrophes	9.4
Member state politics	9
Crime	9
Middle East	6.3
Terrorism	5.8
Social policy and issues	5.8
US politics	4.9
Culture	4.9
EU politics	4
Science and environment	4
Celebrities	2.7
Not applicable	1.3

(Adapted from Garcia-Blanco and Cushion 2010)

agenda differed from many national or international news channels (see Table 6.6). When all political stories were combined, they accounted overall for 11 in 20 items examined.

By contrast, news stories about crime, terrorism, social issues/policy and natural disasters were, between them, less apparent on Euronews than many other 24-hour news channels. Moreover, there were far fewer celebrity-driven or culture-led stories, the kind of infotainment found – as seen later – in more commercially saturated markets such as the US and India.

We now look at national 24-hour news channels in more detail, evaluating whether state, public or commercial influences have shaped the nature of journalism in a smaller geographic region but perhaps more competitive market-place of rolling news stations.

Branding "fair and balanced" journalism: how have public and market-driven rolling news channels evolved around the world?

Within the US, CNN did not face any major domestic rolling news competition until the mid-1990s when MSNBC and Fox News were launched in 1996. Many state or local dedicated news channels have also started up but it is difficult to ascertain how many are operating at any given time, with resources varying considerably from one station to the next. While the 1990s saw many public broadcasters begin to develop 24-hour news channels, no publicly funded or subsidized dedicated rolling news channels have been launched in the US (with the exception of C-Span, of course, which is not a news-gathering channel).

In the US the rise of three national cable news channels – CNN, MSNBC and Fox News – has attracted critical attention over the last decade or so. For while the network news bulletins have long attracted the biggest US television news audiences – and today, between them, have five times as many viewers as the cable news channels (Pew Research Center Project for Excellence in Journalism 2010) – primetime audiences for CNN, MSNBC and Fox News have increased from approximately 1.25 million viewers to over 3.5 million between 1998 and 2008 (Pew Research Center Project for Excellence in Journalism 2009).

Enhanced market share has not been the only reason why cable news channels have been receiving critical attention. Editorially, content analyses of cable news channels over the last decade or so have shown MSNBC and Fox News, in particular, increasingly pursuing a more explicitly motivated political agenda in news coverage generally, but heightened in the run-up to elections and during times of war (Cushion 2012). As Chapter 4 evidenced, systematic analyses of Fox News have repeatedly found political bias, with Republicans being favoured over Democrats while rival mainstream media are routinely denigrated for ostensibly promoting a liberal agenda. And, as

Chapter 5 pointed out, in the aftermath of 9/11 and during the wars in Afghanistan and Iraq, Fox News stood out as being the most patriotic and pro-war. While critics of Fox News have scorned its brand slogan – "Fair and Balanced" – this editorial claim should be interpreted in the context of correcting the liberal bias the channel views as being pervasive in mainstream US news media.

Over the last decade or so, Fox News's populist appeal has attracted more viewers, most of conservative persuasion, raising fears about a "Fox effect" or a "Foxification" of values spreading to rival channels. These terms have been coined to represent a journalistic departure from balance or the pursuit of objectivity and an encouragement of more comment, speculation and politicization (Cushion 2012). There is evidence that these values are rubbing off on cable news competitors. The 2010 *State of the News Media* analysis of cable news stated that MSNBC was the "mirror image of Fox" and had taken on the "role as a left-leaning prime time channel" (Pew Research Center Project for Excellence in Journalism 2010). The 2011 report showed both channels were reinforcing their partisan personalities by employing either right- or left-wing commentators. It was also observed that, in primetime slots, the continuous rolling format was increasingly displaced by opinion-based programming, allowing contributors to wax lyrical on their own political opinions and prejudices. Beyond party politics, Frost and Phillips's (2011) systematic content analysis of crime reporting on CNN, Fox News and MSNBC found criminologists or other academic experts rarely featured on screen. More opinionated and less qualified guests discussed crime without addressing causation or control (Frost and Phillips 2011). Crime coverage could therefore be seen as tacitly encouraging a more punitive response to criminal behaviour, since alternative solutions to crime prevention did not routinely feature.

With no regulatory presence to enforce impartiality, broadcast journalism was able to pursue a more partisan direction, with US cable news channels exercising their own version of objectivity and balance. Fox News and MSNBC, of course, began life after the Fairness Doctrine was abolished in 1987 (FCC regulation requiring broadcasters to balance opinions – see Chapter 1). But they arrived at a time when online news was emerging and, moreover, the blogosphere was cultivating a new form of journalism where news and comment increasingly merged. The culture of news, in other words, appeared to be changing and news channels – most strikingly Fox News – changed with it, carving out a conservative brand in order to compete in an increasingly crowded market-place of news. The absence of US regulatory structures and the changing culture of journalism are returned to at the end of the chapter.

In the 1990s, shifting regulatory structures and intense market competition in India have also had an impact on the nature of the country's rolling news channels. For dedicated news channels have rapidly expanded there since deregulation in 1992 allowed more foreign investment into the market to fund new commercial ventures. The state decided no longer to hold a monopoly on broadcasting, opening up a potentially lucrative commercial market in the largest democracy in the world. It is estimated that 70 commercial news channels have been launched since 1998, broadcasting in 11 different languages (Metha 2010).

But consumer choice has not necessarily translated into editorial diversity and, according to many observers, the rise of commercial Indian news channels has led to the deterioration of journalistic standards. While there have been no systematic comparative content analysis studies of Indian 24-hour news channels, many accounts have noted the downmarket trend in editorial content. Thussu (2007: 91–112) has argued that Indian news channels have undergone a "Bollywoodization", with news and entertainment fused together to produce celebrity-driven infotainment. Drawing primarily on journalistic interpretations within India, he has written that Indian journalists have witnessed a

> noticeable change in style and content away from a considered professional approach to a flashier and visually more dynamic presentation; the emphasis seems to be not on the journalistic skills of news anchors and reporters but on how they look on camera, with style taking precedence over substance. (Thussu 2007: 104)

Likewise, Metha (2010) has concluded that "In a market where more than 70 news channels are competing for advertising, the structural economy of television forces many channels to focus on content with the lowest common denominator that will register on television rating panels" (Metha 2010: 324). While news channels have established a self-regulatory code of conduct under the News Broadcasters Association (NBA), this has not instilled confidence that editorial standards will be maintained (Joshi 2007). The absence of regulatory controls, market competition and the failure to transform the Indian state broadcaster into a more independent public body will form a discussion about the evolution of 24-hour channels later in the chapter.

While there have been limited cross-national comparative studies of rolling news channels around the world, Thussu's (2007: 88) examination of a celebrity-related story – Shilpa Shetty, an Indian actress being racially abused on the UK version of *Celebrity Big Brother* – revealed how Indian news channels reported it with more gusto than many other countries. Since the actress was a famous Bollywood star, it would of course be a newsworthy story in India and the UK, where the show was aired live. But while it dominated the English tabloid press and Ofcom received 40,000 complaints about the racist exchange in the reality game show, it was Indian news channels that ran the most footage of the incident (see Table 6.7), representing, in Thussu's view (2007: 90), their appetite for "global infotainment fare".

Table 6.7 Time spent reporting racism row on *Celebrity Big Brother* in 2007 on national UK news bulletins and international 24-hour news channels

Channel	*Where based*	*Duration*
Star News	India	8 hours 20 minutes
BBC World News	UK	7 hours
NDTV 24x7	India	6 hours 5 minutes
Channel 4 News	UK	5 hours
Al-Jazeera English	Qatar	4 hours and 30 minutes
ITN	UK	3 hours and 25 minutes
Sky News	UK	3 hours and 5 minutes
CNN International	US	2 hours and 15 minutes
France 24	France	1 hour and 40 minutes
DW-TV	Germany	1 hour and 20 minutes
Russia Today TV	Russia	1 hour
Euronews	Brussels	30 minutes

(Adapted from Thussu 2007)

Table 6.8 Types of programme on n-tv in 1997 and 2007 and on N24 in 2007 (% of air time)

	n-tv 1997	*n-tv 2007*	*N24 2007*
News	63	35	26
Commercial	11	11	9
Magazine	7	19	26
Documentary/feature	6	25	34
Weather	5	1	1
Discussion/talk	4	3	1
Programme trailer/other	3	3	1
Live coverage of events	1	2	2
Advice programme	1	2	–

(Adapted from Reinemann and Fawzi 2010: 304 drawing on Krüger's research)

Market forces have also been held responsible for shifting news values in other parts of the world. In Germany, home to one of the largest and best-resourced public service broadcasters around the globe, it was once again a commercial station that established the first dedicated rolling news channel, n-tv, in 1992. The German public broadcaster launched a news service – N24 – eight years later. N-tv's news agenda has been traced longitudinally and, over a ten-year period, has shifted from presenting rolling news to running more documentaries or more general scheduled programming (see Table 6.8).

While n-tv still carried more news than N24, by 2007 both commercial news channels in Germany were running a schedule where between approximately a third and quarter of their time was spent in a continuous news

Table 6.9 Stories on the German public and commercial nightly news bulletins and commercial 24-hour news channels in 2007 (%)

	Public service channels		*Commercial channels*		*24-hour news channels*	
	ARD	*ZDF*	*RTL*	*Sat.1*	*N24*	*n-tv*
Politics	49	38	19	20	20	31
Economy	7	7	5	8	14	21
Sport	8	11	18	8	6	13
Accidents/disasters	4	5	8	10	13	11
Crime	2	3	7	8	27	8
Weather	7	8	7	5	7	5
Society/judiciary	11	10	9	10	–	–
Science/culture	5	6	4	6	n/a	n/a
Human interest	2	5	16	20	3	–
Other	5	7	6	5	11	10

(Adapted from Reinemann and Fawzi 2010: 307 drawing on Krüger's research)

format. According to Reinemann and Fawzi (2010: 303–4), the downsizing of rolling news was partly due to financial constraints as rolling news is expensive to fund. However, it was also due to N24 expanding "the number and schedule of their renowned newscasts. Consequently, n-tv turned to pre-produced content that was cheaper and attracted larger audiences". Content analyses of public and commercial news bulletins as well as the rolling channels in 2007 demonstrated that a more serious, harder news agenda was pursued on ARD and ZDF (see Table 6.9). By contrast, the German 24-hour news channels tended to report softer news stories, such as accidents, disasters or crime, although they covered more economic stories than the conventional news bulletins.

In the UK, where public and commercial 24-hour news channels have been in competition since 1996, both BBC News and Sky News have adopted a more conventional continuous rolling format. While there is some specialist programming, primetime news hours primarily revolve around news bulletins, updates, live or breaking stories (Lewis *et al.* 2005). Three systematic studies in 2003, 2004/5 and 2007 of Sky News and BBC News revealed how longitudinally the public broadcaster has maintained a more serious news agenda (see Table 6.10).

In 2004 19 per cent of Sky News coverage was crime-related as against 8 per cent dedicated to celebrity and entertainment. In 2007 these percentages were more or less reversed, with 8 per cent of coverage devoted to crime and 20 per to celebrity and entertainment. By contrast, BBC News increased coverage of topics traditionally viewed as harder news including social issues/policy, business and economy stories. While Sky News appeared to have overtaken BBC News on the international agenda, a breakdown of stories reveals most – close

Table 6.10 Percentage of time spent on news excluding sports on BBC News and Sky News in 2004, 2005/6 and 2007

	BBC News (2004)	*BBC News (2005/6)*	*BBC News (2007)*	*Sky News (2004)*	*Sky News (2005/6)*	*Sky News (2007)*
Celebrity and entertainment	5.3	3.3	8.7	8.3	9.5	19.7
Crime	11.1	16.6	11.5	18.9	21.2	8.4
Business and economy	7	8.4	17.2	5.4	3.3	8.6
Social issues/policy	16	16.2	26.1	14.5	13.3	18
Politics	21.3	18.2	7.7	17.9	26.2	11.7
Disasters/accidents	5.8	14.4	6.6	2.3	12.6	9.3
International/foreign policy	31.2	21.1	19.7	28.7	12.7	22.4
Other	2.5	1.7	2.4	4.2	1.2	1.9

(Adapted from Cushion and Lewis 2009)

to a third – emanate from the US (many of which were celebrity-based). The public broadcaster, by contrast, spent a similar proportion of time covering international news from the US, Europe, Asia and Iraq. However, the study concluded that both channels routinely spent a reasonable amount of time covering international stories even when there was little major to report (Cushion and Lewis 2009).

By comparison, many other national news channels have agendas that are far more domestically orientated, such as US cable channels (Pew Research Center Project for Excellence in Journalism 2010) or the French France 24 (Kuhn 2010: 273– 4). Moreover, not only do these channels have a nationally discursive character, they have also been seen as spreading Western values to the rest of the world. Sky News, in this respect, might have a more domestically focused news agenda compared to BBC News, but the channel perhaps covers more foreign stories than many commercial news channels in other countries. Since its main competitor is a public service news channel, the BBC's presence and popularity (it has the highest audience share) could have had a knock-on effect, making Sky reluctant to abandon the reporting of international affairs.

The rise of live and "breaking news" coverage: does the need for speed compromise the quality of journalism on different media systems?

Over the last two decades, many media observers and scholars have explored the fast-paced world of 24/7 media and its broader impact on the information environment (Bromley 2010; Lewis 2010; Richardson and Meinhof 1999;

Rosenberg and Feldman 2008). While dedicated rolling news channels have formed part of this analysis, the Internet and, more recently, remote online devices on mobile phones and tablets have further quickened the pace of news and information delivery. Many studies have focused on the production of journalism in busy multimedia newsrooms, ethnographically observing how journalists operate to supply immediate information (Baisnée and Marchetti 2006; Born 2004; Cottle 1999; Domingo and Patterson 2011; MacGregor 1997; Matthews 2010; Steensen 2009). Having to respond instantly to round-the-clock news media, many scholars have alternatively addressed how politicians and spin doctors have become attuned to a 24/7 culture of media reporting (Cohen 2008; Jones 2003). Less attention has been focused on systematically tracing the content of immediate news, however, including the conventions used to report instant or disposable journalism and evaluating its democratic value. This final section explores the convention of live reporting and "breaking news" on 24-hour channels, examining the editorial value of these approaches to journalism across public and commercially driven news media.

The conventional image of a rolling news channel is a live, breaking 24-hour service, living up to the tradition established by CNN into the 1980s and 1990s. But while this CNN-ization of news values has spread to many national channels (Thussu 2003), many transnational rolling news stations do not routinely rely on live or breaking news conventions. So, for example, Euronews has no regular breaking news service, nor does it operate at the frenetic speed of most 24-hour news channels. While its schedule is punctuated with half-hour news bulletins and regular weather forecasts covering the whole of Europe, there is some lifestyle and magazine programming in between these times. Another distinctive feature of Euronews is its use of live news. Whereas most news channels run live coverage of events, with journalists interpreting the visual images, Euronews streams raw footage, sometimes live, without any commentary. As argued elsewhere (Baisnée and Marchetti 2006; Garcia-Blanco and Cushion 2010), this is partly out of necessity, since the channel is broadcast in five languages and translation would be highly costly. Journalists, most of the time, present through voice-overs with their on-screen presence reduced by the absence of anchors.

Likewise, the transnational, French public broadcaster, France 24, does not share the same characteristics as many dedicated commercial news channels. According to a close observer:

> France 24 does not confine itself to a repetitive rolling news approach … it accords relatively low priority to breaking news when it comes to modifying its scheduling … . Compared to most rolling news channels, the visual presentation is kept simple, with just one band of alternative changing news text at the bottom of the screen. (Kuhn 2010: 274)

China's state news channel, CCTV, has undergone several editorial revamps in recent years to enhance its international reputation. While these primarily relate to demonstrating that the channel can operate independently of the state, there have also been attempts to reduce documentary-type scheduling and produce faster, continuous news more in tune with Western conventions (see Jirik 2010: 288–9). Al-Jazeera, likewise, has begun to adopt many Western news practices including the use of live and breaking news conventions (Painter 2008). However, interviews with senior management and editorial staff members revealed a conscious effort not to employ these conventions because this could potentially lead to shared news values and live footage from Western broadcasters. Figenschou's (2011: 8) analysis of interviews with Al-Jazeera journalists concluded that "there has been a tendency to emphasize the alternative pre-planned over the breaking news of the day". Moreover, "privileging breaking news events is difficult because AJE [Al-Jazeera English] risks ending up with the same headlines as CNN and BBC – the mainstream Western news networks they aim to be alternative to" (Figenschou 2011: 9). Since live pictures tend to be supplied by largely Western news agencies (Patterson 2010), conscious editorial selection is required to ensure these channels offer an alternative interpretation of world events.

Without the necessary resources or ambition to remain distinct entities, Patterson (2010) has argued that Western news channels have increasingly relied on news agencies to produce immediate, live, breaking news footage. Since CNN's live reporting of the First Gulf War, many scholars have traced the channel's breaking coverage and its impact not just on the next generation of rolling news channels (Cushion 2010a; Huxford 2007; Marriott 2007; Thussu and Freedman 2003) but on the wider culture of US network and local broadcast journalism (Cushion 2012; Tuggle and Huffman 2001; Tuggle *et al.* 2010). So, for example, Livingston and Bennett (2003: 375) examined CNN stories reported by the international desk between 1994 and 2001 and "found that as the decade progressed, more of CNN's coverage was live". Studies elsewhere have confirmed that other US cable news channels – MSNBC and Fox News – have continued to improve their reporting of live events (Seib 2002). To reinforce their live, visual coverage of events, network and cable television news channels have also extended their delivery of immediate breaking news updates by the use of more sophisticated online technologies. A systematic review of ABC, CBS, CNN, Fox and MSNBC email news alerts found hundreds sent by each broadcaster although with some variation (Bajkiewicz and Smith 2007). While CNN sent 104 emails over a week, Fox News supplied 196, ABC 219 and MSNBC delivered 230. This suggested that decisions about what constitutes breaking news can vary from one broadcaster to the next, since no major incident, event or issue was present over the sample period. It might, in other words, be more of a commercial than public service decision, used to symbolize a news organization's fast, breaking news brand.

Indeed, in the highly competitive 24-hour world of Indian news channels, several observers have noted how breaking news has become increasingly sensationalist during major terrorist attacks. Jain (2010) has suggested that sectarian riots in Gujarat during 2002 trigged a profound shift in how 24-hour rolling news reported subsequent dramatic and unfolding events. While the state channel, DD News, censored some of its coverage, the commercial channels' "extensive 24-hour news reportage of the Gujarat genocide was unambiguously marked by intent to lend visibility to the violence, and showing the failing of the nation-state" (Jain 2010: 166). If this – not long after India had opened up the broadcast market – could be celebrated as a significant democratic breakthrough, since commercial media could be critical of the state without reprisal, towards the end of the decade many critics argued that the intense competition among rolling stations had diminished the quality of journalism and ushered in a new era of commercial Western news values (Thussu 2007). In particular, the live coverage of the Mumbai terrorist attacks lasting over 60 hours in 2008 among the 70-odd news Indian channels has been interpreted as unnecessarily salacious and voyeuristic. With each channel attempting to carve out its own identity, market choice, according to P. N. Vasanti, has cultivated an "extraordinary pressure to sensationalize, claim specious 'exclusives' and do almost anything else to attract attention" (cited in Magnier 2009). A survey examining public attitudes to news media coverage of the Mumbai terrorist attacks found three-quarters of respondents "felt that the reportage-presentation was theatrical" (Thakuria 2008). DD News, however, was interpreted as being the most measured, choosing (or censoring) potentially offensive material for audiences. The state broadcaster "was observed to be the least sensational" (Thakuria 2008).

Many Western studies of live or breaking news have also tended to focus on atypical moments as opposed to more routine periods of time. The immediate aftermath of the terrorist atrocities in New York, London or Madrid, for example, have been explored from a variety of perspectives (Nacos 2003; Reynolds and Barnett 2003). Juntunen (2010) has examined how journalists reacted to breaking online news about school shootings in Finland during 2007 and 2008, renegotiating their ethical codes to be first with information even if this compromised accuracy. Young (2007: 404), meanwhile, has observed that Sky News in Australia established a reputation for its live and breaking coverage of bushfires in 2007, and a mine collapse and rescue lasting 14 days in Beaconsfield. Of course, three years later many international news channels spent considerable time covering the rescue of the Chilean miners live, including the BBC, which sent 26 staff to South America at a cost of more than £100,000 (Halliday 2010).

But even in routine periods, a longitudinal content analysis of national UK television 24-hour news channels established that breaking news had become an increasingly familiar convention over the past decade. Both the public broadcaster, BBC News, and its commercial competitor, Sky News, increased the time they spent on breaking news coverage (Table 6.11). While Sky News

Table 6.11 Percentage of time spent on breaking news items as a proportion of news time (including sport) overall on BBC News and Sky News

	BBC News (2004)	*BBC News (2005/6)*	*BBC News (2007)*	*Sky News (2004)*	*Sky News (2005/6)*	*Sky News (2007)*
Percentage of stories designated breaking news	3	11	11.2	4.5	13	11
Percentage of news time spent on breaking stories	2.4	8.3	11	7.3	21.4	13

(Adapted from Cushion and Lewis 2009)

aired marginally more breaking news in 2007, the commercial channel also employed a "news alert" – another tag to label urgent news borrowed from its sister channel in the US, Fox News – that was not included in the analysis (Cushion and Lewis 2009). The moniker "news alert" was included in pre-scheduled events such as a live press conference and, in the 2005/6 sample, the very high proportion of time Sky News devoted to breaking news was largely due to its lengthy coverage of a few "live" events (Lewis and Cushion 2007).

In each period of analysis, "breaking news" involved following up or repeating a story already labelled as "breaking", rather than reporting something new for the first time. This was particularly the case for Sky News. However, by 2007 BBC News spent approximately half the time reporting first breaking stories as it did on follow-up reports. Since BBC News spent more time explaining a news story when it first broke, this suggested that it had more information before it labelled a story "breaking" compared to Sky News which, at this stage, informed viewers with less knowledge to hand. Indeed, a breakdown of first breaking news stories in 2007 found Sky News had no sources informing coverage whereas BBC News had three sources – an NGO and two business sources. When a story was revisited on Sky News it had nine sources overall, compared to 12 on BBC News.[23] There was also a difference in the nature of the coverage between the public and commercial channels, with the BBC adopting a more cautious tone and measured use of language while Sky News was less circumspect and potentially misleading. So, for example, when a suspected bomb on a flight out of Sydney was found out to be a hoax, both channels reported it as breaking news but the BBC promptly withdrew its on-screen breaking status whereas Sky continued to brand it that way for the next hour or so.

Sky's urgent need to break news first is reflected in its aggressive marketing and editorial ambitions. As the then new head of Sky News – John Ryley – put it in 2006: "Sky News customers know that we are only a heartbeat away from breaking news" (Ryley 2006: 10). The value of breaking news has been extended by social media, including Twitter, with Sky News the first broadcaster in the

Table 6.12 Percentage of time spent on breaking news items on BBC News and Sky News in 2004, 2005/6 and 2007

	BBC News			*Sky News*		
	2004	*2005/6*	*2007*	*2004*	*2005/6*	*2007*
First Breaking	29.2	22.5	49.9	16.7	42.1	25.8
Return to breaking news story	70.8	77.5	50.1	83.3	57.9	74.2

(Adapted from Lewis and Cushion 2009)

UK to appoint a dedicated Twitter correspondent in 2009 (before its use became more widespread among broadcast journalists). Even though the editor of Sky News online has conceded that it is more difficult to substantiate the verification of sources on Twitter, its value has largely been in enabling the commercial broadcaster to break news first (see Beckett 2010: 9–10). Likewise, Nick Pollard (2009: 121), who was head of Sky News for over 15 years, has admitted that technology "drove an increasing demand for liveness, which became one of the dominating features of the medium". But he has pointed out that:

> there clearly is room for debate about the now-routine inclusion of live reporting from the site of nearly all news stories, particularly when little fresh is happening … . The complaint (voiced by plenty of reporters themselves) is that there's a real danger of them ending up as 'satellite jockeys', tied to a live presentation sport and unable to go off and gather fresh facts.

While the BBC approach to breaking news has some qualities that distinguish it from its commercial competitor, as with Sky, its decision to cover more breaking news over the last decade or so has brought editorial consequences. Breaking news stories generally have fewer sources than non-breaking stories and they favour certain categories of news over others – with politics and social policy issues being downsized for stories about crime and natural disasters/accidents (Lewis and Cushion 2009). Moreover, to remain competitive with Sky, there is evidence that the BBC editorial guidelines have been relaxed to allow anchors to be more speculative during breaking news drama (Cushion 2010b). In doing so, the BBC news channel's breaking news philosophy might not be consistent with the public broadcaster's editorial guidelines on accuracy (Cushion 2012: 80–1).

UK television news culture, of course, is not alone in having its ethical code challenged by the pace of rolling news journalism. According to Reinemann and Fawzi (2010: 310) "The speeding up of news cycles, increasing self referentiality, and – as a result – a decay of ethical principles and the quality of journalism have been concerns in Germany." They have argued that this speeding up coincided with the arrival of dedicated news channels, even if they were not exclusively responsible for accelerating the pace of much television news journalism. They concluded, however, that:

> it seems likely that the appearance of the news channels, and especially the foundation of n-tv, at least contributed to them [speeded-up news cycles] ... the fact that the major public service channels added more and more editions of their newscasts to their morning, afternoon, and nightly programmes in the late 1990s very likely is a reaction to the constant flow of TV news provided by n-tv. (Reinemann and Fawzi 2010: 311)

The competition among news channels, in other words, appears to have encouraged a shared journalistic thirst for speed, delivering live, breaking news action as it happens. While this section has shown that some public service media have been more restrained when reporting live or breaking news than their commercial rivals, at the same time both media systems have entered into the competitive spirit to break news first.

Conclusions

The chapter began by asking which media systems had most influenced the creation and development of dedicated rolling news channels. An empirical map of 24-hour news stations around the world was drawn on to demonstrate that for every public/state or not-for-profit 24-hour news channel, over two and a half more commercial stations were currently in operation. Of course, the first dedicated 24-hour news channel was launched by CNN in 1980. The commercial channel defined the genre since it enjoyed a decade without competition until the late 1980s and early 1990s when new satellite platforms with more transnational reach began to be launched beyond America into European, Latin American and Asian markets.

It was in this era public service rolling news stations began to emerge. The chapter sought to compare different news channels' form, style, conventions and, importantly, if public or state-owned stations offered a 24-hour news view of the world that was distinct from that of the commercial broadcasters. Systematic studies demonstrated that, between them, an alternative window on the world to CNN was being conveyed by many publicly funded news channels across regions of the world. Many public service 24-hour news channels contained more scheduled programming and did not necessarily operate at the frenetic pace familiar to commercial rolling news stations. To different degrees, it was found that public rather than commercial 24-hour news channels with an international reach had acted as the "agents of the new visibility" Orgad (2008: 301) has suggested transnational channels make possible.

But while several of the most well-respected international public service news channels diminished the power of CNN on the world stage in the 1990s, it was arguably the arrival of Al-Jazeera that most disrupted the status quo by challenging the hegemonic weight exerted by Western news over the previous decade or so. Painter's (2008: 71) content studies of international news channels concluded that Al-Jazeera was similar to CNN and BBC World News in that each followed "journalistic values such as balance and plurality of opinion". Comparative studies revealed Al-Jazeera reported parts of the world long marginalized by Western news values and framed coverage more in tune with Arab hearts and minds. Since Middle Eastern journalism has been subject to considerable state interference – and in many countries, of course, this has remained the case – Al-Jazeera's claimed editorial freedom as a state broadcaster has not only helped to democratize this region but has had repercussions on the wider international stage.

Other parts of the world historically censored by repressive state forces or reliant on Western news channels have also launched stations in recent years. Unlike Al-Jazeera, however, government-funded channels such as TeleSUR, RT and CC-TV have been unable to break free as public service rather than state broadcasters. While each channel can to a larger extent avoid the commercial constraints imposed on many Western stations, their agendas remain tied to state interests without robust independent impartiality checkpoints. Needless to say, Al-Jazeera – and, for that matter, many other Western broadcasters – display "cultural bias in the stories they choose to report and in the perspective they offer on those stories" (Painter 2008: 72) but they appear less susceptible to market or state influences. As El-Nawawy and Powers (2010: 62) put it when examining the impact of Al-Jazeera English: "it is dominated by neither geopolitical nor commercial interests, and is the first of its kind to have the resources, mandate and journalistic capacity to reach out to typically isolated and ignored audiences throughout the world". They quoted senior editorial figures working for Al-Jazeera who claimed it "may be the last bastion of public broadcasting" (cited in Hanley 2007 by El-Nawawy and Powers 2010: 73) and that the channel was "not driven by the dollar or constrained by commercialisation pressures as many other news networks. And this gives us great liberty in the way we approach our stories" (Zayed 2008 cited by El Nawawy and Powers 2010: 73).

If the success of Al-Jazeera has been its ability to resist market pressure, this differed from most commercial 24-hour news channels that outweigh their public service competitors in national and local contexts. Since the origins of 24-hour news channels can be traced back to commercial broadcasters, the dominant academic critique made about their editorial conventions is that they eschew values associated with the democratic value of news (see Chapters 1 and 2). Much like the culture of fast food, 24-hour news has long been viewed as a service that values immediacy over substance, sacrificing accuracy and analysis in order to show breaking news and broadcast live pictures as events unfold. We should not overlook the important role 24-hour news channels play during a natural disaster or terrorist attack, however, supplying regular updates and alerting viewers to emergency phone lines. New social media, most notably Twitter, have enabled the dissemination of news even more instantly, straight into viewers' computers and mobile phones. But even experienced editors of 24-hour news channels and websites have conceded that live or breaking news conventions have become too normalized a rolling news practice, preventing journalists from exploring another perspective to a story and thus audiences from understanding the wider context to an event or issue. As rolling news channels have competed more intensely in a far more competitive market-place over the last decade or so, this chapter has shown that many of these market-led conventions have been hyped up and subject to less regulatory oversight.

So, for example, CNN's pioneering live approach to rolling news has been emulated more widely by US 24-hour news channels with "breaking news" or "news alerts" becoming standard fare even in routine periods. But this goes beyond the US market-driven rolling news culture, since the "thirst to be first" appears as irresistible an urge for public service broadcasters such as the BBC as for commercial operators like Fox News. However, the BBC and other more transnational public service broadcasters have a more restrained ethos of breaking news policy (France 24 and Euronews, for example) than their commercial competitors. But even when exercising caution, a detailed analysis of breaking news stories on Sky News and BBC News revealed that breaking news conventions can compromise the quality of journalism. Put simply, breaking news traffic consisted of more soft than hard news, including greater priority towards crime and natural disasters, referenced fewer sources than non-breaking stories and, in the case of the BBC, reported fast-moving news that could be viewed as inconsistent with its own editorial guidelines on accuracy. The strict editorial standards upheld by public service broadcasters have not, in other words, considered the role of breaking news on 24-hour news channels or developed adequate regulatory checkpoints exercised in other forms of journalism.

Moreover, many 24-hour channels have been able to develop their journalistic conventions and carve out their editorial agendas in an environment where fewer regulatory obligations have been imposed on them than previously experienced by television news journalists, most strikingly in the US. For example, the FCC's relaxation of the Fairness Doctrine in 1987 – that ensured broadcasters balanced every news story – allowed channels such as Fox News to air more opinion-based journalism and abandon the requirement to cover the world "objectively".

The freedom to define the character of 24-hour news in an increasingly deregulatory environment has been evident elsewhere. Since the Indian government ended its monopoly of broadcasting in the 1990s and opened up a commercial market-place for news, it has been observed that news media could report more freely without state interference. But this democratic victory, according to observers, was short-lived. Self-regulating their own editorial standards, the competition among a myriad of Indian news channels in the 2000s is seen to have encouraged the pursuit of sensationalist and voyeuristic live coverage of terrorist attacks. According to Joshi (2007),

> gradual privatization and deregulation have resulted in increased entertainment-driven rather than public service oriented news channels in India. In other words, rather than being a news channel, they are trying to become wholesome entertainment channels even though there are other channels for this purpose.

Within the UK, the strict impartiality laws have, by contrast, reduced the likelihood of the commercial broadcaster – Sky News – being able to adopt the highly partisan and sensationalist approach followed by Fox News in America (Cushion and Lewis 2009). Moreover, the presence of a popular public service broadcaster – the BBC – has arguably created a journalistic culture that, as Sky News editors have claimed previously, would actively resist breaching values of impartiality if Rupert Murdoch – owner of BSkyB – imposed them on the organization. As previous chapters have concluded, the knock-on effect public service media can have on their commercial rivals, together with the more formally imposed regulatory requirements, have arguably combined to safeguard standards of 24-hour news journalism in some countries. But their impact must be put into perspective. For while public broadcasters and more robust regulation can be seen to have restrained the possibility of a full-blown Fox-style journalism being imported to other regions of the world, the commercial conventions that first defined the 24-hour news genre, such as live or breaking news, continue to exert their influence on many broadcasters, commercial *and* public.

The final chapter now turns to a review of studies examining the audience impact of commercial and public service news on people's knowledge, civic participation and trust in journalism. For while the previous four chapters have focused on the editorial content of public and market-driven news, the last part of the book evaluates the democratic value of news from the perspective of its role in enhancing informed and active citizenship.

Protecting the democratic value of news

Chapter 7

Why public service media matter

Introduction

This final chapter draws together the evidence amassed throughout the book, establishing whether public service news can be editorially distinguished from that on other media systems. However, it not only considers the content of news, it reviews empirical studies that have assessed whether different types of media systems have enhanced people's knowledge and understanding of particular issues, encouraged citizens to participate in civic life or earned the trust of audiences. The intention of this chapter, in other words, is to evaluate the contribution made by different media systems in engendering an active and informed citizenry.

The significant conclusions established in the book are then brought together to generate a wider discussion about the role of news produced by different media systems in contemporary journalism. In brief, the chapter asks whether, in an increasingly crowded commercial media landscape, public service media matter to the future of news and whether citizens should continue to subsidize journalism when an abundance of news is already supplied by the commercial market.

The impact of different media systems: comparing empirical studies of public knowledge, civic participation and audience trust

While the focus in the book so far has been on comparing news content produced under competing funding models or regulatory responsibilities, it is now necessary to compare how different media systems have impacted on people's knowledge, civic participation or the level of trust held towards journalism. After all, if the health of a liberal democracy relies on people being informed about the world or in maintaining an active citizenry, then information supplied by media alone cannot convey whether news has democratic value or not. Public service broadcasters, in particular, have long claimed to deliver programming with civic value in the Reithian spirit to "inform, educate and entertain". Indeed, as Chapter 1 pointed out, in the US watching public television has become associated with being a "good citizen", since some viewers believe it delivers the wholesome diet of news and current affairs necessary for a healthy democracy (Ouellette 2002). But beyond well-intentioned claims made by broadcasters or general impressions from audiences, what empirical evidence is there that particular media systems help generate an active and informed citizenry?

At the turn of the millennium, when new commercial stations were beginning to attract audiences away from public broadcasters, Holtz-Bacha and Norris (2001) carried out representative surveys in 14 European countries to explore whether the proliferation of media channels had enhanced people's knowledge about politics and public affairs as some liberal pluralists had claimed they would. While they were cautious in claiming direct causation, on the basis of plausibility they found that respondents who watched more public than commercial television news were more knowledgeable about political matters. To explain why, they suggested that a "virtuous circle" had been created whereby the "more politically aware may well turn on the news and watch current affairs documentaries on public TV, but, in turn, repeated exposure to these programs also increases people's levels of civic information" (Holtz-Bacha and Norris 2001: 138). By way of conclusion, Holtz-Bacha and Norris (2001: 138) speculated that, if the increased flow of information were to supplement public TV viewing rather than replace it in the future, then "there may be less cause for concern about the democratic implications".

Several years into the new millennium, Prior's (2007) detailed analysis of the routine media consumption habits of US audiences revealed that enhanced consumer choice on television, cable and the Internet had, in fact, resulted in *more* people turning away from news and documentary programming, choosing instead to watch, read and listen to more entertaining genres online, or on print and broadcast platforms. In other words, there *is* cause for democratic concern since fewer people are exposed to the political information considered vital to the maintenance of informed citizenship. Prior's (2007) research, however, was limited to the US, one of the most commercialized media landscapes in the world, with a multi-channel culture that delivers an abundance of programming for viewers to choose from.

Consequently, it has been observed that even regular viewers of one of the most informative genres – news programming – have been influenced by the plethora of commercial channels available in the US. So, for example, Morris and Forgette (2007: 94) coined the phrase "news grazing" to characterize viewers of television news who "watch the news with remote control in hand, clicking to other stations when a disinteresting topic comes up". They established that news viewers defined as grazers had less knowledge about hard news stories compared to non-grazers but did have the same understanding of soft news. In understanding why, they discovered grazers most regularly watched cable news and concluded that it could be that they are switching over when a hard news topic arises or, alternatively, that cable news contained little to no hard news. They suggested that future research should ascertain "how much of the news on cable news is policy orientated and how much is entertainment" (Morris and Forgette 2007: 105). But, as previous chapters have demonstrated, this has already been empirically established: the longitudinal answer is increasingly the latter, since cable news contains a high volume of soft news with diminishing reliability about its accuracy or objectivity (see Chapter 6). In other words, the more commercialized and less regulated the editorial environment in which cable news channels operate (relative to the longer history of network television news) could encourage viewers to actively avoid watching hard news topics.

By contrast, Aalberg *et al.* (2010) found that the flow of hard news remained relatively high in countries where a public service infrastructure had remained in place and a more regulated environment had protected journalism at peak times. They carried out a schedule analysis of television news programming in six countries and identified that, with the exception of commercial US channels – which ran "hardly twenty minutes" of air time – Belgium, the Netherlands, Norway, Sweden and the UK had all maintained their primetime commitment to news and current affairs programming (Aalberg *et al.* 2010: 262). This, they argued, was largely due to the presence of public service media and a more regulated environment than in the US. Of course, the presence of public media alone cannot be celebrated since – as Table 7.1 shows – the amount of people watching either public or commercially driven television news differs cross-nationally. Thus, while Aalberg *et al.*'s (2010) schedule analysis revealed that every public broadcaster supplied more news and current affairs than their commercial counterparts within each country examined, since the entire audience for PBS programming in the US (not just for news content) is 3 per cent overall (Miller 2010: 62), its impact is far more limited when compared to Norway, Sweden, Belgium and, to a lesser extent, the UK.

To explore whether different media systems impacted on public knowledge, Curran *et al.* (2009) developed an internationally comparative study of television news in the US, UK, Denmark and Finland. They established that hard news including international affairs was most frequently reported in countries where public service media dominated and regulation was more robustly policed (e.g. Finland and Denmark) than in the mixed public–commercial system in the UK or in the market-dominated culture of the US (consistent with other content studies drawn on in Chapter 3). They then carried out representative surveys of the population in each country to answer questions about domestic and international affairs and generated data that, in their words, "suggest a connection between patterns of news coverage and levels of public knowledge" (Curran *et al.* 2009: 14). Despite controlling for

Table 7.1 Percentage of viewers watching the main evening public and commercial TV news channels in 1997 and 2007

	1997	*2007*
Belgium		
Main public service evening news	8.6	12
Main commercial evening news	13.6	10
Netherlands		
Main public service evening news	9.4	9.8
Main commercial evening news	5.8	6.1
Norway		
Main public service evening news	20.4	15.4
Main commercial evening news	12.7	10.7
Sweden		
Main public service evening news	16.8	11.2
Main commercial evening news	5.2	5.4
UK		
Main public service evening news	8.9	7.9
Main commercial evening news	9.9	6.1
US		
Main NBC evening news	3.9	2.7
Main ABC evening news	3.7	2.7

(Adapted from Aalberg *et al.* 2010)

other variables that could have impacted on public knowledge, such as varying educational or income levels, interest in politics and public affairs or a sense of civic duty, they established that the Scandinavian respondents were more informed than those in the UK and, in respect of the US, *far* more knowledgeable about hard news topics and international news more generally. In the case of the US, this was reinforced by – as Chapter 3 identified – the routine diet of soft news on network television news and the low visibility of international affairs.

Iyengar *et al.* (2009) compared public knowledge about international affairs in just the US and Switzerland, and they likewise linked high news media exposure with a greater understanding of news and current affairs. Based on a representative survey of both nations they identified that the Swiss possessed far more knowledge about soft and hard international news than Americans, with a 30 per cent gap in knowledge, on average, leading them to argue that many Americans remained ignorant about foreign affairs. Once again, while they controlled for other potential variables likely to enhance an understanding of international affairs, they suggested that the "cross-national knowledge chasm is attributable in part to differences in the supply of information" (Iyengar *et al.* 2009: 354). In their words:

> The Swiss learn more about international affairs because their media are not driven entirely by considerations of profit maximization. The presence of a strong public broadcaster and the tradition of regular public affairs programming by commercial broadcasters create a more reliable supply of international news. Americans, on the other hand, must depend on commercial news outlets that are not required to deliver any minimal level of news programming. (Iyengar *et al.* 2009: 354)

Put simply, regular exposure to regulated public service broadcast news appears to increase people's knowledge about the world.

At the same time, journalism has the ability to *mis*inform people, obscuring rather than enlightening audiences about world events. Of all the case studies explored in this book, US commercial news coverage during the 2003 war in Iraq arguably displayed the most partial and, at times, misleading examples of journalism evaluated. Fox News, in particular, was singled out for its highly patriotic and opinionated coverage, abandoning any aspirations to report impartially about military or diplomatic matters. Consequently, a 2003 representative survey of US television news audiences revealed that regular viewers of Fox News, most strikingly, held many misconceptions about the purpose of and context to the US's military action in Iraq. It discovered many viewers falsely believed that Iraq supported Al-Qaeda; that Iraq played a role in the terrorist attacks of 9/11; and that world opinion, despite many countries being bitterly opposed to the conflict, was largely supportive of the war in Iraq (Kull 2003). Regular viewers of CBS, ABC, NBC and CNN also held these misconceptions but not to the same degree as viewers of Fox News. While only watched by a very small part of the audience overall, it was regular viewers of PBS news who were the least likely to share any of these misconceptions (Kull 2003). In summary, without having to satisfy impartiality requirements or abide by an editorial mission to enhance public knowledge, some US commercial television news outlets cultivated *misinformed* citizenship during coverage of the war in Iraq.[24]

Beyond generally informing people about the world, broadcasters also aim to encourage people's participation in civic affairs or, put another way, promote active and engaged citizenship. This relationship, fundamental to democratic theory, is most critically celebrated at election times – when citizens, more than ever, need reliable information in order to cast an informed vote at the ballot box. As Chapter 4 argued, political news during election time is often subjected to considerable empirical scrutiny, not least because research councils or government bodies tend to award generous grants for reviews into how media reported the campaign. Less understood, however, is the impact different media systems have had in encouraging people to vote or in enhancing an understanding of policies ahead of an election.

Baek (2009) has explored whether the presence of a public broadcaster impacted on levels of electoral turnout cross-nationally. Drawing on survey data comparing media systems and electoral participation in 74 countries, it was revealed that "State/public systems have the highest turnout level, and private systems have the lowest ... the average turnout rate of private systems is significantly lower than that of state/public and mixed system – by 13%" (Baek 2009: 384). In addition, Baek (2009) discovered that voting increased in countries when parties paid for political advertising but only where a public broadcaster existed. However, when a private system was dominant – most notably in the US – paid-for advertising decreased voter turnout. It was concluded that "the negative effect of private broadcasting systems indicates that the free market approach to media regulations does not create an ideal setting for the 'marketplace of ideas' in fostering an engaged and participatory citizenry" (Baek 2009: 388). Public broadcasting, by contrast, appears to enhance citizen involvement in elections and campaign mobilization.

Popescu and Tóka (2009) have drawn on a range of survey data to explore whether watching public or private broadcasters or no television at all had an impact on public knowledge during the 1999 and 2004 European elections. While they determined that television viewing did enhance an understanding of election issues generally, exposure to just commercial or public television consumption did not follow a uniform cross-national pattern. However, Popescu and Tóka believed that a relationship between public and commercial broadcasters could have influenced the acquisition of public knowledge during both elections. They suggested that viewers of public/state broadcasters turned to commercial news when they suspected the former were being editorially influenced by government forces. They identified that public understanding of elections was positively correlated with commercial television when press freedom and autonomy were weaker. Popescu and Tóka's (2009) survey also suggested that the impact of television news on citizen knowledge went beyond the "virtuous circle" (Norris 2000) of politically engaged and regular consumers of news. Their conclusions are worth quoting at length:

> the most politically interested citizens seem to learn about politics whether or not they attend to political news, probably because they actively seek out information through other channels [television], not least the newspapers. It is only for the less interested for whom the encounter with political information on television really matters ... . This finding would seem to support a core assumption behind public broadcasting, namely that it would actually make some difference if people were provided a programming that is richer in information than the kind of programming that market demand for television programs themselves would generate in the absence of publicly funded and regulated broadcasters. (Popescu and Tóka 2009)

This appears to contradict the suggestion that citizens not typically attentive to politics and public affairs might better understand news produced by commercial programming because it is perceived as being more entertaining, if not informative. Indeed, from another perspective, it can be observed that public media can positively engage voters' attention during a campaign when compared to commercial outlets.

Strömbäck and Shehata's (2010) analysis of three waves of panel data during the 2006 election in Sweden revealed the impact of public media during the campaign in generating political interest. This is in spite of the increasingly commercial television landscape in Sweden since TV4 was introduced in the 1990s. The study established that public service television news and radio had a "stronger impact on political interest than exposure to commercial news" (Strömbäck and Shehata 2010: 589). In examining voter interest at critical moments before, on the eve of and immediately after the election, their three broadly representative polls of the Swedish population demonstrated that repeated consumption of public rather than commercial news can have a measurable impact on sustaining viewers' attention to election news programming.

That there was no uniform pattern of public and commercial broadcast impact on public knowledge across Europe (Popescu and Tóka 2009) could be due not only to the diversity of citizens across the continent but also, as Strömbäck and Shehata's study (2010) showed, to the institutional differences across media systems. This points to the limits of internationally comparative studies since the type, regulation, funding and editorial freedom of particular media can vary from one country to the next. The impact of media influence, in other words, also needs to be understood in national contexts and in the informational environment beyond broadcasting. So, for example, drawing on the Norwegian 1997–2001 election survey panel data, Jenssen (2008: 261) pointed out "that there are no significant differences between being exposed to the news and campaign debates on either NRK [public broadcaster] or TV2 [commercial broadcaster], simply because neither has any significant effect on the level of factual political knowledge". According to Jenssen (2008), the most significant variables related, above all, to levels of education, but interest in politics and age were also factors likely to more meaningfully enhance political knowledge than exposure to a particular type of media system. While, at face value, the role of NRK could be dismissed for not enhancing knowledge, it could – as discussed in Chapter 4 – be due to Norway's public broadcasting traditions, which have had a knock-on effect on how TV2 reported the election. Since TV2 election coverage was "almost identical [with NHK] in terms of volume and format" (Jenssen 2008: 261), the impact of the public broadcaster could have had an *indirect* influence by maintaining the editorial standards of its main competitor.

In Belgium, another country with a robust public service media infrastructure watched by a significant proportion of the population (see Table 7.1), Hooghe's (2002) representative survey revealed that, while watching public service television did not necessarily increase civic engagement or political participation, neither did it diminish them. Commercial television's fix of entertainment programming, by contrast, contributed "to the cultivation of a culture of political cynicism, insecurity and isolation" (Hooghe 2002: 101). By way of conclusion, Hooghe suggested "a strong public broadcasting corporation could be a crucial policy instrument for any effort to strengthen or maintain social cohesion in Western societies" (2002: 101).

There are, of course, many ways in which media establish either a connection with or disconnect from their audiences (see Couldry *et al.* 2007). Since the genre of news purports to tell the "truth" or be an accurate "window on the world", most broadcast news aims to establish what Gunter (2005: 395) calls a "trust bond" with its viewers. After all, the democratic value of news lies in informing people about the world and, while audiences might be engaged or entertained, if they cannot trust what is reported, the value of journalism diminishes.

Before the rise of multi-channel television and the emergence of the Internet, audiences had little choice about who to put their faith in. But contemporary news culture offers an unparalleled range of sources on an extending menu of platforms, making trust a far harder commodity to earn among many more competitors. And yet, while the nature of journalism has diversified over the last decade or so, the level of trust the public invests in journalists is often interpreted *generally* without distinguishing between media systems. In doing so, received wisdom is that *all* journalists are viewed suspiciously and mistrusted (Cushion 2009). On closer inspection, however, when polls ask people about journalists, the stereotype of a dishonest, opportunistic and sensationalist reporter derives, most prominently, from the tabloid newspaper industry. So, for example, a longitudinal survey from 2003–2011 in the UK found striking differences in the levels of trust between the print and broadcast industry (see Table 7.2).

Despite all journalists achieving lower levels of trust between 2003–2011 (a trend, although not as sharp, in many other professions too), broadcasters consistently ranked higher than print practitioners, most notably tabloid

Table 7.2 Percentage of public trust in the UK that journalists tell "the truth" "a great deal" or a "fair amount" from 2003–2011

	Feb–March 2003	*July 2003*	*April–May 2006*	*April 2007*	*March 2008*	*August 2010*	*July 2011*	*Change 2003–2011*
BBC journalists	81	63	71	62	61	60	58	−23
ITV journalists	82	65	67	54	51	49	47	−35
Broadsheet journalists	65	–	62	43	43	41	35	−30
Mid-market journalists	36	–	36	20	18	21	16	−20
Tabloid journalists	14	–	12	7	15	10	6	−15

(Adapted from *Economist*/You Gov poll 2011)

journalists. In light of the phone-hacking scandal that dominated the headlines in July 2011 and led to Lord Leveson's judicial review into press regulation (among other things) public trust in tabloid journalists had sunk to a record low (see Table 7.2). But during times when the BBC has faced harsh criticism, public confidence has remained broadly supportive of the public broadcaster compared to other media systems. During the 2003 Hutton Inquiry, for example, when the BBC was subject to close scrutiny after it had accused the government of "sexing up" the case for war (see Chapter 5) the public service broadcaster remained the most trusted media source and was six times more trusted than the government itself (Gunter 2005: 395). During the coverage of the Iraq war, the BBC was also interpreted as the most objective and trusted broadcaster, for both pro- and anti-war factions (Lewis *et al.* 2006: 171–3).

In countries such as the US, where public media have historically received limited financial support and their audience size is relatively meagre, polls have likewise shown them to be more trusted than their commercial counterparts. So, for example, in 2010 a representative poll named PBS as America's most trusted news organization for the seventh consecutive year. The survey indicated that Americans trusted PBS a great deal (45 per cent) compared to the commercial broadcast television networks (17 per cent), newspaper publishing companies (11 per cent) and cable television networks (9 per cent) (Roper Opinion Poll 2010). Ostertag (2010) has more qualitatively researched how people in the US use news media and why they choose one source over another, drawing on 47 semi-structured interviews with regular consumers of news media. PBS, in particular, generated widespread discussion and was seen to represent a "news safety net", an "honest and ideologically neutral news outlet in a land of problematic commercial news outlets" (Ostertag 2010: 610). At the same time, many interviewees recognized the structural limitations of PBS, such as the institution having no regular supply of income, or having sometimes to comply with corporate pressure in order to remain financially stable. While they valued and trusted PBS above commercial news sources, Ostertag (2010: 611) viewed his interviewees as having to "rely on a news resource that is as fundamentally and structurally flawed in many of the same ways as the news outlets they seek to escape". Thus, despite PBS being the most trusted source of news in the US, its limited financial muscle and corporate constraints have perhaps prevented it from winning enough popular support to challenge – or meaningfully deviate its agenda from – US mainstream news media.

These higher levels of trust in public or state television than market-driven systems are evident beyond the US and UK. In a 2006 BBC/Reuters representative survey carried out in Brazil, Egypt, Germany, India, Indonesia, Nigeria, Russia and South Korea, respondents were asked unprompted which news source they trusted most (Table 7.3). This method of snap polling sheds some insight into which television news sources people *instinctively* trust.

Table 7.3 Television news sources mentioned as being trustworthy

Country	*News sources spontaneously mentioned as trustworthy*
Brazil	Rede Globo (mentioned by 52%), TV Records (3%)
Egypt	Al-Jazeera (mentioned by 59%), Channel 1 Egypt TV (12%) and Nile News (4%)
Germany	ARD (mentioned by 22%), ZDF (7%), n-tv/N24 (6%), RTL (4%) and Deutsche Welle (1%)
India	AAJ TAK (mentioned by 11%), Doordarshan television (10%), Dainik Jagran (7%), Sun TV (5%), Star News (4%), NDTV (4%) and Zee News (2%)
Indonesia	RCTI television (mentioned by 27%), SCTV (17%), Metro TV (14%), Trans TV (11%), Indosiar (8%) and TPI television
Nigeria	Channels TV, NTA television (both mentioned by 16%), AIT television (10%), Silver Bird TV (7%), CNN (4%) and BBC World (1%)
Russia	ORT television (mentioned by 36%), NTV (16%) and RTR television (15%)
South Korea	KBS television (mentioned by 18%), MBC television (9%), South Korea's national TV station and YTN television (both 3%)

(Adapted from BBC/Reuters Media Center 2006)

While the dominant commercial channel, Rede Globo, in Brazil was considered the most trustworthy news source (52 per cent), in environments where public/state and commercial broadcasters co-exist more competitively the differences were much closer. The Indian public service channel, Doordarshan, inspired broadly the same degree of trust as the commercially funded AAJ TAK (10 per cent and 11 per cent respectively). Levels of trust for the commercial (Channels TV) and state broadcaster (NTA television) in Nigeria were also held in equal measure (16 per cent). Yet elsewhere – in Germany, Russia and South Korea – public or state-run broadcasters were trusted above their commercial competitors. Even if these countries have different broadcast models, with some subjected to editorial interference from state powers, public trust appears less likely to be granted to commercial television news.

Overall, then, in comparing whether people's knowledge, civic participation or levels of trust have been enhanced by a particular media system, on all measures the evidence points towards public service media playing a stronger civic role than their commercial counterparts across many countries around the world. Put another way, the empirical supply and reception of public service journalism appears the most likely media system to cultivate active and informed citizenship. In light of these conclusions, the final part of this chapter generates a broader discussion about the democratic value of news and makes the case for why the future of public service media should be safeguarded to maintain high journalistic standards in the face of commercial competition and further deregulation of the media industries.

The systemic impact of public service values: upholding editorial standards in an increasingly commercialized media landscape

As the opening chapters explored, the dominance of state or public service broadcasting on national media cultures has increasingly diminished since the 1980s and 1990s. While the tension between, on the one hand, state ownership and intervention and, on the other hand, market freedom and liberalization has long existed, the pendulum in many regions around the world has swung decidedly in the favour of the market in recent decades. Over a decade into the 2000s, the shift from analogue to digital platforms accelerated the pace of commercial penetration into the broadcast market, allowing many more commercial stations to launch without necessarily having to fulfil public service obligations. In most multi-channel television and radio schedules today commercial stations far outnumber public broadcasters.

At the same time, however, public service media have demonstrated remarkable resilience in the face of commercial competition (Curran 2003). After all, while the vast majority of commercial channels launched in recent years are watched by a minuscule share of the audience, many channels with public funding or public service obligations remain popular. Indeed, many national governments and legislative bodies – notably in European countries and by the EU – have made concerted efforts to maintain the position of public broadcast institutions to prevent unfettered market dominance and to regulate the commercial flow of information. But for all the regulatory efforts to protect public service media from the free market, legislators have found it difficult to safeguard public service institutions and principles in an increasingly commercialized era of media policy-making.

Of course, setting up a crude dichotomy between public or commercially driven media fails to appreciate the hybrid nature of many media systems around the world. As Chapter 1 outlined, national broadcast ecologies have unique characteristics, with different funding systems, available resources, levels of political interference, editorial autonomy, ethical standards, regulatory frameworks, technological capabilities, journalistic cultures and audience expectations. Some public or state media, for example, are wholly or partially funded by advertising, whereas others are entirely funded by the public via mechanisms such as the licence fee, general taxation or a government grant. Likewise, commercial media are not always able to operate as entirely free private companies and could be required to adhere to public service obligations agreed upon when obtaining a broadcast licence. These stations operate as commercial public service media, delivering programming that might not be commercially lucrative but that is required by their public service commitments.

As national governments seek to reduce public spending in the aftermath of the global financial crisis, many public service broadcasters have had to oversee cuts to their services, including to news and current affairs journalism.

Given the hybrid funding formulae for public, state and commercial media systems, the financial impact on individual organizations will differ according to their funding arrangements with the state. The varying levels in annual budgets between public service media cross-nationally will have an influence on the quality of news as assessed throughout this book, such as training and staffing costs, manning overseas bureaus, maintaining technical equipment and editing facilities, along with other pressures on journalistic resources. But while public service media are by no means shielded from market forces, compared to the commercial sector, they are not as directly influenced by the financial crisis nor the reduction in advertising streams in recent years. Wholly funded public service media, in other words, have a more reliable form of income and, in many cases, more resources at their disposal than many of their commercial competitors.

But while acknowledging the inherent differences in media systems operating under varying funding models, in achieving the book's primary aim – to evaluate the democratic value of news produced by competing media systems – the quality of journalism was not always related to the resources available at a news organization. The many empirical studies drawn upon throughout this book suggested that media with *some degree* of public service obligations could be distinguished from wholesale market-driven media. So, for example, longitudinal studies of news coverage on ITV and Channel 4 – two UK commercial public service broadcasters – revealed that both generally featured fewer hard news topics than the non-commercial public broadcaster, the BBC. But when compared to news on the fully fledged commercial US network channels, both UK commercial and public service broadcasters devoted a considerably higher proportion of their agenda to hard news such as the reporting of international affairs (see Chapter 3). It is Five news bulletins on the most recently launched commercial broadcaster that are beginning to resemble US network coverage. Longitudinal studies identified an increasingly "soft" agenda compared to rival BBC, ITV, Channel 4 and Sky News bulletins. With very limited public service commitments, Five's licence arrangements have allowed the new station owner, Richard Desmond, to significantly cut the budget dedicated to news and current affairs, to editorially downsize its journalistic resources by asking on-air journalists to edit their own footage, as well as to limit foreign coverage entirely to the 2012 US presidential elections (Halliday 2010).

When broadcasters operating with commercial input are subject to tough public service obligations, the evidence throughout this book established that news of democratic value was more likely to be produced. BBC World News, for instance, is a news channel broadcast beyond the UK around the world and is a commercial subsidiary of the BBC i.e. it is a commercial public service broadcaster. But empirical studies have shown that its journalism remains committed to values of impartiality and accuracy, and that it continues to pursue an in-depth and analytical form of reporting rather than adopt a market-friendly agenda of the softer news topics often favoured by wholesale commercial news channels (Cottle and Rai 2008d; c.f. Cushion and Lewis 2010). Even when public broadcasters receive relatively minor contributions from commercial revenue streams, such as some limited funding via advertising, the many empirical studies examined suggest that, if strict public service responsibilities remain in place, the quality of journalism need not necessarily be compromised.

However, *the rise in commercial broadcast media alone should not be simplistically interpreted as having a democratically diminishing effect nor should sweeping statements be made about the adverse impact of journalism from the private sector*. Far from it, since the arrival of commercial competition can be seen to have rejuvenated many public service broadcasters and enhanced democratic culture in many regions. The arrival of ITN in 1955 ended the BBC state monopoly of journalism in the UK and encouraged the public broadcaster to become less elitist, repackaging news to make it more palatable to ordinary viewers (Cushion 2012). It is a trend Curran (2003: 192–3) has observed internationally:

> The old monopoly public broadcasters were often highly paternalistic. The transition from a public broadcasting monopoly to a regulated mixed economy improved the broadcasting system in a number of countries, including Britain, Sweden, Norway, Finland and Denmark. It made public service broadcasting more responsive to the public without detracting from its fundamental purpose.

More recently, the role of Al-Jazeera and other dedicated news channels in regions that have long been under repressive government control have demonstrated how the removal of state media monopolies and the opening up of commercial markets can enhance democratic culture. As Chapter 6 showed, Al-Jazeera's coverage is easily distinguished from Western news organizations. Thus, despite the liberalization of media markets in recent decades having often been pejoratively linked to deteriorating standards in journalism, competition alone should not be assumed to automatically weaken the democratic value of news.

But while the role of commercial competition in shaping contemporary news culture should not be undervalued, nor should the continued impact of the journalistic values inherent in public service media be overlooked. After all, the editorial origins of Al-Jazeera were fashioned not just by former BBC journalists but by long-standing public service principles of independence and impartiality (see Chapter 6). More generally, the comprehensive review of empirical studies in this book suggests that, in countries with a well-resourced infrastructure of public media and robust regulatory structures, the values of public service broadcasting are rubbing off on more commercially produced journalism. To put it another way, the underlying editorial standards and principles of public service media could be having a systemic impact on the commercial sector, acting almost as a shield from market influences and helping to maintain high-quality journalism. So, for example, the well-resourced German public broadcaster, ZDF, has long been committed to reporting international affairs with the result being that commercial outlets appear to have matched its foreign news coverage since audiences expect it as part of the routine agenda (Kolmer and Semetko 2010; Chapter 3).

Likewise, in the UK, the presence of a popular public service broadcaster – the BBC – has arguably created a journalistic culture that has discouraged commercial news channels such as Sky News from abandoning hard news topics like many market-driven outlets in the US and that champions the value of impartiality, when relaxing this requirement could make it more distinct from rival operators in the way that Fox News has successfully done. Or, as noted earlier in the chapter, NRK's influence in Norway could have helped to maintain editorial standards on TV2 during recent elections. In this context, the long-established culture of public service journalism and each national audience's expectations appear to be policing the editorial standards of broadcast journalism.

In countries where market-driven systems dominate, such as in the US, public service media cannot influence their commercial competitors to the same degree as in countries where the editorial values of a well-resourced public service broadcaster persist. In fact, the history and supremacy of US commercial journalism arguably constrain how public media routinely report what is happening in the world. Although previous chapters have shown PBS to be distinct from mainstream US media, the differences are less striking than with public service media internationally. So, for example, studies have suggested that PBS reporting of recent presidential elections broadly replicated the dominant horse-race framing prevalent in commercial media and that the channel failed to publicize the meaningful opposition to the war in Iraq shown by public service media in other countries. Since journalists share what Zelizer (1997) calls "interpretative communities", deviating from long-standing journalistic norms and practices can potentially confuse or turn off viewers within that nation accustomed to that news culture (see Chapter 2). While PBS might not share the same degree of market-driven pressure as the commercial network and cable channels, the deeply ingrained journalistic culture of US news conventions and practices perhaps inhibits how far the public broadcaster can be editorially distinguishable from its commercial counterparts.

It is arguably the emergence and growing popularity of partisan cable news channels throughout the late 1990s and 2000s (and, of course, the more opinionated world of the blogosphere) that are currently impacting most strongly on the culture of US journalism and the professional values of journalists. As explored in Chapter 1, Hanitzsch *et al.*'s (2011) study of journalists across 18 countries identified that, while many countries remain committed to the "ideal of the separation of facts and opinion ... journalists in the United States exhibit a remarkable tendency to let personal evaluation and interpretation slip into news coverage" (Hanitzsch *et al.* 2011: 14–15). With no regulation policing the slippage of views over news, US broadcast anchors and reporters have been allowed the freedom to speculate and offer their opinions when the journalistic tradition has typically been to stick to the facts.

To sum up, in countries where a strong public service culture exists, the presence of public service media and their more robust regulatory obligations have arguably had a knock-on effect making it difficult for rival commercial media to depart from journalistic norms and adopt news practices or conventions that threaten the integrity of a broadcaster's editorial standards.

Market power, journalism and impartiality: the production of news in an increasingly deregulated environment

This book has regarded journalistic conventions that attempt to maintain impartiality, objectivity or even-handed reporting as standards likely to enhance the democratic value of news (see Chapter 2). While journalistic objectivity has long been exposed as a myth, it was suggested that it remains important to assess how far media *attempt* to balance news about politics and public affairs. After all, if the structures and conventions that police the boundaries of how journalists construct balance are entirely abandoned to the relativistic belief that there is no "truth", then the regulatory environment that helps shape what journalism is produced ceases to be important. And, as previous chapters have established, the regulatory environment in which journalists operate can shape the balance and partiality of journalism.

Indeed, Chapter 1 showed that in most advanced democracies broadcasters adhere to some regulatory checks to ensure that their journalism remains impartial and accurate. Needless to say, just because formal regulatory bodies have been set up to monitor competing media systems, it should not be assumed that every system of media management is effectively policed or subject to routine intervention. According to Jones (2003), while the public broadcaster, ABC, is closely regulated in Australia, commercially driven journalism has not been "subjected to the levels of regulation expected of its counterpart in Britain [ITV] but nor even (in the case of news) to the levels expected by the US's former 'fairness doctrine'". Since the Fairness Doctrine was abandoned, however, a FCC commissioner in an interview with BBC America conceded that a lack of regulation has impacted on the production of news:

> American media has a bad case of substance abuse right now ... we are going to be pretty close to denying our citizens the essential news and information that they need to have in order to make intelligent decisions about the future direction of their country.

Of course, one reason why the Fairness Doctrine was first established was "broadcast scarcity" e.g. only a few channels could broadcast at one time, meaning a particular station with bias could potentially wield considerable influence. In an online, multi-channel television and radio culture, "scarcity" has been replaced by "plenty" (Ellis 2000: 162–78). As a result, the conventional wisdom among many US political elites is that regulation policing balance is no longer required, since media audiences have *access* to a plurality of viewpoints in contemporary news culture.

This argument has extended beyond the US but has faced greater resistance from many politicians and media regulators. However, in an increasingly converged commercial media landscape, broadcast regulators around the world have been subjected to increased pressure to relax impartiality requirements, since they do not always apply to newspapers, magazines or, most significantly, online news. So, for example, the right-wing magazine, the *Economist* (2011), has suggested that in the age of the Internet and consumer choice "transparency may count for more than objectivity". In other words, so long as a supplier of news reveals its motivations, audiences can pick and choose from information sources well aware of a potential bias. While openness about potential conflicts of interest has some merit in the online world where a multiplicity of sources co-exist, the choices available for television news viewers are considerably fewer. Despite many countries having access to a range of 24-hour news channels, the primary sources in many nations are often just a few television news bulletins. As in the era of "scarcity" (Ellis 2000: 39–60), without impartiality obligations, these bulletins could regularly carry significant influence on many more viewers than the fragmented world of online audiences.

Indeed, as Chapters 5 and 6 demonstrated, Fox News audiences have grown steadily after its highly patriotic and pro-war coverage of the 2003 war in Iraq. The fact that the channel's upswing in commercial success was achieved by discarding conventional values of balance, according to consecutive Pew Research Center Project for Excellence in Journalism reports this has led other stations such as MSNBC to mimic Fox's partisan approach to news reporting (Cushion 2012). Incidentally, neither cable news channel has been transparent about its underlying partisan loyalties, with Fox News constantly reminding viewers that it is "fair and balanced". Without regulation policing impartiality, America's free market approach to television news programming has helped shape an environment where competition is being driven by more opinionated or partisan journalism.

When statutory media regulation is opposed, self-regulation is often touted as the more effective democratic check, for it allows journalists to act independently of the state and prevents the abuse of government power. Since many countries impose statutory regulation on broadcasters (see Chapter 1), it is an argument most vociferously made for newspapers. And yet, as Natalie Fenton has pointed out, this can distort debates about how to regulate contemporary journalism:

> Self-regulation has become the sacred mantra associated with the freedom of the press – the only means to ensure governments can't interfere in, dictate the terms and thwart the practice of journalism. But this denies the influence and power of a corporate culture that wreaks its own havoc and sets its own agenda often more blatantly than any democratic government would ever dare … . In neoliberal democracies the power of the market is just as significant as the power of government … there is certainly no rush to regulate for a healthy relationship between news media and democracy, yet there is plenty of urgency about the need to deregulate media for the benefit of the market. (Fenton 2011b)

Perhaps understandably, journalists working under imposed statutory regulation typically interpret this as an obstacle to the editorial process of news-making as opposed to a means of safeguarding standards. Or, put more grandly, regulation is seen as hindering journalists from fulfilling their classic democratic function – to expose "the truth" and hold power to account. And yet, regulation can be a constructive rather than destructive force, enhancing rather than impeding democratic culture. As Chapter 3 argued, the BBC Trust's systematic review of BBC news coverage of the nations and regions in the UK and the reporting of devolved politics led to a set of evidence-based recommendations to render its journalism more impartial and accurate (see Cushion *et al.* 2012). The FCC in the US relaxed concentration of ownership laws for local television and radio stations, by contrast, to allow companies to merge, share costs and pool resources in order to strengthen the provision of more localized journalism. However, studies – pre- and post-deregulation – demonstrated that a free market approach had failed to enhance local news, as the bigger the corporation the less likely they were to serve local public interests (Yan and Park 2009).

However, in many countries it must be acknowledged that deregulation has expanded the range of commercial media and cultivated a more competitive market-place for journalism. With markets liberalized, an increasingly deregulated media environment appears to have encouraged more choice and competition, with new digital and online technologies expanding the platforms within which journalism can operate. Consequently, grand claims within media, communication and cultural studies about media diversity have sometimes been advanced without necessarily drawing on evidence to support the argument. So, for example, in Brian McNair's (2006) *Cultural Chaos – Journalism, News and Power in a Globalised World*, it was argued that twenty-first-century news media offer an abundance of choice across many platforms, preventing any dominant ideology from emerging or any media bias from being meaningfully exerted. In making this case, it was stated that the global news media deliver "a chaotic whirl of competing ideas and belief-systems, sitting atop a crowded cultural-commodity marketplace of unprecedented depth, diversity and adversarialism towards elites in all walks of life" (McNair 2006: 204).

From a broad historical perspective, it would be difficult to argue against McNair and many others' interpretation of the media landscape relative to decades before when news sources were limited to just a select few outlets. Of course, more information is globally accessible since the birth of the Internet, and new digital and cable technologies have brought multi-channel television and radio services. But, at the same time, it is important to critically evaluate what is meant by "depth" and "diversity" within contemporary news culture (e.g. McNair 2006: 204). While a free market approach to media policy-making in recent decades has delivered more sources of information and the generic boundaries of news have been extended to cater to a wider constituency of audiences, whether they have extended democratic choice and pluralized contemporary news culture remains open to question. The longitudinal trends drawn on throughout this book suggest that enhanced deregulation and the influx of market-driven media have coincided with a deterioration in the quality of journalism. The increasing marketization of news and its impact on the editorial standards of journalism are revisited in the final section of this chapter.

Safeguarding editorial independence: how public service values inform audience trust and engagement

The evidence contained in this book has shot down many misconceptions about how public service media function in a democracy. In countries where the infrastructure of public media has not been historically funded or maintained, such as the US, it has often been argued that state-subsidized or publicly owned media are unable to maintain editorial independence from the ruling government. Or, put more bluntly, public media cannot be politically independent institutions. Of course, the history of public service media is plagued with examples where the government of the day *attempts* to intervene editorially at sensitive political moments and these continue to happen periodically. So, for example, in November 2011 members of RTVE's board of directors (the Spanish public broadcaster) – who are political appointees representing every party in Parliament – won a vote enabling them to preview editorial material before it had been aired (Tremlett 2011). After public outrage at this decision, days later the board retracted its request.

But while there are occasions when the relationship between public media and political independence is inevitably strained and impartiality tested, for the most part, public service broadcasters around the world have weathered passing storms and avoided state control. Indeed, as previous chapters argued, during critical democratic moments – in times of war or during an election campaign – it was demonstrated that public service media have been no more complicit with the government line than commercial outlets nor have they compromised their journalistic independence. After all, it was – as Chapter 5 pointed out – a wholly public rather than a commercial broadcaster that robustly challenged the UK government during a sensitive political moment in the aftermath of the 2003 Iraq war. This example warrants further reflection, since it reveals not just that public service media can remain independent at highly sensitive political moments or that many people still invest a considerable level of trust in them and the values of an impartial news service, but it also exposes the inadequacies of the unregulated, free market model of journalism practised in the US.

In May 2003 several BBC journalists accused the government of "sexing up" the reasons why the UK had gone to war in Iraq. The BBC faced significant pressure from the government and commercial rivals and, over the following year, its journalism was subject to close scrutiny and condemnation, not least during the Hutton Inquiry. While, at the time, BBC coverage of the government's case for war posed a real threat to the future of public service broadcasting in the UK, years on it has been interpreted as strengthening rather than weakening the editorial independence of BBC journalism. Writing in the aftermath of the controversy surrounding BBC coverage of the Iraq war, Barnett (2005: 340) observed:

> Those who fear for the BBC's independence sometimes confuse two very different imperatives: the need to maintain the highest possible journalistic standards in terms of accuracy, impartiality and fairness and its vulnerability to intervention and pressure from government. There are times when abiding by a strict code of professional journalistic standards to uphold the former can easily be misconstrued as giving into the latter.

The UK public service broadcaster, in other words, withstood significant government pressure because of its own robust regulatory framework and commitment to enforcing journalistic safeguards about its editorial values.

By contrast, it was in the market-driven landscape of US news media where (by many journalists' own admission) independence was sacrificed after the terrorist attacks of 9/11 and the subsequent lead-up to the wars in Afghanistan and Iraq. A sweeping sense of patriotism compromised many broadcasters' commitment to values of impartiality, with journalists reluctant to hold the government to account at a critical moment in American democracy (see Chapter 5). This was compounded by the commercial model of broadcasting, since advertisers did not want to be associated with any programming that could potentially offend American sensibilities at a highly sensitive political moment. With no imposed regulatory impartiality constraints, Chapter 5 drew on many studies to reveal that US broadcast reporting of Afghanistan and Iraq continued to be shaped by patriotism or, on some cable news channels, outright jingoism. All of this suggested that, far from public service media being subservient to the government of the day, market-driven systems with minimal regulatory obligations appeared more compromised when reporting controversial topics.

As this final chapter has also shown, media regulation can also inform the relationship audiences have with a particular news outlet. In the US, where the FCC lightly regulates media content (see Chapter 1), representative surveys of television audiences have shown many viewers are increasingly trusting of news programming broadly consistent with their own ideological beliefs (Pew Research Center for the People and the Press 2011). PBS – a television station with a formal commitment to impartiality – was the source of news most trusted by Americans (Roper Opinion Poll 2010). In countries where a stronger infrastructure of public service media exists and where regulation is more rigorously policed, trust in television news is generally far higher (Cushion 2009). Because the very survival of public broadcasters rests on maintaining continued public funding, this also acts as a useful mechanism to ensure that high editorial standards of impartiality and independence are consistently delivered. Public funding, in other words, holds public service media directly accountable for the journalism they produce.

In maintaining high editorial standards, public broadcasters, such as the BBC, have also had an impact transnationally on the values of news audiences. A study of "opinion formers and customers" in Egypt, Pakistan, Turkey and Kenya revealed that the BBC is more valued than the UK government, promoting a positive image of the country internationally. The then Director General of the BBC, Mark Thompson (2010), claimed this represented "the cool-headed, fair-minded spirit of Britain – and the BBC – at their best ... . The independence and quality of our international news offer is paramount and sacrosanct. Its integrity and reliability is the platform on which every other reputation is built". Within the UK, this reputation, including the requirement of impartiality, is treasured by a large proportion of the population. Petley's (2009) analysis of representative surveys asking people whether they supported impartiality or not revealed that a large majority consistently did. Likewise, Lewis *et al.* (2006: 169) found that during the 2003 war in Iraq 92 per cent of respondents in a representative poll in the UK agreed with the idea that broadcasters should remain impartial and objective during wartime.

However, in industry circles it has been suggested that relaxing "due impartiality" on television news might engage the young or ethnic minorities who are turned off by the formulaic nature of television news (with regulation, for example, that compels all mainstream political parties to be proportionately represented – see Tambini and Cowling 2004). But there is limited evidence that abandoning impartiality requirements is the magic bullet likely to attract viewers currently disengaged with television news (Petley 2009). In fact, when public service responsibilities have been relinquished in recent years or free market principles accepted – in essence, fashioning a more deregulated culture for contemporary news – it has not necessarily engineered either further engagement with news media nor raised viewers' understanding of public affairs. As Curran *et al.*'s (2009: 22) study on the impact different broadcasting environments have had on informed citizenship in the US, UK, Denmark and Finland concluded: "media provision of public information does matter, and continued deregulation of the broadcast media is likely, on balance, to lead to lower levels of public knowledge". This lack of public knowledge was most strikingly exposed in the US, home to one of the most commercial and deregulated media systems around the world. The study showed that, because commercial network television delivered a relatively low volume of news about politics and public affairs in the US compared to television news in countries better served by public service broadcasters, most Americans showed a considerably poorer understanding of the world than people in other advanced democracies.

As the fully fledged commercial media system has held a monopoly on the broadcast industry in the US since its inception (McChesney 1993), the undersourced public broadcaster in the US – PBS – has not been able to establish the same rapport with American audiences as have many public service broadcasters in Western/Northern European countries. Nor has it been able to draw on the resources to help develop an infrastructure of foreign news bureaus around the world long established by many public media organizations. Consequently, Wall and Bicket (2008a) have identified an increased use of British online news media among US audiences seeking news about international affairs. Since mainstream US news media post-9/11 were reluctant to challenge the government's foreign policy plans (see Chapter 5), they argued that British media provided "a window on the wider world" and delivered more liberal perspectives on international news. It is revealing, in this respect, that the British media they cite – the BBC, *Independent* and *Guardian* newspapers, for example – all operate under fewer market imperatives than might govern major commercial news channels such as CBS, MSNBC or Fox News. But it was the BBC that was singled out, since the public service broadcaster "provides the anchor role that underpins the influence of other institutions" (Bicket and Wall 2009: 365). In their view, the BBC's output had begun to "resemble that of a domestic US alternative news source" (Bicket and Wall 2009: 378).

Of course, as Chapter 1 discussed, many European broadcasters including the BBC have had their publicly subsidized online news services legally challenged by commercial rivals. It is argued that public service media operate with a competitive advantage, making it difficult for new commercial online media to break into the market. But while online public media should not restrict commercial competition, their editorially distinct quality should also be protected from market forces. As the rise in US consumption of BBC online news demonstrates, America's heavily commercialized online news provision appears to result in a deficit of international news, causing audiences to turn to an international public service broadcaster for information.

From normative values to empirical judgements: why public service media matter

As the opening chapters to the book acknowledge, the normative role of public service broadcasting has often been defined and understood by drawing on Jürgen Habermas's (1989) concept of the public sphere. According to Habermas, the public sphere represents an idealized space where free and open communication in society is possible if the right democratic conditions and structures are in place. Moreover, the public sphere is widely seen to convey the normative values central to the editorial aims of many public service broadcasters – namely, to deliver programming for all citizens but also to cater to a diverse range of viewpoints, free from state influence or market interference. Public service broadcasting, in other words, is viewed normatively as the media system that can most reliably serve citizens in a democracy.

In making this case, scholarly defences of public service broadcasting and the contribution it makes to civic life and citizenship have often been couched in theoretical terms. But since authoritative scholars in the field, such as Nicholas Garnham (1986), James Curran (1991) and Graham Murdock (1992), connected the normative ideals of public service broadcasting with the rationalistic Habermassian model of democracy and citizenship (see Chapter 1), debates about the value of publicly funded media in a far more crowded commercial landscape have changed gear. So, for example, John Hartley (1999) and Liz Jacka (2003) have questioned the relevance of top-down public service broadcasters and the self-appointed paternalistic role they claim to play within a nation in an increasingly globalized and interconnected world of international communications. Further still, it has been argued that well-intentioned defences of publicly funded media can appear abstract or empirically lacking, invoking highfalutin concepts such as the public sphere, citizenship and democracy without convincingly connecting their relevance to the audience needs (Jacka 2003). While these arguments reflect general criticisms relating to public service programming or the broader philosophical aims of public media, in the supply and delivery of journalism the attention of this book has been to *empirically connect the quality of news with the media systems that produced it*. Or, put another way, the aim has been to assess which media system most regularly delivers news of democratic value.

This research question was prompted by the increasing marketization of media culture in recent decades and the impact of competing political, philosophical and economic aims on different media systems. The supply and content of news have not been immune from this commercial ascendancy. While news was once a morning, lunchtime or early and late evening service, dedicated channels now air 24-hour programming of continuous news, current affairs or documentaries. In this respect, market forces have delivered more news, making information far more readily available than ever before, with broadcasters' online services accessible via home computers and mobile phones. On the face of it, for liberal pluralists this represents a great victory, since a free market-place of information has delivered more choice and competition among news media, conditions interpreted as vital to the maintenance of a healthy democracy and informed citizenry. But while pluralism – a concept often used to champion establishing a diverse culture of news – is often celebrated for delivering choice, it was suggested in Chapter 2 it should be measured not just by the amount of news outlets available to audiences but by the diversity of *news content* produced. Indeed, the production of news under market-driven systems has generated considerable academic debate about whether it is potentially diminishing the quality of information available in the public sphere to aid citizens in remaining informed. The free market has certainly delivered more news, in other words, but has it produced news of democratic value?

Of course, it is not easy to precisely define the normative qualities inherent in news of democratic value. As Chapter 2 indicated, while scholars have long established a set of news values that explain why journalists choose one story over another (Galtung and Ruge 1965; Harcup and O'Neil 2001), evaluating news of democratic value is a more discursive exercise, with editorial judgements about the performance of media less agreed upon (Norris 2000). To constitute news of democratic value it was suggested that, above all, it should have *informative quality*. This was determined by whether *news conveys information likely to enhance people's understanding of the world on issues likely to empower them as citizens in a democracy*.

To assess which media system most regularly delivered news of democratic value, four areas of news were examined:

1 in relatively routine periods;
2 during election campaigns;
3 in moments of war and conflict;
4 and on the medium of 24-hour news channels.

Normative judgements were made about the democratic value of news in each case. So, for example, the democratic value of news was considered enhanced when there was a regular supply of hard news topics (e.g. international news, politics, social affairs etc.) or in-depth journalism (Chapter 3); when there was a high level of election coverage in different electoral contests, as well as news dedicated to matters of policy (Chapter 4); when war reporting was editorially independent, accurate and impartial (Chapter 5); and, for 24-hour television news channels, when a combination of all of these normative qualities were present in a rolling news format (Chapter 6). Needless to say, these normative judgments about the quality of journalism cross-nationally can only generate broad-based conclusions on the evidence amassed. But the comprehensive review of empirical news studies illustrated some distinct editorial trends between competing media systems.

Overall, the book shows that viewers tuning into or surfing the websites of public and commercial news media will most likely find that in day-to-day coverage public service media reflect a more diverse and in-depth picture of the world than their commercial counterparts (Chapter 3). Longitudinal trends of election coverage revealed that, in most countries, public service media tended to report more news over the campaign period than market-driven systems. Moreover, public service media generally covered more policy-related stories than their commercial rivals at election time, with less emphasis on the game or strategy reporting so dominant in the fully fledged US market-driven system (Chapter 4).

In making sense of the events surrounding 9/11, in reporting the most intense phase of the 2003 war in Iraq or in providing a wider context to foreign policy decision-making, the most striking differences were cross-national rather than between media systems. However, the US market-driven system did stand out. Systematic content analyses of US television news suggested that no major broadcaster adequately scrutinized the government's response to 9/11, the existence of WMD and the reasons why military action was taken in Iraq. If this could be explained by the presence of US soldiers leading the wars in Iraq and Afghanistan, UK troops were also involved in military action but neither commercial nor public UK broadcasters indulged in similarly explicit pro-war coverage (Chapter 5).

Finally, in exploring the rise of 24-hours news channels around the world, it has been established that many more commercial than public broadcasters are operating and market-led values are shaping the genre's routine conventions. In countries where a stronger public media infrastructure exists, however, it is suggested that more formally imposed regulatory requirements have safeguarded the editorial standards of 24-hour news journalism, including that of commercial broadcasters (see Chapter 6).

But public service media should not escape criticism. Each chapter cites instances where news practices and conventions typically associated with market-driven systems are present on public service news media. So, for example, many public service media outlets form part of a broader longitudinal trend in market-led journalism that downgrades hard for soft news (Chapter 3). Likewise, several have begun to share some of the commercialized characteristics of election news journalism imported from the US, such as game or campaign strategy reporting (Chapter 4). In war reporting, many public service news outlets too readily accepted Western perspectives during the war in Iraq (as they did in commercial programming too) and failed to challenge the presence of WMD until after military action had commenced (Chapter 5). Finally, some public service news channels were adopting market-led conventions in routine 24-hour news coverage such as hyping up breaking news stories or broadcasting live for sustained periods (Chapter 6). In each case, these trends in journalism or specific elements of news reporting have been interpreted as generally running counter to any objective of advancing public understanding about the salient issues most likely to impact on citizens in a democracy.

But while public service news media do not always produce news of democratic value, *the comprehensive review of evidence in this book suggested that they supplied content more likely to advance informed citizenship than that provided by market-driven systems.* Indeed, as this chapter evidences, market-driven news media tended not to enhance people's understanding of the world, promote civic engagement or engender trust in what is being reported to the same degree as public service media. Put another way, for all the commercial choice and competition in contemporary news culture, public media remain editorially distinct from market-driven news and more effective in engendering active and informed citizenship. Taken together, *the evidence amassed overall in the book suggests that the normative claims that scholars have long associated with the concept of public service broadcasting – that it is the media system that most reliably serves citizens in a democracy – does stand up to empirical scrutiny in the supply of high-quality news.*

In light of the distinctive supply and content of public news media empirically established throughout this book and the regulatory environment that helped to ensure a higher quality of journalism than that produced by market-led systems operating with less regulatory oversight, these conclusions can inform future policy decisions. In the age of commercialized media policy-making, public service media face increasingly intense scrutiny about their value to citizens, with the relative merits of particular programming on websites, radio stations and television channels regularly subject to close inspection, not least by market competitors eager to pounce on evidence of deteriorating standards and to criticize the use of public funds. In doing so, publicly produced programming, including news-making, is most often assessed in economic terms, whether it delivers "value for money" or provides something meaningfully alternative to the commercial media market-place.

The argument put forward in this book has been that the *democratic value of news* should not be excluded from debates about the future of public service media. While it is difficult to put a price on information of public value or sell the significance of an informed and active citizenry, the defence of high-quality news provision must extend beyond the language of the market-place and relate to the broader impact it can have on democratic life. Put simply, a comprehensive review of empirical studies found that the democratic value of news is more likely to be enhanced when it is produced by public service rather than market-driven media. To protect journalism from market forces and to maintain the wider quality of news culture, continuing to empirically establish why public service media matter can only serve to secure their long term future.

Notes

1. It is important to note that the deregulation of the media industries did not follow a uniform pattern around the world. While some countries began deregulating their media industries in the late 1970s, broadly speaking the 1980s and 1990s are viewed as the period of time when many Western governments loosened their control over broadcasting.
2. So, for example, the governments in Spain and the Netherlands have reduced their budget for public broadcasting by €200 million (see Penty 2011 and Henning 2011) while the Catalan government reduced its funds for the public broadcaster by €40 million, a reduction of 13.3 per cent in 2012 (see Coll 2011). The UK government, likewise, cut public service broadcasting by freezing the licence fee for six years. This represents a 16 per cent reduction in the BBC's budget or about £340 million (Spanier 2010). In the US, where the federal government invests proportionately far less than most European countries (see Chapter 1), leading Republicans have proposed cutting *all* public funding for PBS in order to reduce the nation's deficit (Bond 2011).
3. In total well over 450 sources informed the empirical analysis and the wider discussion throughout the book. A full list of references is available in the Bibliography.
4. They drew on the 2009 *Yearbook of the European Audiovisual Observatory* (for European countries), ABC Annual report 2009 (for Australia), the NHK annual report 2010–11 (for Japan), the New Zealand Annual TV Report and New Zealand on the Air Annual Report (for New Zealand) and the Corporation for Public Broadcasting 2008 Annual Report (for the US).
5. For France this included France Télévisions and France Radio.
6. For the UK this included the licence fee and government grants and in the US this includes federal, state and local government funding.
7. Of course, it is important to check the proportion of a public broadcaster's budget allocated to the provision of news. So, for example, the BBC's total news budget is estimated at £61.1 million (Sabbagh and Deans 2012) from an overall budget of £4.8 billion (Foster 2012). But more research is needed into how far cross-nationally public and market-driven media invest in their news services. BSkyB, for instance, has a higher annual turnover of £6.6 billion more than the BBC but has said it cannot match the public service broadcaster's resources (Sabbagh and Deans 2012).
8. The following quotes relating to the ACMA and the policies of public broadcasters from Australia can be found at http://big-issues.org/local-issues/social-community/138-australian-controls-over-news-and-current-affair-presentation, accessed 19 October 2011.
9. To avoid a major story dominating the agenda (and thus distorting the findings) the sampling period included one weekday chosen per week between February, April, June, September and November for every year.

10 The Curran *et al.* 2012 study has not yet been published. I am grateful to Sharon Coen for sharing the findings ahead of publication.
11 The US and Colombia were also included in the Curran *et al.* (2012) study but have been excluded in Table 3.8 due to the difficulty of comparing public and commercial bulletins in these countries.
12 Kaid and Strömbäck (2008) also indicated the rules relating to the reporting of opinion polls in each country but this has been excluded in Table 4.1.
13 Again, this has been generated from Loughborough University's 2010 general election media data set.
14 Data were generated by using SPPS files available at the PIREDEU data centre (www.piredeu.eu). I am grateful to Ingo Linsenmann for her guidance on downloading the relevant data sets.
15 The study examined all 27 EU countries. However, since Luxembourg does not have a public broadcaster, it has been excluded from the comparative analysis.
16 Eurobarometer data sets can be downloaded from http://ec.europa.eu/public_opinion/archives/eb_arch_en.htm.
17 S4C was not included in the sample in the 2004 Local and European Council Election study (Thomas *et al.* 2004b).
18 Funding has not been available to research Welsh news coverage of the 2007 or 2011 Assembly elections.
19 This quote is taken from the BBC's editorial guidelines: see http://www.bbc.co.uk/editorialguidelines/page/guidelines-war-introduction.
20 The study included two time slots of CNN (5–5.30pm and 6–6.30pm). The 6–6.30pm slot has been excluded because it is *The Lou Dobbs Show*, Dobbs being an "outspoken conservative" anchor at CNN (Aday *et al.* 2005a: 8). The interest here is on more conventional/typical rolling CNN coverage of the war.
21 As this analysis was published in 2010, more channels might have been launched or closed down, since – as outlined previously in the chapter – rolling news channels are not commercially stable organizations. So, for example, the Australian public broadcaster's news channel, ABC 24, was launched in 2010, but TVNZ 7 (in New Zealand) will close down in June 2012 after public funding is withdrawn. It was not possible to methodologically replicate the Rai and Cottle (2010) study and accurately update the hundreds of 24-hour news channels around the world. But Tables 6.1 and 6.2 show the commercial dominance of 24-hour television news channels in late 2009.
22 It should be noted too that Rai and Cottle (2007 and 2010) did not list every local/state news channel in every large market such as the myriad of dedicated rolling news channels in the US. More research is needed to unpack local news channels in national markets.
23 These data were generated from studies by Lewis and Cushion (2007) and Lewis and Cushion (2009).
24 It should be acknowledged, of course, that broadcasting alone is not the only source of information that can (mis)inform people about the world. While television news regularly rates as the primary source of information among most advanced democracies, newspapers, radio stations, magazines and, most recently, the Internet (particularly among the young) also play a vital role in the formation of informed citizenship. Indeed, while the focus in this book has been on the comparative strengths of public and market-driven television news, studies have

also established that other media can enhance people's knowledge and understanding of politics and public affairs to a great extent. So, for example, Fraile's (2010) representative survey of Spanish people discovered that knowledge about politics and constitutional affairs was enhanced when daily exposure to newspapers – not television news (although public or commercial stations were not differentiated) – was indicated.

Bibliography

Aalberg, Toril and Curran, James (2011) (eds) *How Media Inform Democracy: A Comparative Approach*. London: Routledge

Aalberg, Toril, Aelst, Peter and Curran, James (2010) "Media Systems and the Political Information Environment: A Cross-national Comparison" in *International Journal of Press/Politics*, Vol. 15(3): 255–71

Aalberg, Toril, Strömbäck, Jesper and De Vreese, Claes H. (2011) "The Framing of Politics as Strategy and Game: A Review of Concepts, Operationalizations and Key Findings" in *Journalism: Theory, Practice and Criticism*, available iFirst 11 November

Aday, Sean (2010) "Chasing the Bad News: An Analysis of 2005 Iraq and Afghanistan War Coverage on NBC and Fox News Channel" in *Journal of Communication*, Vol. 60: 144–64

Aday, Sean, Livingston, Steven and Hebert, Maeve (2005a) "Embedding the Truth: A Cross-cultural Analysis of Objectivity and Television Coverage of the Iraq War" in *Harvard International Journal of Press/Politics*, Vol. 10(1): 3–21

Aday, Sean, Cluverius, John and Livingston, Steven (2005b) "As Goes the Statue, So Goes the War: The Emergence of the Victory Frame in Television Coverage of the Iraq War" in *Journal of Broadcasting and Electronic Media*, Vol. 49(3): 314–31

Aldridge, Meryl (2007) *Understanding the Local Media*. Maidenhead: Open University Press

Allan, Stuart and Thorsen, Einar (eds) (2009) *Citizen Journalism: Global Perspectives*. New York: Peter Lang

Allan, Stuart and Thorsen, Einar (2011) "Journalism, Public Service and BBC News Online" in Meikle, Graham and Redden, Guy (eds) *News Online: Transformations and Continuities*. Basingstoke: Palgrave MacMillan

Allan, Stuart and Zelizer, Barbie (2005a) (eds) *Reporting War: Journalism in Wartime*. London: Routledge

Allan, Stuart and Zelizer, Barbie (2005b) "Rules of Engagement: Journalism and War" in Allan, Stuart and Zelizer, Barbie (eds) *Reporting War: Journalism in Wartime*. London: Routledge

Almiron, Núria, Capurro Robles, María and Santcovsky, Pablo (2010) "The Regulation of Public Broadcasters' News Coverage of Political Actors in Ten European Union Countries" in *Comunicación y sociedad: Revista de la Facultad de Comunicación*, Vol. 23(1): 205–36

Al-Saggaf, Yeslam (2006) "The Online Public in the Arab World: The War in Iraq on the Al-Arabiya Website" in *Journal of Computer Mediated Communication*, Vol. 12(1): 311–34

Altheide, David (2006) *Terrorism and the Politics of Fear*. Lanham, MD: AltaMira Press

Anderson, Simon P. (2005) "Regulation of Television Advertising", http://www.virginia.edu/economics/Workshops/papers/anderson/tvadreg081705.pdf accessed 23 February 2011

Aufderheide, Patricia (1999) *Communications Policy and the Public Interest: The Telecommunications Act of 1996*. New York: Guilford Press

Ayish, Muhammad I. (2010a) "Arab State Broadcasting Systems in Transition: The Promise of the Public Service Broadcasting Model" in *Middle East Journal of Culture and Communication*, Vol. 3: 9–25

Ayish, Muhammad I. (2010b) "Morality vs. Politics in the Public Sphere: How the Al Jazeera Satellite Channel Humanized a Bloody Political Conflict in Gaza" in Cushion, Stephen and Lewis, Justin (eds) *The Rise of 24 Hour News Television*. New York: Peter Lang

Baek, Mijeong (2009) "A Comparative Analysis of Political Communication Systems and Voter Turnout" in *American Journal of Political Science*, Vol. 53(2): 376–93

Baisnée, Oliver and Marchetti, Dominique (2006) "The Economy of Just-in-Time Television Newscasting: Journalistic Production and Professional Excellence at Euronews" in *Ethnography*, Vol. 7(1): 99–123

Bajkiewicz, Timothy and Smith, Jessica (2007) "When the Inbox Breaks: An Exploratory Analysis of Online Network Breaking News E-mail Alerts" in *Electronic News*, Vol. 1(4): 197–210

Baker, Edwin C. (2007) *Media Concentration and Democracy: Why Ownership Matters*. Cambridge: Cambridge University Press

Bakshi, Amar C. (2011) "China's Challenge to International Journalism" in *SAIS Review*, Vol. XXXI(1): 147–51

Banerjee, Indrajit and Seneviratne, Kalinga (2006) (eds) *Public Service Broadcasting in the Age of Globalization*. Singapore: AMIC & Nanyang Technological University

Bardoel, Johannes and d'Haenens, Leen (2008) "Reinventing Public Service Broadcasting in Europe: Prospects, Promises and Problems" in *Media, Culture and Society*, Vol. 30(3): 337–55

Barkho, Leon (2008) "The BBC's Discursive Strategy and Practices vis-à-vis the Palestinian–Israeli Conflict" in *Journalism Studies*, Vol. 9(2), 278–94

Barkin, Steve M. (2003) *American Television News: The Media Marketplace and the Public Interest*. New York: M. E. Sharpe

Barlow, David, Mitchell, Philip and O'Malley, Tom (2005) *The Media in Wales: Voices of a Small Nation*. Cardiff: University of Wales Press

Barnett, Clive (1999) "The Limits of Media Democratization in South Africa: Politics, Privatization and Regulation" in *Media, Culture and Society*, Vol. 21(5): 649–71

Barnett, Steven (2005) "Opportunity or Threat? The BBC, Investigative Journalism and the Hutton Inquiry" in Allan, Stuart (ed.) *Journalism: Critical Issues*. Maidenhead: Open University Press

Barnett, Steven, Seymour, Emily and Gaber, Ivor (2000) *From Callaghan to Kosovo: Changing Trends in British Television News*. London: University of Westminster

Barnhurst, Kevin G. and Steele, Catherine A. (1997) "Image Bite News: The Coverage of Elections on U.S. Television, 1968–1992" in *Harvard International Journal of Press/Politics*, Vol. 2(1): 40–58

BBC/Reuters Media Center (2006) "Trust in the Media: Media More Trusted than Governments – Poll", http://www.globescan.com/news_archives/bbcreut.html, accessed 10 August 2011

BBC Trust (2009/2010) *BBC Trust's Review and Assessment*. London: BBC Trust

Beam, Randal A., Brownlee, Bonnie J., Weaver, David H. and Di Cicco, Damon T. (2009) "Journalism and Public Service in Troubled Times" in *Journalism Studies*, Vol. 10(6): 734–53

Beckett, Charlie (2010) *The Value of Networked Journalism*. London: London School of Economics

Beer, Arnold S. (2010) "News from and in the 'Dark Continent'" in *Journalism Studies*, Vol. 11(4): 596–609

Bek, Mine Gencel (2004) "Research Note: Tabloidization of News Media: An Analysis of Television News in Turkey" in *European Journal of Communication*, Vol. 19(3): 371–86

Bennett, Lance W. (2007) *News: The Politics of Illusion*, 7th edn. New York: Pearson Longman

Bennett, Lance W. and Iyengar, Shanto (2008) "A New Era of Minimal Effects? The Changing Foundations of Political Communications" in *Journal of Communication*, Vol. 58: 707–31

Bennett, Lance W., Lawrence, Regina G. and Livingston, Steven (2007) *When the Press Fails: Political Power and the News Media from Iraq to Katrina*. Chicago, IL: University of Chicago Press

Benoit, William and Currie, Heather (2001) "Innaccuries in Media Coverage of Presidential Debates" in *Argumentation and Advocacy*, Vol. 38: 28–39

Benson, Rodney and Powers, Matthew (2010) *Public Media and Political Independence: Lessons for the Future of Journalism from around the World*. New York: Free Press

Berkey-Gerard, Mark (2011) "Public Broadcasters Venture into Online Hyperlocal News: A Case Study of NewsWorks". Paper presented at the International Symposium on Online Journalism, Austin, Texas, 1 April, http://www.slideshare.net/markbg/berkey-gerardhyperlocal, accessed 28 April 2011

Berleson, Bernard (1952) *Content Analysis in Communication Research*. New York: Hafner

Bicket, Douglas and Wall, Melissa (2009) "BBC News in the U.S.A.: A 'Super-alternative' News Medium Emerges" in *Media, Culture and Society*, Vol. 31(3): 365–84

Bignell, Jonathan (2002) *Media Semiotics: An Introduction*, 2nd edn. Manchester: Manchester University Press

Bird, Elizabeth (2010) "Introduction: The Anthropology of News and Journalism: Why Now" in Bird, Elizabeth (ed.) *The Anthropology of News and Journalism: Global Perspectives*. Bloomington: Indiana University Press

Blumler, Jay and Gurevitch, Michael (1995) (eds) *The Crisis of Public Communication*. London: Routledge

Boehlert, Eric (2009) "Auld Lang Syne: Farewell to Another Decade of 'Liberal media bias'" in *Media Matters*, 22 December, http://mediamatters.org/columns/200912220005, accessed 16 June 2011

Bond, Paul (2011) "Matt Romney Claims He'll Cut off Funding for PBS, Says He Wants Advertisements on *Sesame Street*" in *Hollywood Reporter*, 28 December, http://www.hollywoodreporter.com/news/mitt-romney-pbs-big-bird-sesame-street-276555, accessed 13 January 2012

Born, Georgina (2004) *Uncertain Vision: Birt, Dyke and the Reinvention of the BBC*. London: Secker and Warburg

Boulton, Adam and Roberts, Tom D. C. (2011) "The Election Debates: Sky News' Perspective on Their Genesis and Impact on Media Coverage" in Wring, Dominic, Mortimore, Roger and Atkinson, Simon (eds), *Political Communication in Britain*, Basingstoke: Palgrave Macmillan

Boyd-Barrett, Claudia and Boyd-Barrett, Oliver (2010) "24/7 News as Counter-hegemonic Soft Power in Latin America" in Cushion, Stephen and Lewis, Justin

(2010) (eds) *The Rise of 24-Hour News Television: Global Perspectives*. New York: Peter Lang

Brants, Kees and Praag, Philip Van (2006) "Signs of Media Logic: Half a Century of Political Communication in the Netherlands" in *Javnost: The Public*, Vol. 13(1): 25–40

Brevini, B. (2010) "Towards PSB 2.0? Applying the PSB Ethos to Online Media in Europe: A Comparative Study of PSBs' Internet Policies in Spain, Italy and Britain" in *European Journal of Communication*, Vol. 25(4): 348–65

Brighton, Paul and Foy, Dennis (2007) *News Values*. London: Sage

Bromley, Michael (2010) "'All the World's a Stage': 24/7 News, Newspapers, and the Ages of Media" in Cushion, Stephen and Lewis, Justin (eds) *The Rise of 24-Hour News Television: Global Perspectives*. New York: Peter Lang

Brookes, Rod, Lewis, Justin and Wahl-Jorgensen, Karin (2004) "The Media Representation of Public Opinion: British Television News Coverage of the 2001 General Election" in *Media, Culture and Society*, Vol. 26(1): 63–80

Brugger, Niels and Burns, Maureen (2011) *Public Service Broadcasting on the Web: A Comprehensive History*. New York: Peter Lang

BSA (2009) *Free-to-Air Television Code of Broadcasting Practice*. Wellington: BSA

Buchinger, Christine, Wasserman, Herman and de Beer, Arnold (2004) in Berenger, Ralph D. (ed.) *Global Media Go to War: Role of News and Entertainment Media during the 2003 Iraq War*. Washington: Marquette Books LLC

Caldwell, John T. (1995) *Televisuality: Style, Crisis, and Authority in American Television*. New York: Rutgers University Press

Calhoun, Craig (ed.) (1992) *Habermas and the Public Sphere*. London: MIT Press

Cappella, Joseph N. and Jamieson, Kathleen Hall (1997) *Spiral of Cynicism*. New York: Oxford University Press

Carruthers, Susan L. (2008) "No One's Looking: The Disappearing Audience for War" in *Media, War and Conflict*, Vol. 1(1): 70–6

Carruthers, Susan L. (2011) *The Media at War*, 2nd edn. Basingstoke: Palgrave Macmillan

Chadwick, Andrew (2011) "Britain's First Live Televised Party Leaders' Debate: From the News Cycle to the Political Information Cycle" in *Parliamentary Affairs*, Vol. 64(1): 24–44

Chalaby, Jean K. (2009) *Transnational Television in Europe*. London: I.B. Tauris

Chamberlin, Bill F. (1978) "The FCC and the First Principle of the Fairness Doctrine: A History of Neglect and Distortion", *Federal Communications Law Journal*, Vol. 31(3): 361–411

Chang, Tsan-Kuo, Himelboim, Itai and Dong, Dong (2009) "Open Global Networks, Closed International Flows: World System and Political Economy of Hyperlinks in Cyberspace" in *International Communication Gazette*, Vol. 71(3): 137–59

Christians, Clifford G. (1999) "The Common Good as First Principle" in Glasser, Theodore L. (ed.) *The Idea of Public Journalism*. New York: Guilford Press

Christians, Clifford G., Glasser, Theodore L., McQuail, Dennis, Nordenstreng, Kaarle, and White, Robert A. (2009) *Normative Theories of the Media: Journalism in Democratic Societies*. Urbana: University of Illinois Press

Clark, Caroline (2009) "Wide Angles and Narrow Views: The Iraq Conflict in Embed and Other War Zone Reports" in Haarman, Louann and Lombardo, Linda (eds) *Evaluation and Stance in War News: A Linguistic Analysis of American, British and Italian Television News Reporting of the 2003 Iraqi War*. London: Continuum

Clausen, Lisbeth (2003) "Global News Communication Strategies – 9.11. 2002: Around the World" in *Nordicom Review*, (3), fall edition, Göteborg: Nordicom

Cohen, Jeffrey E. (2008) *The Presidency in the Era of 24-Hour News*. Princeton, NJ: Princeton University Press

Cohen, Jeffrey (2010) *Going Local: Presidential Leadership in the Post-broadcast Age*. Cambridge: Cambridge University Press

Coleman, Stephen (2000) *Televised Election Debates: International Perspectives*. Basingstoke: Macmillan

Coleman, Stephen, Steibel, Fabro and Blumler, Jay G. (2011) "Media Coverage of the Prime Ministerial Debates" in Coleman, Stephen (ed.) *Leaders in the Living Room: The Prime Ministerial Debates of 2010: Evidence, Evaluation and Some Recommendations*. Oxford: Reuters Institute for the Study of Journalism

Coll, Gaspar Pericay (2011) "The Catalan Public Television and Radio Broadcaster Will Have Its Budget Drastically Cut", Catalan News Agency, 25 December, http://www.catalannewsagency.com/news/politics/catalan-public-television-and-radio-broadcaster-will-have-its-budget-drastically-cut, accessed 16 January 2012

Collins, Richard (2002) *Media and Identity in Contemporary Europe: Consequences of Global Convergence*. Bristol: Intellect

Collins, Richard (2004) "'ISES' AND 'OUGHTS': Public Service Broadcasting in Europe" in Allan, Robert and Hill, Annette (eds) *The Television Studies Reader*. London: Routledge

Communications Committee (2009) *Public Service Broadcasting: Short-term Crisis, Long-term Future*. London: House of Lords. Second Report

Comrie, Margie (1996) "The Commercial Imperative in Broadcast News: TVNZ from 1985 to 1990", unpublished doctoral dissertation, Massey University, Palmerston North

Comrie, Margie (1999) "Television News and Broadcast Deregulation in New Zealand" in *Journal of Communication*, Vol. 49(2): 42–54

Comrie, Margie and Fountaine, Susan (2005) "'Knowing' through the News" in *International Journal of Humanities*, Vol. 3(8): 181–8

Convergence (2008) special edition on public service broadcasting, Vol. 14(3)

Cooper, Mark (2004) "Hyper-commercialism and the Media: The Threat to Journalism and Democratic Discourse" in Skinner, D., Compton, J. R and Gasher, M. (eds) *Converging Media, Diverging Politics: A Political Economy of News Media in the United States and Canada*. Lanham, MD: Lexington Books

Corner, John (1998) *Studying Media: Problems of Theory and Method*. Edinburgh: Edinburgh Press

Cottle, Simon (1999) "From BBC Newsroom to BBC Newscentre: On Changing Technology and Journalist Practices", *Convergence: The Journal of Research into New Media Technologies*, Vol. 5(3): 22–43

Cottle, Simon (2006) *Mediatized Conflict: Developments in Media and Conflict Studies*. Maidenhead: Open University Press

Cottle, Simon (2009) *Global Crisis Reporting: Journalism in a Global Age*. Maidenhead: Open University Press

Cottle, Simon and Matthews, Julian (2011) "Television News Ecology in the United Kingdom: A Study of Communicative Architecture, Its Production and Meanings" in *Television and New Media*, available on iFirst, 13 April

Cottle, Simon and Rai, Mugdha (2006) "Between Display and Deliberation: Analyzing TV News as Communicative Architecture" in *Media, Culture and Society*, Vol. 28(2): 163–89

Cottle, Simon and Rai, Mugdha (2007) "Australian TV News Revisited: News Ecology and Communicative Frames" in *Media International Australia*, (122): 43–58

Cottle, Simon and Rai, Mugdha (2008a) "Television News in Singapore: Mediating Conflict with Consent" in *Asian Journal of Social Science*, Vol. 36(3–4): 638–58

Cottle, Simon and Rai, Mugdha (2008b) "Television News in South Africa: Mediating an Emerging Democracy" in *Journal of Southern African Studies*, Vol. 34(2): 343–58

Cottle, Simon and Rai, Mugdha (2008c) "Television News in India: Mediating Democracy and Difference" in *International Communication Gazette*, Vol. 70(1): 76–96

Cottle, Simon and Rai, Mugdha (2008d) "Global 24/7 News Providers: Emissaries of Global Dominance or Global Public Sphere?" in *Global Media and Communication*, Vol. 4(2): 157–81

Couldry, Nick, Livingstone, Sonia and Markham, Tim (2007) *Media Consumption and Public Engagement: Beyond the Presumption of Attention*. Basingstoke: Palgrave Macmillan

Crisell, Andrew (1997) *An Introductory History of British Broadcasting*, 2nd edn. London: Routledge

Croteau, David and Hoynes, William (2001) *The Business of Media: Corporate Media and Public Interest*. Thousand Oaks, CA: Pine Forge

Curran, James (1991) "Mass Media and Democracy: A Reappraisal" in Curran, James and Gurevitch, Michael (eds) *Mass Media and Society*. London: Edward Arnold

Curran, James (2003) *Media and Power*. London: Routledge

Curran, James (2011) *Media and Democracy*. London: Routledge

Curran, James and Park, Myung-Jin (2000) *De-Westernizing Media Studies*. London: Routledge

Curran, James, Iyengar, Shanto, Lund, Anker Brink and Salovaara-Moring, Inka (2009) "Media Reporting, Public Knowledge and Democracy: A Comparative Study" in *European Journal of Communication*, Vol. 24(1): 5–26

Curran, James *et al.* (2012) "Media Systems, Political Culture and Public Knowledge: An 11-Nation Comparative Study" Unpublished material at present

Cushion, Stephen (2008) "Truly International? A Content Analysis of Journalism: Theory, Practice and Criticism and Journalism Studies" in *Journalism Practice*, Vol. 2(2): 280–93

Cushion, Stephen (2009) "From Tabloid Hack to Broadcast Journalist: Which News Sources Are the Most Trusted?" in *Journalism Practice*, Vol. 3(4): 472–81

Cushion, Stephen (2010a) "Three Phases of 24-hour News Television" in Cushion, Stephen and Lewis, Justin (eds) *The Rise of 24-hour News Television: Global Perspectives*. New York: Peter Lang

Cushion, Stephen (2010b) "Rolling Service, Market Logic: The Race to Be 'Britain's Most Watched News Channel'" in Cushion, Stephen and Lewis, Justin (eds) *The Rise of 24-hour News Television: Global Perspectives*. New York: Peter Lang

Cushion, Stephen (2012) *Television Journalism*. London: Sage

Cushion, Stephen and Lewis, Justin (2009) "Towards a 'Foxification' of 24 Hour News Channels in Britain? An Analysis of Market Driven and Publicly Funded News Coverage" in *Journalism: Theory, Practice and Criticism*, Vol. 10(2): 131–53

Cushion, Stephen and Lewis, Justin (2010) (eds) *The Rise of 24-hour News Television: Global Perspectives*. New York: Peter Lang

Cushion, Stephen, Lewis, Justin and Groves, Chris (2009a) "Prioritizing Hand-shaking over Policy-making: A Study of How the 2007 Devolved Elections Was Reported on BBC UK Network Coverage", *Cyfrwng: Media Wales Journal*, Vol. 6

Cushion, Stephen, Franklin, Bob and Court, Geoff (2006) "Citizens, Readers and Local Newspaper Coverage of the 2005 General Election" in *Javnost: The Public*, Vol. 13(1): 41–60

Cushion, Stephen, Lewis, Justin and Groves, Chris (2009b) "Reflecting the Four Nations? An Analysis of Reporting Devolution on UK Network News Media" in *Journalism Studies*, Vol. 10(5): 655–71

Cushion, Stephen, Lewis, Justin and Ramsay, Gordon (2010) *Four Nations Impartiality Review Follow Up: An Analysis of Reporting Devolution*. London: BBC Trust

Cushion, Stephen, Lewis, Justin and Ramsay, Gordon (2012) "The Impact of Interventionist Regulation in Reshaping News Agendas: A Comparative Analysis of Public and Commercially Funded Television Journalism" in *Journalism: Theory, Practice and Criticism*, available on iFirst

Dahlgren, Peter (1995) *Television and the Public Sphere: Citizenship, Democracy and the Media*. London: Sage

D'Angelo, Paul and Kuypers, Jim A. (2010) (eds) *Doing News Framing Analysis*. New York: Routledge

De Vreese, Claes H. (2003) "Television Reporting of Second Order Elections" in *Journalism Studies*, Vol. 4(2): 183–98

De Vreese, Claes H. (2008) "Media Logic and Floating Voters" in Strömbäck, Jesper and Kaid, Lynda Lee (eds) *The Handbook of Election News Coverage around the World*. New York: Routledge

De Vreese, Claes H. and Elenbaas, Matthijs (2002) "Cynical and Engaged: Strategic Campaign Coverage, Public Opinion and Mobilization in a Referendum" in *Communication Research*, Vol. 29(6): 615–41

De Vreese, Claes H., Banducci, Susan A., Semetko, Holli A. and Boomgaarden, Hajo G. (2006) "The News Media Coverage of the 2004 European Parliamentary Election Campaign in 25 Countries" in *European Union Politics*, Vol. 7(4): 477–504

Deacon, David and Wring, Dominic (2011) "Reporting the 2010 General Election: Old Media, New Media – Old Politics, New Politics" in Wring, Dominic, Mortimore, Roger and Atkinson, Simon, *Political Communication in Britain*. Basingstoke: Palgrave Macmillan

Deacon, David, Golding, Peter and Billig, Michael (2001) "'Real Issues' and Real Coverage in the 2001 Campaign", *Parliamentary Affairs*, Vol. 54(4): 666–78

Deacon, David, Wring, Dominic, Golding, Peter (2006) "Same Campaign, Differing Agendas: Analysing News Media Coverage of the 2005 General Election" in *British Politics*, Vol. 1(2): 222–56

Debrett, Mary (2010) *Reinventing Public Service Television for the Digital Future*. Bristol: Intellect

Demertzis, Nicolas and Pleios, George (2008) "Election News Coverage in Greece: Between Two Logics" in Strömbäck, Jesper and Kaid, Lynda Lee (eds) *The Handbook of Election News Coverage around the World*. New York: Routledge

Deuze, Mark (2006) "The Changing Context of News Work: Liquid Journalism and Monitorial Citizenship" in *International Journal of Communication*, Vol. 2(5): 848–65

D'Haenens, Leen and Saeys, Frieda (2007) (eds) *Western Broadcast Models: Structure, Conduct and Performance*. New York: Mouton de Gruyter

Dimitrova, Daniela V. and Connolly-Ahern, Colleen (2007) "A Tale of Two Wars: Framing Analysis of Online News Sites in Coalition Countries and the Arab World during the Iraq War" in *Howard Journal of Communications*, Vol. 18(2): 153–68

Dimitrova, Daniela V. and Neznanski, Matt (2006) "Online Journalism and the War in Cyberspace: A Comparison between US and International Newspapers" in *Journal of Computer-mediated Communication*, Vol. 12(1): 248–63

Dimitrova, Daniela V. and Strömbäck, Jesper (2010) "Exploring Semi-structural Differences in Television News between the United States and Sweden" in *International Communication Gazette*, Vol. 72(6): 487–502

Dimitrova, Daniela V., Kaid, Lynda Lee, Williams, Andrew Paul and Trammell, Kaye D. (2005) "War on the Web: The Immediate News Framing of Gulf War II" in *Harvard International Journal of Press/Politics*, Vol. 10(1): 22–44

Djerf-Pierre, Monika (2001) "Squaring the Circle: Public Service and Commercial News on Swedish Television 1956–99" in *Journalism Studies*, Vol. 1(2): 239–60

Dobek-Ostrowska, Boguslawa, Glowacki, Michal, Jakubowicz, Karol and Sükösd, Miklós (2010) (eds) *Comparative Media Systems: European and Global Perspectives*. Budapest: CEU and COST A30 publication

Domingo, David and Patterson, Chris (eds) (2011) *Making Online News: Newsroom Ethnography in the Second Decade of Internet Journalism*, 2nd edn. New York: Peter Lang

Donders, Karen and Pauwels, Caroline (2010) "What if Competition Policy Assists the Transfer from Public Service Broadcasting to Public Service Media? An Analysis of EU State Aid Control and Its Relevance for Public Broadcasting" in Gripsrud, Jostein and Moe, Hallvard (eds) *The Digital Public Sphere: Challenges for Media Policy*. Gotenborg: Nordicom

Douglas, Susan J. (1987) *Inventing American Broadcasting, 1899–1922*. Baltimore, MD: Johns Hopkins University Press

Downing, John and Davidson, Scott (2005) "The Internet and the UK General Election" in Deacon, David, Wring, Dominic, Billig, Michael, Downey, John, Golding Peter and Davidson, Scott, "Reporting the 2005 U.K. General Election". A study conducted on behalf of the Electoral Commission by the Communication Research Centre, Department of Social Sciences, Loughborough University

Dumisani, Moyo and Siphiwe, Hlongwane (2009) "Regulatory Independence and the Public Interest: The Case of South Africa's ICASA" in *Journal of African Media Studies*, Vol. 1(2): 279–94

Dunaway, Joanna (2008) "Markets, Ownership, and the Quality of Campaign News Coverage" in *Journal of Politics*, Vol. 70(4): 1193–202

Dwyer, Tim (2010) *Media Convergence*. Maidenhead: McGraw Hill, Open University Press

Economist/You Gov (2011) "Whom Does the Public Trust?" website, http://labs.yougov.co.uk/publicopinion/archive, accessed July 2011

Economist (2011) "The Foxification of News", 7 July, http://www.economist.com/node/18904112, accessed 10 August 2011

Edelman, M. J. (1964) *The Symbolic Uses of Politics*. London: University of Illinois Press

Edy, Jill A. and Meirick, Patrick C. (2007) "Wanted, Dead or Alive: Media Frames, Frame Adoption, and Support for the War in Afghanistan" in *Journal of Communication*, Vol. 57: 119–41

Ellis, John (2000) *Seeing Things: Television in the Age of Uncertainty*. London: I. B. Tauris

El-Nawawy, Mohammed and Powers, Shawn (2010) "A Conciliatory Medium in a Conflict-driven Environment?" in *Global Media and Communication*, Vol. 6(1): 61–84

Engel, Matthew (2002) "US Media Cowed by Patriotic Fever, Says CBS Star" in *Guardian*, 17 May, http://www.guardian.co.uk/media/2002/may/17/terrorismandthemedia.broadcasting, accessed 13 June 2011

Enli, Sara Gunn (2008) "Redefining Public Service Broadcasting Multi-platform Participation" in *Convergence: The International Journal of Research into New Media Technologies*, Vol. 14(1): 105–20

Entman, Robert M. (1993) "Framing: Toward Clarification of a Fractured Paradigm" in *Journal of Communication*, Vol. 43(4): 51–8

Esser, Frank (2008) "Dimensions of Political News Cultures: Sound Bite and Image Bite News in France, Germany, Great Britain and the United States" in *International Journal of Press/Politics*, Vol. 13(4): 401–28

Esser, Frank and Hemmer, Katharina (2008) "Characteristics and Dynamics of Election News Coverage in Germany" in Strömbäck, Jesper and Kaid, Lynda Lee (eds) *The Handbook of Election News Coverage around the World*. New York: Routledge

Euronews (2008) "Presentation to the European Parliament", http://www.europarl.europa.eu/document/activities/cont/200806/20080609ATT31165/20080609ATT31165EN.pdf, accessed 2 August 2011

Fahmy, Shahira S. and Al Emad, Mohammed (2011) "Al-Jazeera vs Al-Jazeera: A Comparison of the Network's English and Arabic Online Coverage of the US/Al Qaeda Conflict" in *International Communication Gazette*, Vol. 73(3): 216–32

Farnsworth, Stephen J. and Lichter, Robert S. (2007) *The Nightly News Nightmare: Television's Coverage of U.S. Presidential Elections, 1988–2004*, 2nd edn. Lanham, MD: Rowman & Littlefield

Farnsworth, Stephen J. and Lichter, Robert S. (2008) "Trends in Television Network News Coverage of U.S. Elections" in Strömbäck, Jesper and Kaid, Lynda Lee (eds) *The Handbook of Election News Coverage around the World*. New York: Routledge

Farnsworth, Stephen J. and Lichter, Robert S. (2011) "Network Television's Coverage of the 2008 Presidential Election" in *American Behavioural Scientist*, Vol. 55(4): 354–70

Fehrman, Craig (2011) "The Incredible Shrinking Sound Bite" in *Boston Globe*, 2 January, http://www.boston.com/bostonglobe/ideas/articles/2011/01/02/the_incredible_ shrinking_sound_bite/?page=full, accessed 28 April 2011

Fenton, Natalie (2009) (ed.) *New Media, Old News: Journalism and Democracy in the Digital Age*. London: Sage

Fenton, Natalie (2011a) "Deregulation or Democracy? New Media, News, Neoliberalism and the Public Interest" in *Continuum: Journal of Media and Cultural Studies*, Vol. 25(1): 63–72

Fenton, Natalie (2011b) "News of the World: We Need More than a Public Inquiry" in *Red Pepper*, 8 July, http://www.redpepper.org.uk/notw-more/, accessed 9 August 2011

Ferguson, Galit and Hargreaves, Ian (1999) *Wales in the News: Monitoring of Network News July & September 1999*. A Wales Media Forum working paper

Figenschou, Tine Ustad (2010) "A Voice for the Voiceless? A Quantitative Content Analysis of Al-Jazeera English's Flagship News" in *Global Media and Communication*, Vol. 6(1): 85–107

Figenschou, Tine Ustad (2011) "The South Is Talking Back: With a White Face and a British Accent – Editorial Dilemmas in Al-Jazeera English" in *Journalism: Theory, Practice and Criticism*. Published on iFirst, 14 June 2011

Fitzsimmons, Caitlin (2009) "Seventeen Regions into Nine: How the Updated ITV Local News Services Will Run" in *Media Guardian*, 17 February, http://www.guardian.co.uk/media/organgrinder/2009/feb/16/seventeen-regions-into-nine-itv-news, accessed 28 April 2011

Flew, Terry (2011) "Rethinking Public Service Media and Citizenship: Digital Strategies for News and Current Affairs at Australia's Special Broadcasting Service" in *International Journal of Communication*, Vol. 5: 215–32

Flew, Terry and Wilson, Jason (2010) "Journalism as Social Networking: The Australian Youdecide Project and the 2007 Federal Election" in *Journalism: Theory, Practice and Criticism*, Vol. 11(2): 131–47

Flournoy, Don M. and Stewart, Robert K. (1997) *CNN Making News in the Global Market*. Luton: John Libbey Media

Foster, Patrick (2012) "BBC 'Should Not Axe Services as Part of Ofcom Media Plurality Review'" in *Media Guardian*, 5 January, http://www.guardian.co.uk/media/2012/jan/05/bbc-ofcom-media-plurality-review, accessed 16 January 2012

Fountaine, Susan, Comrie, Margie and Cheyne, Christine (2005) "Empty Heartland: The Absent Regions on New Zealand Television" in *Media International Australia*, Vol. 117: 100–9

Fox, Julia R. and Park, Byungho (2006) "The 'I' of Embedded Reporting: An Analysis of CNN Coverage of the 'Shock and Awe' Campaign" in *Journal of Broadcasting and Electronic Media*, Vol. 50(1): 36–51

Fraile, Marta (2011) "Widening or Reducing the Knowledge Gap? Testing the Media Effects on Political Knowledge in Spain (2004–2006)" in *International Journal of Press/Politics*, Vol. 16(2): 163–84

Franklin, Bob (2004) *Packaging Politics: Political Communications in Britain's Media Democracy*. London: Routledge

Franklin, Bob (2005) "McJournalism? The McDonaldization Thesis, Local Newspapers and Local Journalism in the UK" in Allan, Stuart (ed.) *Journalism Studies: Critical Essays*. Milton Keynes: Open University Press

Franklin, Bob (2006) (ed.) *Local Journalism and Local Media: Making the Local News*. London: Routledge

Franklin, Bob and Cushion, Stephen (2007) "Amateurs or Adversaries?: Local Journalists' Coverage of the UK Non-general Election" in Wring, Dominic, Green, Jane, Mortimore, Roger and Atkinson, Simon (eds) *Political Communications: The General Election Campaign of 2005*. Basingstoke: Palgrave Macmillan

Franklin, Bob and Richardson, John (2002) "A Journalist's Duty? Continuity and Change in Local Newspapers' Coverage of Recent UK General Elections" in *Journalism Studies* Vol. 3(1): 35–52

Friedman, Wayne (2001) "Commercial-free TV: Cost $400 Mil" in *Advertising Age*, 17 September, http://adage.com/article/news/commercial-free-tv-cost-400-mil/53836/, accessed 13 June 2011

Frisch, Karl (2010) "Obama: '24/7 Media ... Exposes Us to All Kinds of Arguments, Some of Which Don't Always Rank That High on the Truth Meter'" in *Media Matters for America*, 9 May, http://mediamatters.org/blog/201005090011, accessed 9 August 2011

Frost, Natasha A. and Phillips, Nickie D. (2011) "Talking Heads: Crime Reporting on Cable News" in *Justice Quarterly*, Vol. 28(1): 87–112

Fuller, Jack (2010) *What Is Happening to News: The Information Explosion and the Crisis in Journalism*. Chicago, IL: Chicago University Press

Galtung, Johan and Ruge, Mari M. (1965) "The Structure of Foreign News" in *Journal of International Peace Research*, Vol. 1: 64–90

Gamson, William (2002) "Promoting Political Engagement" in *Mediated Politics: Communication in the Future of Democracy*, Cambridge: Cambridge University Press

Gans, Herbert (1979) *Deciding What's News*. New York: Pantheon Books

Gans, Herbert (2009) "Can Popularization Help the News Media?" in Zelizer, Barbie (ed.) *The Changing Faces of Journalism: Tabloidization, Technology and Truthiness*, New York: Routledge

Garcia-Blanco, Inaki (2011) "The Journalistic Construction of Voters in the Spanish General Election Campaign 2008" in *Journalism Practice*, Vol. 5(2): 177–92

Garcia-Blanco, Inaki and Cushion, Stephen (2010) "A Partial Europe without Citizens or EU-level Political Institutions: How Far Can Euronews Constitute a European Public Sphere" in *Journalism Studies*, Vol. 11(3): 393–411

Garnham, Nicholas (1986) "Media and the Public Sphere" in Golding, Peter, Murdock, Graham and Schlesinger, Philip, *Communicating Politics*, Leicester: Leicester University Press

Garnham, Nicholas (1990) *Capitalism and Communication*. London: Sage

Gidengil, Elisabeth (2008) "Media Matter: Election Coverage in Canada" in Strömbäck, Jesper and Kaid, Lynda Lee (eds) *The Handbook of Election News Coverage around the World*. New York: Routledge

Glasser, Theodore (1999) *The Idea of Public Journalism*. New York: Guilford Press

Golding, Peter and Elliott, Phillip (1979) *Making the News*. Harlow: Longman

González Martín, Pedro (1995) *Euronews: Una television pública para Europa*, Barcelona: Icaria

Grabe, Maria Elizabeth and Bucy, Erik Page (2009) *Image Bite Politics: News and the Visual Framing of Elections*. New York: Oxford University Press

Gunter, Barrie (2005) "Trust in the News on Television", *Aslib Proceedings: New Information Perspectives*, Vol. 57(5): 384–97

Gurevitch, Michael, Coleman, Stephen and Blumler, Jay G. (2009) "Political Communication – Old and New Media Relationships" in *Annals of the American Academy of Political and Social Science*, Vol. 625(1): 164–81

Haarman, Louann (2009) "Decoding Codas: Evaluation in Reporter and Correspondent News Talk" in Haarman, Louann and Lombardo, Linda (eds) *Evaluation and Stance in War News: A Linguistic Analysis of American, British and Italian Television News Reporting of the 2003 Iraqi War*. London: Continuum

Haarman, Louann and Lombardo, Linda (2009) (eds) *Evaluation and Stance in War News: A Linguistic Analysis of American, British and Italian Television News Reporting of the 2003 Iraqi War*. London: Continuum

Habermas, Jürgen (1989) *Structural Transformation of the Public Sphere*. Cambridge: Polity Press

Hall, Jim (2001) *Online Journalism: A Critical Primer*. London: Pluto

Halliday, Josh (2010) "BBC Alters Link Guidelines for Online Articles" in *Media Guardian*, 8 October, http://www.guardian.co.uk/media/pda/2010/oct/08/bbc-link-guidlines, accessed 28 April 2011

Halliday, Josh (2010) "Chile Miners: BBC World News Editor Defends Overspend" in *Guardian*, 14 October, http://www.guardian.co.uk/media/2010/oct/14chile-miners-bbc-overspend-?INTCMP=SRCH, accessed 29 June 2011

Halliday, Josh (2011) "Channel 5 News to Relaunch with Reporters Editing Their Own Footage" in *Media Guardian*, 6 December, http://www.guardian.co.uk/media/2011/dec/06/chanel-5-news, accessed 8 December 2011

Hallin, Daniel C. (1986) *The "Uncensored War": The Media and Vietnam*. Oxford: Oxford University Press

Hallin, Daniel C. (1992) "Sound Bite News: Television Coverage of Elections, 1968–1988" in *Journal of Communication*, Vol. 42(2): 5–24

Hallin, Daniel C. (1994) *We Keep America on Top of the World: Television Journalism and the Public Sphere*. New York: Routledege

Hallin, Daniel C. and Mancini, Paolo (2004) *Comparing Media Systems: Three Models of Media and Politics*. New York: Cambridge University Press

Hallin, Daniel C. and Mancini, Paolo (2010) "Preface" in Dobek-Ostrowska, Boguslawa, Głowacki, Michal, Jakubowicz, Karol and Sükösd, Miklós (eds) *Comparative Media Systems: European and Global Perspectives*. Budapest: CEU and COST A30 publication

Hamilton, James T. (2010) "The (Many) Markets for International News: How News from Abroad Sells at Home" in *Journalism Studies*, Vol. 11(5): 650–66

Hanitzsch, Thomas *et al.* (2011) "Mapping Journalism Cultures across Nations: A Comparative Study of 18 Countries" in *Journalism Studies*, Vol. 12(3): 273–93

Harcup, Tony and O'Neil, Deirdre (2001) "What Is News? Galtung and Ruge Revisited" in *Journalism Studies*, Vol. 2(2): 261–80

Hargreaves, Ian and Thomas, James (2002) *New News, Old News*. London: ITC

Harrison, Jackie (2000) *Terrestrial TV News in Britain: The Culture of Production*. Manchester: Manchester University Press

Harrison, Jackie (2010) "User-generated Content and Gatekeeping at the BBC Hub" in *Journalism Studies*, Vol. 11(2): 243–56

Hartley, John (1982) *Understanding News*. London: Routledge

Hartley, John (1999) *Uses of Television*. London: Routledge

Hartley, John (2005) "Creative Identities" in Hartley, John (ed.) *Creative Industries*. Oxford: Blackwell

Hartley, John and Cunningham, Stuart (2010) *The Uses of Digital Literacy*. Queensland: University of Queensland

Haynes, Danny and Guardino, Matt (2010) "Whose Views Made the News? Media Coverage and the March to War in Iraq" in *Political Communication*, Vol. 27(1): 59–87

Henning, Dietmar (2011) "Netherlands Budget Cuts Hit Social Services" World Socalist Web Site, 12 July, http://www.wsws.org/articles/2011/jul2011/neth-j12.shtml, accessed 16 January 2012

Hibberd, Matthew (2008) *The Media in Italy*. Milton Keynes: Open University Press

Himelboim, Itai (2010) "The International Network Structure of News Media: An Analysis of Hyperlinks Usage in News Web Sites" in *Journal of Broadcasting and Electronic Media*, Vol. 54(3): 373–90

Holtz-Bacha, Christina and Norris, Pippa (2001) "'To Entertain, Inform and Educate': Still the Role of Public Television" in *Political Communication*, Vol. 18(2): 123–40

Hood, Lee (2007) "Radio Reverb: The Impact of 'Local' News Reimported to Its Own Community" in *Journal of Broadcasting & Electronic Media*, Vol. 51(1): 1–19

Hooghe, Marc (2002) "Watching Television and Civic Engagement: Disentangling the Effects of Time, Programs, and Stations" in *International Journal of Press/Politics*, Vol. 7(2): 84–104

Hopmann, David Nicolas, van Aelst, Peter and Legnante, Guido (2011) "Political Balance in the News: A Review of Concepts, Operationalizations and Key Findings" in *Journalism: Theory, Practice and Criticism*, available on iFirst, 18 November

Hoskins, Andrew (2004) *Television War: From Vietnam to Iraq*. London: Continuum

Hoynes, William (1994) *Public Television for Sale: Media, the Market, and the Public Sphere*. Boulder, CO: Westview Press

Hoynes, William (2003) "Branding Public Service: The 'New PBS' and the Privatization of Public Television" in *Television and New Media*, Vol. 4(2): 117–30

Humphreys, Peter (1996) *Mass Media and Media Policy in Western Europe*. Manchester: Manchester University Press

Huxford, John (2007) "The Proximity Paradox: Live Reporting, Visual Proximity and the Concept of Place in the News" in *Journalism: Theory, Practice and Criticism*, Vol. 8(6): 657–74

Interactions: Studies in Communication & Culture (2010) Special edition on "Whither the Public Interest in the New Political Economy?", Vol. 1(2)

Iosifidis, Petros (2010) (ed.) *Reinventing Public Service Communication: European Broadcasters and Beyond*. London: Palgrave Macmillan

Irwin, Galen A. and Van Holsteyn, Joop J. M. (2008) "'What Are They Waiting For?' Strategic Information for the Late Deciding Voters" in *International Journal of Public Opinion*, Vol. 20(4): 483–93

Iskandar, Adel and El-Nawawy, Mohammed (2004) "Al-Jazeera and War Coverage in Iraq: The Media's Quest for Contextual Objectivity" in Allan, Stuart and Zelizer, Barbie (eds) *Reporting War: Journalism in Wartime*. London: Routledge

Iyengar, Shanto (1991) *Is Anyone Responsible? How Television Frames Political Issues*. Chicago, IL: University of Chicago Press

Iyengar, Shanto, Norpoth, Helmut and Hahn, Kyu S. (2004) "Consumer Demand for Election News: The Horserace Sells" in *Journal of Politics*, Vol. 66(1): 157–75

Iyengar, Shanto, Hahn, Kyu S., Bonfadelli, Heinz and Marr, Mirko (2009) "'Dark Areas of Ignorance' Revisited: Comparing International Affairs Knowledge in Switzerland and the United States" in *Communication Research*, Vol. 36(3): 341–58

Jacka, Elizabeth (2003) "'Democracy as Defeat': The Impotence of Arguments for Public Service Broadcasting" in *Television and New Media*, Vol. 4(2): 177–91

Jain, Anuja (2010) "'Beaming It Live': 24-hour Television News, the Spectator and the Spectacle of the 2002 Gujarat Carnage" in *South Asian Popular Culture*, Vol. 8(2): 163–79

Jenssen, Anders Todal (2008) "Does Public Broadcasting Make a Difference? Political Knowledge and Electoral Campaigns on Television" in *Scandinavian Political Studies*, Vol. 32(3): 247–71

Jirik, John (2010) "24-Hour Television News in the People's Republic of China" in Cushion, Stephen and Lewis, Justin (2010) (eds) *The Rise of 24-Hour News Television: Global Perspectives*. New York: Peter Lang

Jones, Nicholas (2003) "24 Hours Media" in *Journal of Public Affairs*, Vol. 3(1): 27–32

Jones, Paul (2003) "Regulating for Freedom: Media Lessons from Australia" in *Open Democracy*, 17 September, http://www.opendemocracy.net/media-globalmedia ownership/article_1492.jsp#, accessed 4 March 2011

Jones, Steve (2008) "Television News: Geographic and Sources Biases, 1982–2004" in *International Journal of Communication*, Vol. 2: 223–52

Joshi, Prem Lal (2007) "Adherence of Indian News Channels to Cardinal Principles of Broadcasting: A Survey of the Perceptions of Persian Gulf-based Indians", http://www.worldpress.org/Asia/2696.cfm, accessed 2 August 2011

Juntunen, Laura (2010) "Explaining the Need for Speed: Speed and Competition as Challenges to Journalism Ethics" in Cushion, Stephen and Lewis, Justin (2010) (eds) *The Rise of 24-hour News Television: Global Perspectives*. New York: Peter Lang

Kaid, Lynda Lee (2006) "Political Advertising in the United States" in Kaid, Lynda Lee and Holtz-Bacha, Christina (eds), *The Sage Handbook of Political Advertising*. London: Sage

Kaid, Lynda Lee and and Strömbäck, Jesper (2008) "Election News Coverage around the World: A Comparative Perspective" in Strömbäck, Jesper and Kaid, Lynda Lee (eds) *The Handbook of Election News Coverage around the World*. New York: Routledge

Karlsson, Michael and Strömbäck, Jesper (2010) "Freezing the Flow of Online News: Exploring Approaches to the Study of the Liquidity of Online News" in *Journalism Studies*, Vol. 11(1): 2–19

Katz, Elihu and Warshel, Yael (2001) *Election Studies: What's Their Use?* Boulder, CO: Westview Press

Kellner, Douglas (2004) "Media Propaganda and Spectacle in the War on Iraq: A Critique of U.S. Broadcasting Networks" in *Cultural Studies, Critical Methodologies*, Vol. 4(3): 329–38

Kerbel, Matthew R. and Apee, Sumaiya and Ross, Marc Howard (2000) "PBS Ain't So Different: Public Broadcasting, Election Frames and Democratic Empowerment" in *Harvard International Journal of Press/Politics*, Vol. 5(4): 8–32

Knightley, Philip (2004) *The First Casualty: The War Correspondent as Hero and Myth-Maker from the Crimea to Iraq*. Baltimore, MD: Johns Hopkins University Press

Kolmer, Christian and Semetko, Holli A. (2009) "Framing the Iraq War: Perspectives from American, U.K., Czech, German, South African, and Al-Jazeera News" in *American Behavioral Scientist*, Vol. 52(5): 643–56

Kolmer, Christian and Semetko, Holli A. (2010) "International Television News" in *Journalism Studies*, Vol. 11(5): 700–17

Kperogi, Farooq A. (2011) "Cooperation with the Corporation? CNN and the Hegemonic Cooptation Citizen Journalism through iReport.com" in *New Media Society*, Vol. 13(2): 314–29

Kuhn, Raymond (2010) "France 24: Too Little, Too Late, Too French?" in Cushion, Stephen and Lewis, Justin (2010) (eds) *The Rise of 24-hour News Television: Global Perspectives*. New York: Peter Lang

Kull, Stephen (2003) *Misconceptions, the Media and the Iraq War*. Programme on International Policy Attitudes (PIPA) Research Report

Lasorsa, Dominic L., Lewis, Seth C. and Holton, Avery E. (2011) "Normalizing Twitter" in *Journalism Studies*, accessed via iFirst

Lawson, Chappell (2008) "Election Coverage in Mexico: Regulation Meets Crony Capitalism" in Strömbäck, Jesper and Kaid, Lynda Lee (eds) *The Handbook of Election News Coverage around the World*. New York: Routledge

Lazarsfeld, P., Berelson, B. and Gaudet, H. (1948) *The People's Choice*. New York: Columbia Press

Lee-Wright, Peter (2008) "Virtual News: BBC News at a 'Future Media and Technology' Crossroads" in *Convergence: The International Journal of Research into New Media Technologies*, Vol. 14(3): 249–60

Lehman-Wilzig, Sam N. and Seletzky, Michal (2010) "Hard News, Soft News, 'General' News: The Necessity and Utility of an Intermediate Classification" in *Journalism: Theory, Practice and Criticism*, Vol. 11(1): 37–56

Leurdijk, Andra (2006) "Public Service Broadcasting's Dilemmas and Regulation in a Converging Media Landscape", paper presented at RIPE conference, November, London

Lewis, Justin (1991) *The Ideological Octopus: An Exploration of Television and Its Audience*. New York: Routledge

Lewis, Justin (2004) "Television, Public Opinion and the War in Iraq: The Case of Britain" in *International Journal of Public Opinion Research*, Vol. 16(3): 295–310

Lewis, Justin (2006) "News and the Empowerment of Citizens" in *European Journal of Cultural Studies*, Vol. 9(3): 303–19

Lewis, Justin (2010) "Democratic or Disposable? 24-Hour News, Consumer Culture, and Built-in Obsolescence" in Cushion, Stephen and Lewis, Justin (2010) (eds) *The Rise of 24-hour News Television: Global Perspectives*. New York: Peter Lang

Lewis, Justin and Cushion, Stephen (2007) *An Analysis of 24 Hour News in the UK*. BBC internal research

Lewis, Justin and Cushion, Stephen (2009) "The Thirst to Be First: An Analysis of Breaking News Stories and Their Impact on the Quality of 24-hour News Coverage in the UK" in *Journalism Practice*, Vol. 3(3): 304–18

Lewis, Justin, Cushion, Stephen and Thomas, James (2005) "Immediacy, Convenience or Engagement? An Analysis of 24 Hour News Channels in the UK" *Journalism Studies*, Vol. 6(4): 461–78

Lewis, Justin, Inthorn, Sanna and Wahl-Jorgensen, Karin (2005) *Citizens or Consumers? What the Media Tell Us about Political Participation*. Maidenhead: Open University Press

Lewis, Justin, Williams, Andy and Franklin, Bob (2008) "A Compromised Fourth Estate? UK News Journalism, Public Relations and News Sources" in *Journalism Studies*, Vol. 9(1): 1–20

Lewis, Justin, Brookes, Rod, Mosdell, Nick and Threadgold, Terry (2006) *Shoot First and Ask Questions Later: Media Coverage of the 2003 Iraq War*. New York: Peter Lang

Livingston, Steven (1997) *Clarifying the CNN Effect: An Examination of Media Effects according to Type of Military Intervention*. A Harvard University John F. Kennedy School of Government Research Paper R-18

Livingston, Steven and Bennett, W. Lance (2003) "Gatekeeping, Indexing and Live-Event News: Is Technology Altering the Construction of News?" *Political Communication*, Vol. 20(4): 363–80

Livingstone, Sonia (2003) "On the Challenges of Cross-national Comparative Media Research" in *European Journal of Communication*, Vol. 18(4): 477–500

Löffelholz, Martin and Weaver, David (2008) (eds) *Global Journalism Research*. New York and London: Blackwell Press

Lombardo, Linda (2009) "The News Presenter as Socio-cultural Construct" in Haarman, Louann and Lombardo, Linda (eds) *Evaluation and Stance in War News: A Linguistic Analysis of American, British and Italian Television News Reporting of the 2003 Iraqi War*. London: Continuum

Lowe, Gregory Ferrell (2010) (ed.) *The Public in Public Service Media*. Gotenborg: Nordicom

Lowe, Gregory Ferrell and Bardoel, Jo (2008) (eds) *From Public Service Broadcasting to Public Service Media*. Gotenborg: Nordicom

Lowe, Gregory Ferrell and Jauert, Per (2005) (ed.) *Cultural Dilemmas in Public Service Broadcasting*. Gotenborg: Nordicom

Lule, Jack (2004) "War and Its Metaphors: News Language and the Prelude to War in Iraq, 2003" in *Journalism Studies*, Vol. 5(2): 179–90

MacGregor, Brent (1997) *Live, Direct and Biased: Making Television News in the Satellite Age*. London: Arnold

Magnier, Mark (2009) "Indian News Channels Criticized for Mumbai Coverage" in *Los Angeles Times*, 9 January, http://articles.latimes.com/2009/jan/18/world/fg-mumbai-tv18?pg=2, accessed 2 August 2011

Marriott, Stephanie (2007) *Live Television: Time, Space and the Broadcast Event*. London: Sage

Mason, Paul (2006) "Rolling News RIP" in *Media Guardian*, 16 January, http://www.guardian.co.uk/media/2006/jan/16/mondaymediasection, accessed 22 June 2011

Matheson, Donald and Allan, Stuart (2009) (eds) *Digital War Reporting*. New York: Peter Lang

Matthews, Julian (2010) *Producing Serious News for Citizen Children: A Study of the BBC's Children's Programme, Newsround*. New York: Edwin Mellen Place

McCauley, Michael P., Peterson, Eric E., Artz, Lee B. and Halleck, DeeDee (2003) *Public Broadcasting and the Public Interest*. New York: M. E. Sharpe

McChesney, Robert (1993) *Telecommunications, Mass Media and Democracy: The Battle for the Control of U.S. Broadcasting, 1928–1935*. New York: Oxford University Press

McChesney, Robert (2000) *Rich Media, Poor Democracy: Communication Politics in Dubious Times*. New York: New Press

McChesney, Robert (2004) *The Problem of the Media: US Communication Politics in the Twenty-first Century*. New York: Monthly Review Press

McGuigan, Jim (1992) *Cultural Populism*. London: Routledge

McManus, John H. (2009) "The Commercialization of News" in Wahl-Jorgensen, Karin and Hanitzsch, Thomas (eds) *Handbook of Journalism Studies*. Mahwah, NJ: Lawrence Erlbaum Associates

McNair, Brian (2006) *Cultural Chaos – Journalism, News and Power in a Globalised World*. London: Routledge

McQuail, Dennis (1987) *Mass Communication Theory*, 2nd edn. London: Sage

McQuail, Dennis (2005) *McQuail's Mass Communication Theory*, 5th edn. London: Sage

Meade, Geoff (1999). "Brussels Rejects Sky Complaint against BBC 24-hour News" in *Independent*, http://www.independent.co.uk/news/media/brussels-rejects-sky-complaint-against-bbc-24hour-news-738877.html, accessed 22 June 2011

Meier, Werner A. (2011) "From Media Regulation to Democratic Media Governance" in Trappel, Josef, Meir, Werner, A., d'Haenens, Leen, Steemers, Jeanette and Thomass, Barbara, *Media in Europe Today*. Bristol: Intellect

Metha, Nalin (2010) "India Live: Satellites, Politics, and India's TV News Revolution" in Cushion, Stephen and Lewis, Justin (2010) (eds) *The Rise of 24-hour News Television: Global Perspectives*. New York: Peter Lang

Miles, Hugh (2005) *Al Jazeera: How Arab TV News Challenged the World*. London: Abacus

Miller, Toby (2010) *Television: The Basics*. London: Routledge

Moe, Hallvard (2008) "Public Service Media Online? Regulating Public Broadcasters' Internet Services – A Comparative Analysis" in *Television & New Media*, Vol. 9(3): 220–38

Moe, Hallvard (2010) "Governing Public Service Broadcasting: 'Public Value Tests' in Different National Contexts" in *Communication, Culture and Critique*, Vol. 3: 207–23

Moe, Hallvard (2011) "Defining Public Service beyond Broadcasting: The Legitimacy of Different Approaches" in *International Journal of Cultural Policy*, Vol. 17(1): 52–68

Moe, Hallvard and Syvertsen, Trine (2009) "Researching Public Service Broadcasting" in Wahl-Jorgensen, Karin and Hanitzsch, Thomas (eds) *Handbook of Journalism Studies*, New York and London: Routledge

Moeller, Susan D. (2004) *Media Coverage of Weapons of Mass Destruction*. College Park, MD: Center for International and Security Studies at Maryland

Montgomery, Martin (2007) *The Discourse of Broadcast News: A Linguistic Approach*. London: Routledge

Morris, Jonathan S. and Forgette, Richard (2007) "News Grazers, Television News, Political Knowledge, and Engagement" in *Harvard International Journal of Press/Politics*, Vol. 12(1): 91–107

Murdock, Graham (1992) "Citizens, Consumers and Public Culture" in Skovmand, Michael and Schroder, Kim Christian, *Media Cultures: Reappraising Transnational Media*. London: Routledge

Murdock, Graham (2005) "Building the Digital Commons: Public Broadcasting in the Age of the Internet" in Lowe, Gregory Ferrell and Jauert, Per (eds) *Cultural Dilemmas in Public Service Broadcasting*. Gotenborg: Nordicom

Murray, Simone (2009) "Servicing 'Self-scheduling Consumers' Public Broadcasters and Audio Podcasting" in *Global Media and Communication*, Vol. 5(2): 197–219

Nacos, Brigitte I. (2003) "Terrorism as Breaking News: Attack on America" in *Political Science Quarterly*, Vol. 118(1): 23–52

Negrine, Ralph (1989) *Politics and the Mass Media in Britain*. London: Routledge

Newman, Ric (2010) "#UK Election2010, Mainstream Media and the Role of the Internet: How Social and Digital Media Affected the Business of Politics and Journalism", Working Paper for Reuters Institute for the Study of Journalism

Nikolaev, Alexander G. and Hakanen, Ernest A. (2006) (eds) *Leading to the 2003 Iraq War: The Global Media Debate*. Basingstoke: Palgrave Macmillan

Nissen, Christian (2006) *Making a Difference: Public Service Broadcasting in the European Media Landscape*. Eastleigh: John Libbey

Nord, Lars W. and Strömbäck, Jesper (2006) "Reporting More, Informing Less: A Comparison of the Swedish Media Coverage of September 11 and the Wars in Afghanistan and Iraq" in *Journalism: Theory, Practice and Criticism*, Vol. 7(1): 85–110

Norris, Pippa (2000) *A Virtuous Circle? Political Communications in Post-industrial Democracies*. Cambridge: Cambridge University Press

Norris, Pippa, Curtice, John, Sanders, David, Scammell, Margaret and Semetko, Holli (1999) *On Message: Communicating the Campaign*. London: Sage

Ofcom (2007) *New News, Future News*. London: Ofcom

Ofcom (2009) ICMR CHARTS, http://stakeholders.ofcom.org.uk/binaries/research/cmr/ICMRcharts.pdf, accessed 9 August 2011

Ofcom (2010a) *International Communications Report*. London: Ofcom

Ofcom (2010b) *Report on Public Interest Test on the Proposed Acquisition of British Sky Broadcasting Group Plc by News Corporation*. London: Ofcom

Ofcom (2011) *The Ofcom Broadcasting Code*. London: Ofcom

O'Malley, Tom (2011) "Wales, ITV and Regulation" in *Cyfrwng: Wales Media Journal*, Vol. 8: 7–22

O'Neil, Deirdre and Harcup, Tony (2009) "News Values and Selectivity" in Wahl-Jorgensen, Karin and Hanitzsch, Thomas (eds) *The Handbook of Journalism Studies*. London: Routledge

Orgad, Shani (2008) "'Have You Seen Bloomberg?': Satellite News Channels as Agents of the New Visibility" in *Global Media and Communication*, Vol. 4(3): 301–27

Ostertag, Stephen (2010) "Establishing News Confidence: A Qualitative Study of How People Use the News Media to Know the News-world" in *Media, Culture and Society*, Vol. 32(4): 597–614

Ottosen, Rune and Figenschou, Tine Ustad (2007) "September 11 in Norwegian Media: Images of the Local Threat" in Pludowski, Tomasz (ed.) *How the World's News Media Reacted to 9/11: Essays from around the World*. Washington, DC: Marquette Books

Ouellette, Laurie (2002) *Viewers like You? How Public TV Failed the People*. New York: Columbia University Press

Padovani, Cinzia and Tracey, Michael (2003) "Report on the Conditions of Public Service Broadcasting" in *Television and New Media*, Vol. 4(2): 131–53

Painter, James (2008) *Counter-hegemonic News: A Case Study of Al-Jazeera English and Telesur*. Oxford: Reuters

Patterson, Chris (2010) "The Hidden Role of Television News Agencies: 'Going Live' on 24-hour News Channels" in Cushion, Stephen and Lewis, Justin (2010) (eds) *The Rise of 24-hour News Television: Global Perspectives*. New York: Peter Lang

Patterson, Thomas E. (2000) *Doing Well and Doing Good: How Soft News and Critical Journalism Are Shrinking the News Audience and Weakening Democracy – and What News Outlets Can Do about It*. Harvard: John F. Kennedy School of Government

Paz, Marìa Antonia and Avilés, José Alberto Garcia (2009) "Demonizing the Tyrant: Saddam Hussein's Image in Spanish News Programs during the Second Persian Gulf War" in *International Journal of Contemporary Iraqi Studies*, Vol. 3(1): 53–74

Penty, Charles (2011) "Spain Raises Taxes, Cuts Spending to Trim Deficit: Highlights" Bloomberg News in Bloomberg.com/news/2011-12-30/spain-raises-taxes-cuts-spending-to-trim-deficit-highlights?category=, accessed 16 January 2012

Petley, Julian (2009) "Impartiality in Television News: Profitability versus Public Service" in Allan, Stuart, *The Routledge Companion to News and Journalism*. London: Routledge

Pew Research Center for the People and the Press (2007) "Public Knowledge of Current Affairs Little Changed by News and Information Revolutions", http://people-press.org/2007/04/15/public-knowledge-of-current-affairs-little-changed-by-news-and-information-revolutions/, accessed 9 August 2011

Pew Research Center for the People and the Press (2011) "Beyond Red vs. Blue: Political Typology", http://people-press.org/2011/05/04/beyond-red-vs-blue-the-political-typology/, accessed 10 August 2011

Pew Research Center Project for Excellence in Journalism (1998) "Changing Definitions of News", Pew Project for Excellence report, http://www.journalism.org/node/1090, accessed 27 April 2011

Pew Research Center Project for Excellence in Journalism (2005) *The State of the News Media: An Annual Report on American Journalism*

Pew Research Center Project for Excellence in Journalism (2009) *The State of the News Media: An Annual Report on American Journalism*

Pew Research Center Project for Excellence in Journalism (2010) *The State of the News Media: An Annual Report on American Journalism*

Pew Research Center Project for Excellence in Journalism (2011) *The State of the News Media: An Annual Report on American Journalism*

Pfau, Michael *et al.* (2005) "Embedded Reporting during the Invasion and Occupation of Iraq: How the Embedding of Journalists Affects Television News Reports" in *Journal of Broadcasting & Electronic Media*, Vol. 49(4): 468–87

Philo, Greg and Berry, Mike (2004) *Bad News from Israel*. London: Pluto Press

Philo, Greg and Berry, Mike (2011) *More Bad News from Israel*. London: Pluto Press

Piazza, Roberta (2009) "News Is Reporting What Was Said: Techniques and Patterns of Attribution" in Haarman, Louann and Lombardo, Linda (eds) *Evaluation and Stance in War News: A Linguistic Analysis of American, British and Italian Television News Reporting of the 2003 Iraqi War*. London: Continuum

Piazza, Roberta and Haarman, Louann (2011) "Toward a Definition and Classification of Human Interest Narratives in Television War Reporting" in *Journal of Pragmatics*, Vol. 43: 1540–9

Pludowski, Tomasz (ed.) (2007) *How the World's News Media Reacted to 9/11: Essays from around the World*. Washington, DC: Marquette Books

Plunkett, John (2010) "BBC iPhone Apps Given Green Light" in *Media Guardian*, 23 July, http://www.guardian.co.uk/media/2010/jul/23/bbc-iphone-apps-green-light, accessed 7 March 2011

Pollard, Nick (2009) "Non-stop Deadlines: 24-hour News" in Owen, John and Purdey, Heather (eds), *International News Reporting: Frontlines and Deadlines*. London: Wiley-Blackwell

Popescu, Marina and Tóka, Gábor (2009) "Public Television, Private Television and Citizens' Political Knowledge", paper presented at the 2009 EPCR Joint Sessions in Lisbon, 15–19 April

Price, Monroe Edwin and Raboy, Marc (2003) *Public Service Broadcasting in Transition: A Documentary Reader*. The Hague; New York: Kluwer Law International

Prior, Marcus (2007) *Post-broadcast Democracy: How Media Choice Increases Inequality in Political Involvement and Polarizes Elections*. Cambridge: Cambridge University Press

Rai, Mugdha and Cottle, Simon (2007) "Global Mediations: On the Changing Ecology of Satellite Television News" in *Global Media and Communication*, Vol. 3(1): 51–78

Rai, Mugdha and Cottle, Simon (2010) "Global News Revisited: Mapping the Contemporary Landscape of Satellite Television News" in Cushion, Stephen and Lewis, Justin (eds), *The Rise of 24-Hour News Television: Global Perspectives*. New York: Peter Lang

Rao, Shakuntala (2009) "Glocalization of Indian Journalism" in *Journalism Studies*, Vol. 10(4): 474–88

Reese, Stephen D. (2010) "Journalism and Globalization" in *Sociology Compass*, Vol. 4(6): 344–53

Reinemann, Carsten and Fawzi, Nayla (2010) "The Shrinking News Agenda: How Market Forces Have Shaped 24-hour Television News Channels in Germany" in Cushion, Stephen and Lewis, Justin (2010) (eds) *The Rise of 24 Hour News Television: Global Perspectives*. New York: Peter Lang

Reinemann, Carsten and Wilke, Jürgen (2007) "It's the Debates, Stupid! How the Introduction of Televised Debates Changed the Portrayal of Chancellor Candidates in the German Press, 1949–2005" in *International Journal of Press/Politics*, Vol. 12(4): 92–111

Reinemann, Carsten, Stayner, James, Scherr, Sebastian and Legnante, Guido (2011) "Hard and Soft News: A Review of Concepts, Operationalizations and Key Findings" in *Journalism: Theory, Practice and Criticism*, available on iFirst on 11 November

Rendall, Steve and Broughel, Tara (2003) "Amplifying Officials, Squelching Dissent" in *Fair*, May/June, http://www.fair.org/index.php?page=1145, accessed 14 June 2011

Reynolds, Amy and Barnett, Brooke (2003) "This Just In ... How National TV News Handled the Breaking 'Live' Coverage of September 11" in *Journalism and Mass Communication Quarterly*, Vol. 80(3): 689–703

Richardson, Kay and Meinhof, Ulrike H. (1999) *Worlds in Common? Television Discourse in a Changing Europe*. London: Routledge

Robinson, Piers (2002) *The CNN Effect: The Myth of News, Foreign Policy and Intervention*. London: Routledge

Robinson, Piers (2005) "The CNN Effect Revised" in *Critical Studies in Media Communication*, Vol. 22(4): 344–9

Robinson, Piers, Goddard, Peter, Parry, Katy and Murray, Craig with Taylor, Philip M. (2010) *Pockets of Resistance: British News Media, War and Theory in the 2003 Invasion of Iraq*. Manchester: Manchester University Press

Roper Opinion Poll (2010) "PBS Roper Poll", http://www.pbs.org/roperpoll2010/PBS_Roper_brochure_2.18.10.pdf, accessed 2 August 2011

Rosenbaum, M. (1997) *From Soapbox to Soundbite: Party Political Campaigning in Britain since 1945*. Basingstoke: Macmillan

Rosenberg, Howard and Feldman, Charles S. (2008) *No Time to Think: The Menace of Media Speed and the 24-hour News Cycle*. New York: Continuum

Ryley, John (2006) "Never Been a Better Time to Be in TV News; Television's Sky News; In the Age of Broadband, Podcasts and Texts, How Can the Small Screen Hope to Keep up?" in *Independent*, 4 September: 10

Sabbagh, Dan and Deans, Jason (2012) "News Corp Urges Ofcom to Not Ignore BBC in Media Plurality Review" in *Media Guardian*, http://www.guardian.co.uk/media/2012/jan/05/news-corp-ofcom-bbc, accessed 16 January 2012

Samuel-Azran, Tal (2010) *Al-Jazeera and US War Coverage*. New York: Peter Lang

Sanders, Tyrone (2008) "American Local Radio Journalism", PhD Dissertation, University of Oregon Graduate School, Eugene, Oregon

Scammell, Margaret and Semetko, Holli (2008) "Election News Coverage in the UK" in Strömbäck, Jesper and Kaid, Lynda Lee (eds) *The Handbook of Election News Coverage around the World*. New York: Routledge

Scannell, Paddy (1989) "Public Service Broadcasting and Modern Public Life" in *Media, Culture and Society*, Vol. 11(2): 135–66

Schejter, Amit M. and Obar, Jonathan A. (2009) "Tell It Not in Harrisburg, Publish It Not in the Streets of Tampa: Media Ownership, the Public Interest and Local Television News" in *Journalism Studies*, Vol. 10(5): 577–93

Schlesinger, Philip (1987) *Putting Reality Together: BBC News*. London: Methuen

Schuck, Andreas, Andreas R. T., Vliegenthart, Rens, Boomgaarden, Hajo, Elenbaas, Matthijs, Azrout, Rachid, Spanje, Joost van (2010) "How Medium, Time and Context Explain Variation in the Media Framing of the 2009 European Parliamentary Elections". Paper presented at the PIREDEU Conference, Brussels, November

Schudson, Michael (1999) *The Good Citizen: A History of American Civic Life*. Cambridge, MA: Harvard University Press

Schudson, Michael (2001) "The Objectivity Norm in American Journalism" in *Journalism: Theory, Practice and Criticism*, Vol. 2(2): 149–70

Schulz, Winfried and Zeh, Reimar (2007) "Changing Campaign Coverage of German Television: A Comparison of Five Elections 1990–2005". Paper presented at the ICA, San Francisco, May

Schwalbe, Carol B. (2006) "Remembering Our Shared Past: Visually Framing the Iraq War on U.S. News Websites" in *Journal of Computer-mediated Communication*, Vol. 12(1): 264–89

Scott, David K. and Gobetz, Robert H. (1992) "Hard News/Soft News Content of the National Broadcast Networks, 1972–1987" in *Journalism Quarterly*, Vol. 69(2): 406–12

Scott, David K., Chanslor, Mike and Dixon, Jennifer (2010) "FAIR and the PBS *NewsHour*: Assessing Diversity and Elitism in News Sourcing" in *Communication Quarterly*, Vol. 58 (3): 319–40

Scott, David K., Gobetz, Robert H. and Chanslor, Mike (2008) "Chain versus Independent Television Station Ownership: Toward an Investment Model of Commitment to Local News Quality" in *Communication Studies*, Vol. 59(1): 84–98

Seib, Philip (2002) *The Global Journalist: News and Conscience in a World of Conflict*. Oxford: Rowman & Littlefield

Semetko, Holli A. and Blumler, Jay G., Gurevitch, Michael and Weaver, David H. (1991) *The Formation of Campaign Agendas: A Comparative Analysis of Party and Media Roles in Recent American and British Elections*. Hillsdale, NJ: Erlbaum

Shenker, Jack (2011) "Egypt's Media Undergo Their Own Revolution" in *Media Guardian*, 21 February, http://www.guardian.co.uk/media/2011/feb/21/egypt-media-revolution, accessed 21 February 2011

Siebert, Fredrick S., Peterson, Theodore and Schramm, Wilbur (1956) *Four Theories of the Press: The Authoritarian, Libertarian, Social Responsibility, and Soviet Communist Concepts of What the Press Should Be and Do*. Urbana and Chicago: University of Illinois Press

Sotirovic, Mira and McLeod, Jack (2008) "Media Coverage of U.S. Elections: Persistence of Tradition" in Strömbäck, Jesper and Kaid, Lynda Lee (eds) *The Handbook of Election News Coverage around the World*. New York: Routledge

Sousa, Helena and Costa e Silva, Elsa (2009) "Keeping up Appearances: Regulating Media Diversity in Portugal" in *International Communication Gazette*, Vol. 71(1–2): 89–100

Spanier, Gideon (2010) "What Will the BBC Cut in Its Budget Cull", *Evening Standard*, 20 October, http://www.thisislondon.co.uk/markets/article/23889636-what-will-the-bbc-cut-in-its-budget-cull.do, accessed 13 January 2012

Sparks, Colin and Tulloch, John (eds) (2000) *Tabloid Tales: Global Debates over Media Standards*. Lanham, MD: Rowman & Littlefield

Steele, Catherine A. and Barnhurst, G. Kevin (1996) "The Journalism of Opinion: Network Coverage in US Presidential Campaigns, 1968–1988" in *Critical Studies in Mass Communication*, Vol. 13(3): 187–209

Steensen, Steen (2009) "The Shaping of an Online Feature Journalist" in *Journalism: Theory, Practice and Criticism*, Vol. 10(5): 702–18

Stevenson, Neil (2010) "Chatting the News: The Democratic Discourse Qualities of Non-Market and Market Political Talk Television" in *Journalism Studies*, Vol. 11(6): 852–73

Stiles, Mark J. and Weeks, Cindy (2006) *Towards an Improved Strategy of Support for Public Service Broadcasting*. New York: UNESCO, http://unesdoc.unesco.org/images/0014/001473/147332e.pdf, accessed 23 February 2011

Street, John (2011) *Mass Media, Politics and Democracy*, 2nd edn. Basingstoke: Palgrave Macmillan

Strömbäck, Jesper (2008) "Swedish Election News Coverage: Towards Increasing Mediatization" in Strömbäck, Jesper and Kaid, Lynda Lee (eds) *The Handbook of Election News Coverage around the World*. New York: Routledge

Strömbäck, Jesper and Dimitrova, Daniela V. (2011) "Mediatization and Media Interventionism: A Comparative Analysis of Sweden and the United States" in *International Journal of Press/Politics*, Vol. 16(1): 30–49

Strömbäck, Jesper and Kaid, Lynda Lee (eds) (2008) *The Handbook of Election News Coverage around the World*. New York: Routledge

Strömbäck, Jesper and Shehata, Adam (2010) "Media Malaise or a Virtuous Circle? Exploring the Causal Relationships between News Media Exposure, Political News Attention and Political Interest" in *European Journal of Political Research*, Vol. 49: 575–97

Strömbäck, Jesper and van Aelst, Peter (2010) "Exploring Some Antecedents of the Media's Framing of Election News: A Comparison of Swedish and Belgian Election News" in *International Journal of Press/Politics*, Vol. 15(1): 41–59

Sussman, Gerald (2005) *Global Electioneering: Campaign Consulting, Communications, and Corporate Financing*. New York: Rowman & Littlefield

Syvertsen, Trine (2003) "Challenges to Public Television in the Era of Convergence and Commercialization" in *Television and New Media*, Vol. 4(2): 155–75

Szalai, Georg (2011) "NPR Executive Ron Schiller Resigns after Calling Tea Party 'Racist'" in *Hollywood Reporter*, 3 March, http://www.hollywoodreporter.com/news/npr-executive-ron-schiller-resigns-165941, accessed 1 August 2011

Tait, Richard (2006) "What Future for Regional Television News" in Franklin, Bob (ed.), *Local Journalism and Local Media*, London: Routledge

Tambini, Damien and Cowling, Jamie (eds) (2004) *From Public Service Broadcasting to Public Service Communications*. London: IPPR

Taylor, Philip M. (1992) *War and the Media: Propaganda and Persuasion in the Gulf War*. Manchester: Manchester University Press

Taylor, Philip M. (2000) *Rewiring Media Studies for the Digital Age: Web Studies*. London: Arnold

Television and New Media (2003) Special edition on "The Struggle for and within Public Television", Vol. 4(2)

Thakuria, Nava (2008) "India: Brickbat for Commercial Channel on Terror Coverage", *News Blaze*, 18 December, http://newsblaze.com/story/20081218152755nava.nb/topstory.html, accessed 28 June 2011

Thomas, James, Jewell, John and Cushion, Stephen (2003) *Media Coverage of the 2003 Welsh Assembly Elections*. Cardiff: Electoral Commission in Wales

Thomas, James, Cushion, Stephen and Jewell, John (2004a) "Stirring up Apathy? Political Disengagement and the Media in the 2003 Welsh Assembly Elections" in *Journal of Public Affairs*, Vol. 4(4): 355–363

Thomas, James, Jewell, John and Cushion, Stephen (2004b) *Media Coverage of the 2004 Welsh Local Elections*. Cardiff: Electoral Commission in Wales

Thomas, Lisa (2011) "Reconstructions of 'Reality'? The Coverage of the Gaza Withdrawal in the British Media" in *Journalism Studies*, iFirst published online 21 April

Thomass, Barbara and Kleinsteuber, Hans J. (2011) "Comparing Media Systems: The European Dimension" in Trappel, Josef, Meir, Werner, A., d'Haenens, Leen, Steemers, Jeanette and Thomass, Barbara (eds), *Media in Europe Today*. Bristol: Intellect

Thompson, John (1995) *The Media and Modernity: A Social Theory of the Media*. Cambridge: Polity Press

Thompson, Mark (2010) "Nation Speaking Peace unto Nation: The BBC's Global Mission – Speech to Chatham House", 11 May, http://www.bbc.co.uk/pressoffice/speeches/stories/thompson_chatham_shtml, accessed 8 December 2011

Thorsen, Einar (2009) "News, Citizenship and the Internet: BBC News Online's Reporting of the 2005 UK General Election", PhD Thesis, Bournemouth University

Thussu, Daya (2002) "Managing the Media in an Era of Round-the-clock News: Notes from India's First Tele-War" in *Journalism Studies*, Vol. 3(2): 203–12

Thussu, Daya (2003) "Live TV and Bloodless Deaths: War, Infotainment and 24-hour News" in Thussu, Daya and Freedman, Des (2003) (eds) *War and the Media: Reporting Conflict 24/7*. London: Sage

Thussu, Daya (2007) *News as Entertainment: The Rise of Global Infotainment*. London: Sage

Thussu, Daya and Freedman, Des (2003) (eds) *War and the Media: Reporting Conflict 24/7*. London: Sage

Tiffen, Rodney (2008) "Australia: Gladiatorial Parties and Volatile Media in a Stable Polity" in Strömbäck, Jesper and Kaid, Lynda Lee (eds) *The Handbook of Election News Coverage around the World*. New York: Routledge

Tracey, Michael (1998) *Decline and Fall of Public Service Broadcasting*. Oxford: University Press

Trappel, Josef (2008) "Online Media within the Public Service Realm? Reasons to Include Online into the Public Service Mission" in *Convergence: The International Journal of Research into New Media Technologies*, Vol. 14(3): 313–22

Trappel, Josef and Enli, Sara Gunn (2011) "Online Media: Changing Provision of News" in Trappel, Josef, Meir, Werner, A., d'Haenens, Leen, Steemers, Jeanette and Thomass, Barbara (eds), *Media in Europe Today*. Bristol: Intellect

Trappel, Josef, Meir, Werner, A., d'Haenens, Leen, Steemers, Jeanette and Thomass, Barbara (2011) *Media in Europe Today*. Bristol: Intellect

Tremlett, Giles (2011) "Governors of Spain's Public Broadcaster Move to Take Editorial Control of News" in *Media Guardian*, 22 September, http://www.guardian.co.uk/media/2011/sep/22/governors-spanish-public-broadcaster-news-control, accessed 8 December 2011

Tuchman, Gaye (1978) *Making News: A Study in the Construction of Reality*. New York: Free Press

Tuggle, C. A. and Huffman, Suzanne (2001) "Live Reporting in Television News: Breaking News or Black Holes?" in *Journal of Broadcasting and Electronic Media*, Vol. 45(2): 335–44

Tuggle, C. A., Casella, Peter and Huffman, Suzanne (2010) "Live, Late-breaking, and Broken: TV News and the Challenge of Live Reporting in America" in Cushion, Stephen and Lewis, Justin (2010) (eds) *The Rise of 24-hour News Television: Global Perspectives*. New York: Peter Lang

Turner, Graeme (2005) *Ending the Affair: The Decline of Television Current Affairs in Australia*. Sydney: University of New South Wales Press

Tworzecki, Hubert and Semetko, Holli A. (2010) "Media Uses and Effects in New Democracies: The Case of Poland's 2005 Parliamentary and Presidential Elections" in *International Journal of Press/Politics*, Vol. 15(2): 155–74

UNESCO (2005) *Public Service Broadcasting: A Best Practices Sourcebook*, http://unesdoc.unesco.org/images/0014/001415/141584e.pdf, accessed 10 August 2011

Van der Veer, Peter and Munshi, Shoma (2004) (eds) *Media, War, and Terrorism: Responses from the Middle East and Asia*. London: Routledge

Volkmer, Ingrid (1999) *News in the Global Sphere: A Study of CNN and Its Impact on Global Communication*. Luton: University of Luton Press

Wall, Melissa and Bicket, Douglas (2008a) "The 'Baghdad Broadcasting Corporation': US Conservatives Take Aim at the British News Media" in *Journalism: Theory, Practice and Criticism*, Vol. 9(2): 123–40

Wall, Melissa and Bicket, Douglas (2008b) "Window on the Wider World: The Rise of British News in the United States" in *Journalism Practice* Vol. 2(2): 163–78

Ward, David (2004) (ed.) *Public Service Broadcasting: Change and Continuity*. Mahwah, NJ: Lawrence Erlbaum

Wardle, Claire and Williams, Andy (2010) "Beyond User-generated Content: A Production Study Examining the Ways in Which UGC Is Used at the BBC" *Media, Culture & Society*, Vol. 32(5): 781–99

Wasserman, Herman and Rao, Shakuntala (2008) "The Glocalization of Journalism Ethics" in *Journalism: Theory, Practice and Criticism*, Vol. 9(2): 163–81

Weaver, David H., Beam, Randal A., Brownlee, Bonnie J., Voakes, Paul S. and Wilhoit, Cleveland G. (2007) *The American Journalist in the 21st Century: U.S. News People at the Dawn of a New Millennium*. Mahwah, NJ: Lawrence Erlbaum

Williams, Kevin (1998) *Get Me a Murder a Day! A History of Mass Communication in Britain*. London: Arnold

Williams, Kevin (2000) "No Dreads, Only Some Doubts: The Press and the Referendum Campaign" in Jones, Barry and Bolsom, Denis (eds), *The Road to the National Assembly for Wales*. Cardiff: University of Wales Press

Williams, Andy, Wardle, Claire and Wahl-Jorgensen, Karin (2011) "'Have They Got News for US?' Audience Revolution or Business as Usual at the BBC" in *Journalism Practice*, Vol. 5(1): 85–99

Wu, Dennis H. (2007) "A Brave New World for International News? Exploring the Determinants of the Coverage of Foreign News on US Websites" in *International Communication Gazette*, Vol. 69(6): 539–51

Yan, Michael Zhaoxu and Napoli, Philip M. (2006) "Market Competition, Station Ownership, and Local Public Affairs Programming on Broadcast Television" in *Journal of Communication*, Vol. 56: 795–812

Yan, Michael Zhaoxu and Park, Yong Jin (2009) "Duopoly Ownership and Local Informational Programming on Broadcast Television: Before-After Comparisons" in *Journal of Broadcasting and Electronic Media*, Vol. 53(3): 383–99

Young, Sally (2007) "Sky News Australia: The Impact of Local 24-hour News on Political Reporting in Australia" in *Journalism Studies*, Vol. 10(3): 401–16

Young, Sally (2010) "Audiences and the Impact of 24-hour News in Australia and Beyond" in Cushion, Stephen and Lewis, Justin (2010) (eds) *The Rise of 24-Hour News Television: Global Perspectives*. New York: Peter Lang

Young, Sally (2011) *How Australia Decides: Election Reporting and the Media*. Melbourne: Cambridge University Press

Zaller, John (2003) "A New Standard of News Quality: Burglar Alarms for the Monitorial Citizen" in *Political Communication*, Vol. 20(2): 109–30

Zayani, Mohamed (2005) (ed.) *The Al-Jazeera Phenomenon: Critical Perspectives on New Arab Media*. London: Pluto Press

Zayani, Mohamed (2010) "The Changing Face of Arab News Media: Ambiguities and Opportunities" in Cushion, Stephen and Lewis, Justin (eds) *The Rise of 24-hour News Television: Global Perspectives*. New York: Peter Lang

Zayani, Mohamed and Ayish, Muhammad I. (2006) "Arab Satellite Television and Crisis Reporting: Covering the Fall of Baghdad" in *International Communication Gazette*, Vol. 68(5–6): 473–97

Zayani, Mohamed and Sahraoui, Sofiane (2007) *The Culture of Al-Jazeera: Inside an Arab Media Giant*. Jefferson, NC and London: McFarland and Company

Zelizer, Barbara (1997) "Journalists as Interpretive Communities" in Berkowitz, Dan (ed.), *Social Meanings of News: A Text-Reader*, London: Sage

Zelizer, Barbara and Allan, Stuart (2002) (eds) *Journalism after September 11*, 1st edn. London: Routledge.

Zelizer, Barbara and Allan, Stuart (2011) (eds) *Journalism after September 11*, 2nd edn. London: Routledge.

Index